SECURING DEMOCRACY

SECURING DEMOCRACY

My Fight for
Press Freedom and Justice
in Bolsonaro's Brazil

GLENN GREENWALD

Published in 2021 by
Haymarket Books
P.O. Box 180165
Chicago, IL 60618
773-583-7884
www.haymarketbooks.org
info@haymarketbooks.org

ISBN: 978-1-64259-450-8

Distributed to the trade in the US through Consortium Book Sales and
Distribution (www.cbsd.com) and internationally through Ingram Publisher Services International (www.ingramcontent.com).

This book was published with the generous support of Lannan Foundation and Wallace Action Fund.

Special discounts are available for bulk purchases by organizations and institutions. Please email info@haymarketbooks.org for more information.

Cover design by Abby Weintraub.

Library of Congress Cataloging-in-Publication data is available.

10 9 8 7 6 5 4 3 2 1

Index available at haymarketbooks.org

For my husband, partner, and soul mate, David Miranda;
our two children, João Vitor and Jonathas; and the country
that gave them, and so much more, to me: Brazil

CONTENTS

Preface

"A ONCE-IN-A-LIFETIME SCOOP"

In March 2015, I traveled to Sweden to participate in an event about journalism with former *Washington Post* reporter Carl Bernstein. Entitled "Greenwald Meets Bernstein: From Watergate to Snowden," it was billed as a discussion between the journalist who broke the biggest story of the prior generation (the Nixon administration's 1972–73 cover-up) and the journalist who broke the biggest story of the current generation (NSA surveillance).

I had never met Bernstein, but we had exchanged a few barbed insults through the media at the start of my Snowden reporting. A few days prior to our trip to Sweden, Bernstein generously reached out to me by email and proposed that we have dinner the night before our event. He suggested that it would be a good opportunity to clear the air of any residual resentment so that we could have a civil, constructive dialogue. I quickly thanked him for the invitation and accepted.

We met at a restaurant on the top floor of the hotel where we were both staying. After exchanging a few pleasantries, he quickly raised the old episodes in which we had criticized one another. By that point, they were already a couple of years old; also, people had said far worse things about both of us on many occasions. So it took only a few minutes for both of us to laugh off those minor affronts, agreeing that we did not take them personally. We then moved on to have a very compelling, interesting, and entertaining dinner discussion.

Truth be told, I was excited to meet him. As a child I was obsessed with Watergate—which happened when I was six or seven years old—and, when I was a few years older, I spent endless hours reading and studying *All the President's Men*, the best-selling book by Bob Woodward and Bernstein about their experience journalistically investigating and exposing the Nixon administration's role in the 1972 break-in of the Democratic National Committee headquarters. I had also repeatedly watched the 1976 film adaptation, in which Woodward is played by Robert Redford and Bernstein by Dustin Hoffman.

Our dinner discussion was wide ranging, but one part of it particularly stuck with me in the years that followed. "I'm sure you already know this," he said to me halfway through the meal, "but I'll emphasize it anyway: this Snowden story is a once-in-a-lifetime scoop. You'll never have anything as big or impactful as this again. So make sure to enjoy it while it lasts."

Though it was a bit jarring to think of it in those terms, I knew there was a good chance he was right. The whole premise of the event in Sweden, after all, was that we had each reported the most important story of our respective generations. By definition, it's unreasonable to expect that any journalist will be able to help break and report multiple stories of that magnitude.

But then, on Mother's Day in 2019, a series of events commenced that once again placed me at the heart of a sustained and explosive journalistic controversy. The reporting I subsequently undertook with a team of young journalists brought to light stunning information about grave corruption, deceit, and wrongdoing by extremely powerful political actors—the crux of the journalistic mission, as I've always seen it. For that very reason, the endeavor also prompted serious risks.

Unlike the Snowden story, which had global implications for Internet-era privacy and entailed reporting in more than two dozen countries, this story was focused almost entirely on one country: Brazil. But in so many ways, this experience was at least as intense, and the consequences of the reporting at least as profound and enduring. I spent the second half of 2019 and the early months of 2020 publishing one highly sensitive story after the next that rocked the political and legal landscape of one of the world's largest, most vibrant, and most violent countries, and then navigating an array of threats and dangers that arose from them.

This series of exposés began just five months after the January 2019 inauguration of Brazil's new far-right president, Jair Bolsonaro. Despite his depiction as the "Trump of the Tropics" by the Western press, Bolsonaro is far more of a throwback to the old US-backed, despotic right-wing leaders of the Cold War than he is representative of the modern right in North America or Europe.

As an army captain during Brazil's murderous twenty-one-year military dictatorship that ended only in 1985, and then as a fringe member of Congress for the twenty-eight years that preceded his election to the presidency, Bolsonaro has long explicitly endorsed the military regime as a superior form of government to Brazilian democracy. He has often said that his only criticism of Brazil's military dictatorship is that it did not kill enough people, torture pervasively enough, or impose the level of repression needed to eradicate the leftist opposition entirely.

Adept at the media game, Bolsonaro has spent years courting the attention of the press with extreme statements. When he was merely a sideshow in Congress, these remarks seemed outlandish; expressed from within the presidential palace, however, they have a more terrifying ring. He has said he'd rather learn that his son was dead than gay, and that the military regime should have killed thirty thousand more people, pointing to the example of Chilean dictator Augusto Pinochet; and, in his last speech before voting began in the 2018 presidential election, he vowed a "cleansing the likes of which has never been seen in Brazilian history"—a jarring vow in a country that has experienced, quite recently, sustained torture and murder of dissidents by its government.

The anonymous source who contacted me on Mother's Day said that he had hacked many years' worth of the communications of some of Brazil's most powerful political officials, claiming that the huge archive he had compiled revealed systematic and grave corruption on their part. In mid-May, the source began uploading to my telephone tens of thousands of hacked documents and chats, which then quickly turned into hundreds of thousands.

Just as the source promised, the hacked materials—which he had downloaded from the officials' telephones and which they had exchanged using the Telegram messaging app—proved that some of Brazil's most admired and influential figures were deeply corrupt. But for so many reasons, the landscape for reporting this archive was fraught with dangers, uncertainties, and obstacles.

To begin with, Brazil—unlike the United States and Europe in the era of the Pentagon Papers, the Panama Papers, WikiLeaks, and Edward Snowden—had never seen a mass unauthorized leak of this kind. Whether any of the country's institutions—its courts, its legal agencies, even its media—would regard our reporting as journalism, as opposed to some sort of criminal action, was quite unclear. There was simply nothing in the culture or history of Brazil that provided a road map for how reporting on such a leaked archive would be received.

More menacingly, the country was now under the rule of the authoritarian Bolsonaro, fresh off a stunning and overwhelming victory for both him and his new far-right party, which overnight became the second-largest party in Congress. The new president had long made explicit that he believed in neither democracy nor a free press. Indeed, in the 2018 speech that featured his now-notorious "cleansing" pledge, he specifically promised that his presidency would usher in a "Brazil without *Folha* of São Paulo," the country's largest newspaper, which, shortly before the election, had earned Bolsonaro's wrath by exposing an illegal funding scheme that propelled his campaign.

More worrying still was that one of the figures most implicated by the archive's contents also happened to be the most influential and popular high official in Bolsonaro's government, someone arguably more powerful than even Bolsonaro himself: his minister of justice and public security, Sérgio Moro. Beginning in 2014, Moro, as a judge in the midsize town of Curitiba, oversaw a sweeping anti-corruption probe dubbed "Operation Car Wash," which sent dozens of the country's richest oligarchs and most influential political leaders to prison for involvement in kickback and money laundering schemes that centered on the state-run oil giant, Petrobras. Under Moro's judicial supervision, the probe eventually spread far beyond Petrobras, sweeping up Brazil's entire petroleum and construction sectors, as well the political leadership of numerous parties.

Moro, a stone-faced, no-nonsense judge who consigned people to prison for years or even decades without seeming to bat an eye, became the public face of this probe. Operation Car Wash was widely viewed as a long-overdue cleansing of politicians who, with virtually absolute impunity, corruptly enriched themselves at the expense of most of the population. Moro also became a symbol of ethical probity and rigid law-and-order values in a country long beleaguered by rampant violence and disorder, fortifying his revered status.

The previously obscure judge was now a folk hero: his massive image was plastered in the form of murals on the sides of city buildings, life-size dolls of him dressed as Superman ("SuperMoro") appeared at political protests, and he was the only Brazilian to be featured in *Time* magazine's 2016 list of the world's one hundred most influential people.

With Moro's unrelenting approval and encouragement, the Operation Car Wash prosecutors used radical, controversial, and previously unprecedented tactics to secure convictions. They imprisoned politicians and businesspeople under harsh conditions for months, and in some cases years, without them being convicted of anything—"preventative imprisonment," they called it—and then made clear that they could exit their cells only if they accused other more powerful people of grave crimes.

Sometimes the accusations these defendants signed to spring themselves from jail were true. Very often they were not. But the Car Wash prosecutors routinely leaked the accusations to a subservient media—even though doing so was itself a crime—destroying reputations and terrorizing potential suspects in the process. It was a media strategy that served to solidify their power and their ability to instill fear.

The Car Wash prosecutors, along with Judge Moro himself, also engaged in both overt campaigning and covert media manipulation to poison public opinion against their targets and bolster their own popularity. Moro ran roughshod over the claims of the most high-profile defendants, aggressively and unapologetically applying the most extreme pro-prosecutorial interpretations to their cases. In the process, he not only earned the contempt of Brazil's criminal defense attorneys, who claimed he was single-handedly corrupting Brazilian justice with baseless precedents, but also gained an almost religious veneration among leading media outlets and the broader public.

By far the most valuable prize of Operation Car Wash was the 2017 conviction on corruption charges of former two-term president Luiz Inácio Lula da Silva, the iconic center-left political leader of the Workers' Party (PT) who was term-limited out of office at the close of 2010 with an 86 percent approval rating, and who—at the time of his conviction by Judge Moro—was the clear front-runner in all polls to regain the presidency in 2018. But Moro's decisive and rapid finding of guilt in Lula's case as the election year approached, followed by an affirmation from an appellate court known for its deference to Moro, resulted in Lula being barred from running for the presidency, paving the way for Bolsonaro to ascend to the presidential palace.

Once Bolsonaro's main obstacle to the presidency—Lula—had been removed by Judge Moro's actions, Bolsonaro turned around and rewarded Moro with a huge promotion, elevating him from his position as one of many trial judges in Curitiba to the nation's top law enforcement official. That Moro would join the very far-right government he had made possible bore the unmistakable stench of a quid pro quo, rattling even many of his supporters—not just in the media but also, as our reporting revealed, inside his ministry and even on the Car Wash task force.

In secret chats we eventually published, prosecutors on the Car Wash task force said that Moro's installation in Bolsonaro's government would forever destroy the legacy of their work. They worried the appointment would vindicate growing criticisms, especially on the left, that Moro was a right-wing ideologue abusing the power of law for political rather than legal ends. In particular, these prosecutors suggested, Moro's decision to join hands with a figure as polarizing and scandal plagued as Bolsonaro fed one of the primary critiques of his use of judicial power. Anti-corruption, his opponents argued, was merely his pretext, while his real goal was one the Brazilian right had tried, without success, to achieve at the ballot box since 2002: namely, the removal of the Workers' Party from the presidency and its ultimate destruction.

——— —— ——— —— —— —— —— ——— —— —

When Bolsonaro was elected president, he needed Moro far more than Moro needed Bolsonaro—particularly due to the crusading judge's popularity among the nation's middle class and his credibility with its elite sectors. Indeed, for Moro, the notion of joining Bolsonaro's government was an extremely risky proposition, since it had the potential to undermine his long-cultivated image as transcendent of either ideology or party. Thus, as Bolsonaro tried to persuade Moro to leave his judicial position and join the new government, Moro had all the leverage. And he used that leverage to extract from Bolsonaro extraordinary concessions that gave him unprecedented power. In particular, Moro sought the consolidation under his command of powers that had previously been dispersed among multiple ministries and agencies, including those of investigation, law enforcement, policing, domestic intelligence, financial monitoring, and electronic surveillance. The functions of the once-separate ministries of justice and of public security were also united into his portfolio.

Bolsonaro agreed to all of Moro's demands. Indeed, when they unveiled Moro's newly created position in November 2018, it was so powerful that the Brazilian press began referring to Moro not as the minister but the "super-minister" of justice. That *this* Bolsonaro official was going to be one of the primary targets of our reporting of a huge archive of hacked telephone conversations made it obvious that we faced serious and unpredictable challenges and dangers.

With his power consolidated, the president's super-justice minister and public security spent most of 2019 and early 2020 loyally supporting Bolsonaro, even when it came to the president's most extreme ideological pronouncements. Most revealingly, Moro steadfastly offered defenses of Bolsonaro when he and his family were repeatedly linked to the same type of corruption on which Moro had built his career by claiming to combat.

Once my anonymous source finally completed the upload of the hacked archive in May 2019, we began working in secret to research, process, and then report these materials. (The archive was so enormous that the Intercept's technology specialists in New York had to construct a new, highly encrypted delivery system to accommodate it.) Among our initial concerns was that Moro and the surveillance and intelligence agencies he now controlled would discover the archive we had been given and use his influence to obtain a prepublication censorship order. Worse, we took very seriously the possibility that Moro could exploit his control over the Federal Police to arrest us by asserting that we had participated in a crime merely by receiving these hacked materials.

Given these concerns, we decided to simultaneously publish three of the most explosive stories we had found in the archive, to make as clear as we could that the materials revealed grave corruption and thus indisputably deserved to be in the public domain. We wanted to leave no doubt that despite their basis in hacked private online chats, the public had a clear right to know about the content of these materials—and that our actions were classic journalism.

On June 9, working with the team of journalists and editors at the Intercept Brasil (a bureau I founded in 2016), I published three long articles based on the hacked conversations, the contents of which outraged even many of Moro's most stalwart defenders. In an editorial explaining the journalistic principles we applied to determine which materials should be made public, we made clear that many more stories would be published in the months to come. Borrowing a safeguard the *Guardian* and I used at the start of the Snowden reporting, we also pointedly made clear in this editorial that our archive was safely stored in several places outside Brazil, meaning it would be impossible for Brazilian authorities to stop the reporting, no matter how extreme the measures they employed.

Each of the June 9 articles detailed, with extensive evidence from the hacked archive, different forms of judicial and prosecutorial corruption by Judge Moro and the Car Wash task force. The first demonstrated that Moro had spent years secretly collaborating and conspiring with prosecutors to construct criminal charges and even to direct the public campaign against the very defendants he was legally and ethically required to judge with neutrality and objectivity—including, most explosively, Lula. The years' worth of chats we published revealed what Moro's critics had long suspected, but he and the Car Wash team had publicly and vehemently denied: Moro was so hell-bent on securing convictions for the most high-profile defendants that he acted as the clandestine chief of the prosecution, going so far as to privately mock defendants with the prosecutors, order public attacks against defendants and their lawyers, and instruct the prosecutors how to design the charges such that they were immunized from challenge on appeal once Moro had issued his guilty findings.

In sum, the article showed that Moro, contrary to his repeated public denials, spoke in secret and continuously with the Car Wash prosecutors, especially chief prosecutor Deltan Dallagnol, and that he participated in and directed—rather than fairly judged and evaluated—the prosecution of the most prominent defendants who appeared before him. As the

New York Times observed, "Moro's legacy suffered a further blow when The Intercept Brasil . . . began reporting in June on a trove of leaked text messages exchanged by federal prosecutors. The messages showed that Mr. Moro had provided guidance to the prosecution in [Lula]'s case." The *Times* added, "the leaked cellphone text messages showed the main judge in the investigation giving strategic guidance to federal prosecutors in what criminal procedure experts saw as a clear violation of legal and ethical guidelines."

Our second story revealed chats in which the corruption task-force members openly plotted how to use their prosecutorial powers to prevent Lula's Workers' Party from winning the 2018 election and returning to power—actions diametrically opposed to their long-standing insistence to the public that they were unfailingly nonpartisan and apolitical. Most incriminating in this article were the frenetic efforts of the Car Wash prosecutors, led by Dallagnol, to overturn a judicial order in the weeks before the election that authorized São Paulo's *Folha* newspaper to interview Lula from prison. When plotting to stop the interview, Dallagnol told a prosecutorial colleague that he was "praying daily" against the "return of [the Workers' Party] to power."

The third article revealed that in the days before they brought the criminal charges against Lula, the prosecutors knew there were fundamental defects in their case—particularly an absence of evidence to support the essential elements of the charges—but brought them anyway, secure in the knowledge that Moro would be the one adjudicating the charges. Even as they privately acknowledged such gaping evidentiary holes in the charges against Lula and others, in public the prosecutors righteously insisted that the cases were airtight.

When we simultaneously published our initial findings in both English and Portuguese, everything changed in Brazil's political world. Longtime media, legal, and academic defenders of Judge Moro and Operation Car Wash said the revelations were gravely disturbing. Some called on Moro and Dallagnol to resign their public offices. Polls showed Moro's popularity declining for the first time in years. As the *Guardian* observed, our exposés "had an explosive impact on Brazilian politics and dominated headlines for weeks . . . appear[ing] to show prosecutors in the sweeping Operation Car Wash corruption inquiry colluding with Sérgio Moro."

That the Supreme Court would be emboldened by our reporting to finally confront Moro's abuses first became evident when the high court issued a remarkable ruling involving myself and Bolsonaro's justice minister. In early July 2019—less than a month after our reporting began—a large news site notorious for being a reliable dumping ground for leaks by Moro and the Car Wash task force, *O Antagonista*, reported that law enforcement agencies under Moro's command had initiated criminal investigations into my personal finances. The ostensible justification was to determine whether I had paid my source(s) to hack the information from the phones of Moro and Car Wash prosecutors. Claims that I had "paid the hackers" became a frequent theme among the far-right, pro-Bolsonaro network of fake news sites agitating for my arrest and imprisonment. If I had paid someone to hack the telephones of Brazilian authorities, that would make me a participant in the criminal conspiracy. But the accusation was completely false.

Whether because of social media bot networks, genuine pro-Moro fanaticism, or both, variants of the hashtags #GlennInJail or #DeportGlenn trended on Brazilian Twitter throughout June and July. Virtually every day that I went to work online, I saw some new prominent call at the top of Twitter's trending topics for punitive acts against me. Evidently, Moro and his allies had decided they would exploit those baseless accusations by launching a formal criminal investigation against me and then leaking news of that investigation to their most loyal website—an investigation that, however specious, aimed to intimidate me and other journalists working on the archive.

Shortly after news of the investigation leaked, the center-left party led by environmentalist and former presidential candidate Marina Silva, Sustainability Network (REDE), acted on its own against Moro by petitioning the Supreme Court to stop any and all investigations by the Federal Police or associated agencies into me or my finances. The REDE party argued that any such investigations were obvious retaliation against my journalism and thus constituted a violation of the constitutional guarantee of a free press.

The Supreme Court quickly accepted REDE's petition, and one of its justices, Gilmar Mendes, issued a stirring and groundbreaking ruling that ordered the Federal Police and all other law enforcement agencies to immediately cease any investigations relating to me or my journalism. Heralding press freedom as a "pillar of democracy," Justice Mendes wrote: "Freedom of expression and the press cannot be vilified by investigative acts directed at the journalist in the regular exercise of his profession."

Then, beginning in August, the Supreme Court—which in the past had reflexively ratified even Moro's most legally dubious transgressions—finally began ruling against him. Three months after we began our reporting, in a case involving one of Moro's most high-profile corruption convictions, against the former president of Petrobras, the high court ruled that Moro had violated the constitutional rights of dozens of Car Wash defendants. In particular, the court found he had refused them the opportunity to address accusations lodged by fellow defendants whose cooperation was secured in exchange for leniency. In another ruling weeks later, the high court ruled that a controversial and harsh practice often employed by Operation Car Wash—the imprisonment of defendants before they had exhausted their appeals—was unconstitutional, potentially freeing dozens of prisoners.

It is hard to overstate how radically the climate changed for Moro and the Car Wash prosecutors once our reporting began. In May, it had been unthinkable that the Supreme Court would confront him in this manner. After June 9, it became commonplace. Virtually overnight, Moro went from being depicted as a superhero into a drastically diminished and scandal-plagued far-right partisan who now depended on Bolsonaro and his movement for his power.

Congress smelled blood in the water and, in the wake of our reporting, dealt Moro one humiliating legislative defeat after the next. It refused to enact the key parts of his signature "anti-crime" package, including a proposal that would allow US-style plea bargains to turn defendants into informants, and another to strengthen the legal immunities police officers enjoy when they kill innocents (a key plank in Bolsonaro's pro-police presidential campaign that he had tapped Moro to implement). Even worse for Moro, Congress enacted several of its own reforms, ones Moro vehemently opposed, aimed at curbing judicial and prosecutorial abuses. As the lead congressional sponsors introduced and then successfully enacted this legislation, they centrally touted our exposés, using our disclosures regarding Moro's improprieties to impose new limits on judges and prosecutors generally and Operation Car Wash specifically.

Additionally, multiple disciplinary proceedings in Congress and the public ministry were brought against Dallagnol, the chief Car Wash prosecutor. In November, he suffered the first of what was predicted to be many disciplinary sanctions, and his removal from his position as Car Wash chief became only a matter of time and pretext. (In mid-2020, it would be announced he was leaving his position, with multiple disciplinary actions pending against him.)

Perhaps the starkest and most dramatic result of our reporting also came in November, when Lula himself walked out of Moro's makeshift prison in a federal building in Curitiba (ironically, the lobby of the building where he was imprisoned bears a plaque with Lula's name, as it was built during his presidency). The order to free Lula was not explicitly tied to the abuses in his prosecution that our reporting revealed; rather, it was a result of the Supreme Court ruling that held it unconstitutional to imprison a defendant before they have exhausted their appeals. Nevertheless, few people had any doubts that our reporting made it politically palatable for Lula to be freed by the Supreme Court. In fact, the media and the legal world had treated the question before the court as a monumental decision about whether to free Lula from Moro's prison. By showing that the process and the officials who imprisoned Lula were corrupt all along, our journalism enabled the court to issue its ruling without popular upheaval.

Chief among those crediting our reporting for his freedom was Lula himself. For most of the roughly eighteen months he sat in his prison cell, Lula was barred from granting interviews and was thus forced to communicate with his country via a series of handwritten letters. On November 8, the day he was widely expected to be released, an aide called me to say that Lula had pointedly decided that his last handwritten letter from his cell in Moro's prison should be written to me. The aide asked if I had any objections. After I said I didn't, I received this letter, which was promptly published by *Folha*. It focused on the work I had done in exposing Moro's corruption, but the first line referenced a widely reported episode from the day before, when I was physically attacked by a pro-Bolsonaro journalist while live on-air on a popular radio and YouTube program.

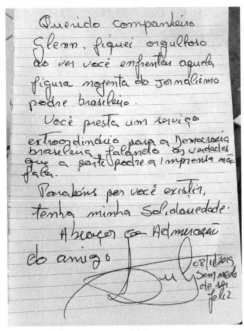

My dear comrade Glenn,

I was so proud watching you confront that nauseating figure of the rotted Brazilian media.
You are providing an extraordinary service to Brazilian democracy, speaking truths that the rotten part of the press won't say.
Congratulations for your existence, you have my solidarity.
Hugs, with admiration from a friend
Lula: not afraid to be happy.

Hours after the letter from Lula arrived, the former president—with thousands of people gathered outside the Curitiba prison, along with film crews from media outlets across the world—strolled out of the building and fell into the embrace of the swelling crowd of highly emotional supporters, as well his fiancée (Lula's wife of forty-three years died shortly before he was imprisoned). That night, from his home in São Paulo, Lula called me. We spoke for roughly twenty minutes. Among other things, he thanked me and my colleagues for our reporting.

In speeches and articles that followed, Lula frequently said that our exposés had revealed the truth, not only about the corruption that drove his prosecution, but the lawlessness of Moro and Operation Car Wash. In a *Washington Post* op-ed published eleven days after he left prison, Lula wrote:

> Throughout the judicial farce, my attorneys proved I was not guilty through overwhelming exculpatory evidence. They also highlighted the coordinated "lawfare" against me—trying to use the law to delegitimize me. With a few honorable exceptions, most of the Brazilian media chose to ignore these facts. It was only in June, with the pub-

lication of an investigation that showed collusion between the prosecution and judges by the Intercept Brazil, that the truth finally began
to emerge. These revelations have rocked Brazilians and the world because they showed that a once acclaimed anti-corruption effort had
been politicized, tainted and illegal.

All of these consequences of the reporting—though gratifying—
had concomitant costs, as is often the case for journalists who expose
serious corruption by society's most powerful actors. Most of the journalists who worked closely on this reporting with me would surely say
that the last half of 2019 was one of the most challenging, high-pressure,
and difficult periods in their lives. That's certainly true for me. Beginning with the publication of the first series of articles on June 9, 2019, an
anonymous website was created with a petition demanding my deportation from Brazil. The next day, the hashtag #DeportaGreenwald rose to
the top of the topics trending on Twitter. From that day through to the
publication of this book, a wave of credible death threats—in a country where political violence is commonplace—poured in, preventing me
from leaving my house without armed guards and an armored vehicle.
Major pro-Bolsonaro fake news sites targeted me, my husband, and our
two young sons with constant lies about our private lives and our past.

When I testified before the lower house of Congress in early July
2019, several members from Bolsonaro's party demanded during the
hearing that I be arrested before I left the building. In a nationwide, multi-
city street protest in support of Moro and Operation Car Wash, far-right
marchers carried angry signs with my picture on them, including one particularly large one that read in English: "Glenn Greenwald, get out of Brazil! You are disgusting." In a July 12 article on the growing controversies,
the Associated Press said of the demands from members of Congress that
I be imprisoned:

> By some accounts that wasn't an empty threat: A conservative website
> reported that federal police had requested that financial regulators in-
> vestigate Greenwald's finances. The Pulitzer Prize–winning journalist
> and his Brazilian husband also say they have been receiving detailed
> death threats, calls for his deportation and homophobic comments in
> an increasingly hostile political environment.

Greenwald, an attorney-turned-journalist who has long been a free-speech advocate, has found himself at the center of the first major test of press freedom under Bolsonaro, who took office on Jan. 1 and has openly expressed nostalgia for Brazil's 1964–1985 military dictatorship—a period when newspapers were censored and some journalists tortured.

Those hostilities were catapulted to a new level entirely when President Bolsonaro himself invoked my name explicitly—on three consecutive days in late July—to say that I would possibly "spend time in the slammer" for my journalism. Bolsonaro also accused me and my husband, David Miranda, who is now a member of Congress from one of Brazil's left-wing parties, of fraudulently marrying one another and illegally adopting our two Brazilian children as a "scam" for me to avoid deportation.

David and I married in 2005, when I was still a lawyer, which would make me the most prescient person in the world under Bolsonaro's "theory." In December 2019, David and I petitioned the Supreme Court to initiate a criminal proceeding against the president for criminal defamation for his remarks about our marriage and children. A Supreme Court justice accepted our petition and quickly gave the president ten days to explain what he meant, withdraw his remarks, or face a criminal inquiry. Bolsonaro responded by claiming he was speaking ironically, and that even as president, he had the free speech right to criticize our actions.

I was the perfect villain for the Bolsonaro right: I'm technically a "foreigner" in Brazil, despite living there for fifteen years; I gained notoriety from my reporting on Snowden's leaked NSA documents; I'm gay; and my husband is a left-wing politician. Even though I was purposely turned into the face of the story, all of the journalists at the Intercept Brasil faced their own levels of serious recriminations and threats.

The Intercept Brasil's editor, Leandro Demori, had his phone cloned by an anonymous account that then published, on Twitter and elsewhere, forged WhatsApp chats in Leandro's name (including some purportedly exchanged with my husband and other left-wing members of Congress). The forged chats purported to show not only various crimes they were plotting, but also ones I had allegedly committed, including a claim that

I had paid Russian hackers to obtain the materials leaked to me. The fake exchanges quickly rose to the top of Twitter's trending topics, not only in Brazil but globally.

A few weeks prior to our Supreme Court petition, I appeared on a highly watched right-wing radio and YouTube program called *Pânico*. At the last moment, they told me I would be joined on the show by a pro-Bolsonaro journalist who had previously called for a child court judge to investigate whether David and I were adequately caring for our two sons—an allegation he made on the grounds that David was working in Brasilia as a member of Congress while I was working on these exposés in Rio de Janeiro. When I confronted him about those comments and called him cowardly for having dragged our children into the public arena in such a demeaning way, he physically assaulted me, slapping my face on live television. Key Bolsonaro allies in Congress, including the president's sons—along with his "guru," US-based pundit Olavo de Carvalho—explicitly cheered this attack on me, and said it should have been more severe.

All of these attacks were designed as a form of sustained intimidation: to make us feel as if our liberty and physical security were endangered, and that such threats would increase if we published more.

In January 2020, I was with David, our two children, and two nephews in the interior of Rio de Janeiro state for a weeklong vacation at a farm. This break came after an indescribably intense and often-trying seven months of reporting that had been accompanied by online attacks and threats of both prosecution and violence. Our reporting on the archive was starting to wind down, and in late December, the Federal Police—which was controlled by Moro—announced it had completed a comprehensive investigation into the hacks. In a 177-page report, an entire section was devoted to their investigation of me, which stated emphatically that there was no evidence of any criminality on my part and that I had been meticulously careful in my work as a journalist never to get near the line of criminality.

That the Federal Police issued such a full-throated public exoneration led us to conclude that one threat that had been lurking for months—criminal prosecution—was over. But on the third day of our vacation, January 21, I was preparing horses to ride with our youngest son, Jonathas, when I looked at my phone and saw "URGENT." The headline read: "Journalist Glenn Greenwald criminally charged by the Public Ministry [roughly equivalent to the US Justice Department] in connection with hacking reporting."

My first reaction was to assume that I had read the Portuguese incorrectly. But over the next twenty minutes, multiple other media outlets reported that I had been formally charged, along with six alleged conspirators, as part of a criminal conspiracy—and was accused of committing 121 felonies that could lead to hundreds of years in prison if I were found guilty.

The international repercussions of the charges were instant—news outlets around the world almost universally condemned the charges—but I knew that the Bolsonaro government was immune to such pressures. That the *New York Times* and European press freedom groups were condemning my prosecution was of no concern to reactionary forces in Brazil.

Weeks after the charges were filed, a federal judge dismissed them. But when he did so, he made clear his belief that my work with my sources could constitute serious crimes—ones that, in his words, could even justify "preventative imprisonment" pending my trial. The judge said that, notwithstanding his view of the evidence, he was forced to reject the charges only because of the Supreme Court ruling from the prior year that barred any criminal prosecution of me in connection with my journalism. Still, the prosecutor who brought the charges appealed this dismissal, asking an appellate court to reinstate the charges. He and others inside the public ministry also began working to try to convince the Supreme Court to reverse its ruling—the only thing standing between me and a prison cell, according to the judge. As of this writing, that appeal is still pending.

Throughout our work, the Intercept and its parent company, First Look Media, provided all the protection we could have asked for—physical security, a team of the best possible lawyers, a network to combat lies and fake news. This was not an abstract or theoretical concern. The eighteen months prior to our revelations were marked by political violence. For my family, the darkest moment of this period was the brutal assassination of a close family friend, Rio de Janeiro city council member Marielle Franco, in March 2018. We also knew that Sérgio Moro was an authoritarian in control of repressive police powers, and that he was more than willing to use them to punish his enemies.

Yet if I had the chance to travel back in time and choose again, I would choose exactly the same course of action. Like so many others, I became a journalist to report stories like this one. And this is easily among the most gratifying work I've ever done in my life.

— — — — — — — — — —

I was enchanted by Brazil—its beautiful, extraordinary, vibrant, and unique history, culture, diversity, and people—the first time I visited in the mid-1990s. I've lived in the country since I met and fell in love with my Brazilian husband in 2005. Brazil is the country that has given me everything I have in my life: my marriage, my children, my career as a journalist and writer, and a new way of thinking about life and the world.

I'm grateful that the power of a free press, the privilege of my public platform, and the ability of journalism to shine a cleansing light on corrupt and powerful actors gave me the opportunity to give something back to my second homeland. I would certainly not say that everything we did was perfect. This reporting was highly complex and fraught with difficulties, and we made some mistakes in our choices and in our reporting, which I will explore in the pages that follow. But I have no doubt that the revelations we were able to bring to the public strengthened Brazilian democracy in an enduring and fundamental way. I believe we righted wrongs, reversed injustices, and exposed grave corruption. In many ways, I regard the dangers and threats we faced as vindication that we fulfilled our core function as journalists: to unflinchingly confront those who wield power with transparency, accountability, and truth.

Chapter 1

THE BATTLEGROUND: BRAZIL

N orth American and Western European nations pay far more attention to one another than they do other parts of the world, with the
possible exception of the Middle East, where their "attention" typically manifests as various forms of internal control and violent interference designed to maintain dominance over the region's energy resources.
But over the last several years, the West has devoted more attention to
Brazil, with good reason.

In all circumstances, what happens in Brazil matters to the world,
whether or not the world takes notice. Its size alone is one major reason.
With a population of 213 million people, it is the sixth-most populous
country on the planet, the second-largest in the hemisphere, and by far the
most influential in Latin America. As one of the last countries to legally
eliminate slavery, it both enjoys remarkable racial diversity and suffers from
enduring systemic racism: whites are now a minority in a country where
nonwhites remain largely excluded from most halls of power and wealth.
Then there are the country's natural assets, including its massive oil reserves, which helped make Brazil the world's seventh-largest economy. And
it is the custodian of the most environmentally and economically valuable
forests in the world, found in the Amazon.

For all of those reasons, the country was a major focal point for the
Cold War battles between the Soviet Union and the United States. In the

1

1950s and 1960s, Brazil struggled to avoid being swallowed by either of the two hostile superpowers, remaining generally neutral as it slowly built a measure of independence. Its 1946 constitution and the institutions it spawned became the basis for an imperfect yet burgeoning modern democracy, while the document came to serve as a regional model for guaranteeing modern civil liberties and democratic rights.

All of that came crashing down in April 1964, when right-wing factions of the Brazilian military, backed by multiple layers of support from the US Central Intelligence Agency and Pentagon, used physical force and intimidation, along with the threat of further violence, to oust the democratically elected center-left president. Amid hollow promises of a quick transition back to democracy, they imposed a twenty-one-year regime of military dictatorship that used murder, torture, and harsh repression to rule the country.

Three years prior to the coup, Brazilians had elected a ticket composed of the center-right Jânio Quadros as president and the center-left João Goulart as vice president. After Quadros resigned in August 1961—largely as a tactical bet, ultimately unsuccessful, that the population would rise up and demand his return, thereby strengthening him—Goulart assumed the presidency by constitutional mandate. When Brazilian oligarchs and military leaders resisted Goulart's ascension to the presidency, asserting he was too left-wing, a compromise was reached in which Goulart would preside over a parliamentary system that, by design, significantly weakened the presidency. But in 1963, a national referendum that restored the presidency model overwhelmingly passed, serving as ratification of Goulart's popular legitimacy and governance.

Contrary to the accusations made against him by Brazil's elite classes, Goulart was nothing close to an actual communist. He was more of a soft, European-style socialist devoted to mild reforms of Brazil's notoriously harsh systems that maintained massive wealth and income inequality. But at the hyper-paranoid peak of the Cold War in the 1960s, even an unthreatening center-left incrementalist, particularly one who had made some friendly gestures toward Moscow, was intolerable to Washington as president of the largest country in Latin America—a continent the United States, more or less continuously since the 1823 enactment of the Monroe Doctrine, has regarded as its "backyard," subject only to its interference and control.

The Monroe Doctrine, written by then secretary of state and future president John Quincy Adams, was a declaration against European colonialism in Latin America (in exchange for a renunciation by the United States of colonialism in European spheres of interest). Despite such lofty language of noninterference, it was widely understood at the time of its enactment, and by US officials for the next two centuries, to be motivated not by anti-colonialist sentiments but their opposite: namely, the US government's determination to exercise exclusive control over the continent nearest its homeland.

Any residual doubts about the core purpose of the doctrine were dispelled in 1895, when the United States objected to British behavior in a conflict with Venezuela over control of a nearby territory. President Grover Cleveland's secretary of state, Richard Olney, threatened the United Kingdom with serious reprisals if it did not cease its coercive efforts, issuing one of the clearest understandings of the powers bestowed by the doctrine: "The United States is practically sovereign on this continent, and its fiat is law upon the subjects to which it confines its interposition."

Three years later, the Monroe Doctrine again served as the express basis for US conflict with a European power over control of Latin America, this time in a much more serious way. In 1898, the US government supported Cuba in its war for independence against Spain; after winning the war and placing Cuba squarely within its sphere of control, the United States also "won" Puerto Rico, Guam, and the Philippines from the Spanish.

Throughout the Cold War, US policymakers explicitly invoked the Monroe Doctrine as justification for their support in Latin America of coups, domestic repression, and other means of ensuring that governments friendly to US interests wielded power while those that did not paid the price. As recently as 2018, John Bolton, then President Donald Trump's national security adviser, said the doctrine allowed the United States to overthrow the government of Venezuela if it so chose (and as Bolton advocated).

Under that well-established historical framework, US support for the violent 1964 overthrow of Brazil's democratically elected center-left president, and the aid it provided to the military regime that followed, was nothing unusual. If anything, such a refusal to tolerate any form of leftism in Latin America's largest country—even if it meant the imposition of despotism where democracy had been taking root—was virtually inevitable.

As he grew in confidence and stature following the 1963 referendum that fortified his power, President Goulart had increasingly angered the oligarchical class of both the United States and Brazil, the CIA, as well as Western institutions of capital that were lending Brazil money, including the International Monetary Fund. The three policies of President Goulart that had particularly provoked their ire addressed Brazil's historically brutal wealth inequality: rent control, modest land reform programs, and a nationalization plan for some of Brazil's oil fields. On the other hand, Goulart's reforms had bolstered his popularity among the Brazilian people (whose opinions, after all, should have mattered to anyone purporting to favor "democracy"). Indeed, in 2014, Brazilian journalist Mário Magalhães unearthed polling data from the leading firm IBOPE from March 1964, which showed that President Goulart enjoyed widespread support in key regions around the country:

If President João Goulart could also run for president would you vote for him?

	Would vote for him	Would not	Don't know
Fortaleza	57%	34%	9%
Recife	60%	28%	12%
Salvador	59%	32%	9%
Belo Horizonte	39%	56%	5%
Rio de Janeiro	51%	44%	5%
São Paulo	40%	52%	8%
Curitaba	41%	45%	14%
Porto Alegre	52%	44%	4%

Source: IBOPE polls, March 9–26, 1964.

Under President Lyndon Johnson, the CIA, working with right-wing factions in the Brazilian military, successfully launched the military coup against the Goulart presidency, forcing the elected leader, under threat of house arrest and violence, to flee to Uruguay in April 1964. With Goulart out of the country, the military seized control and forced a scared and compliant Congress to legalize its coup.

Though the coup seemingly transpired in rapid and dramatic fashion—just a few days elapsed between US-backed Brazilian forces' initial march on Rio de Janeiro and Goulart's departure from the country—the administration of John F. Kennedy had determined two years earlier, in 1962, that Goulart could lead Brazil into Moscow's orbit and even into communism, which warranted the covert plot against him. A 1963 visit to Goulart by Attorney General Robert Kennedy—designed to pressure the Brazilian president to become more pro-American and more capitalist-friendly, or face heightened economic sanctions—had been regarded in Washington largely as a failure. After that, covert CIA and Pentagon plotting with Brazil's paramilitary forces against Goulart had intensified. The joint US–Brazilian military coup had thus been in the works for at least two years before it was finally executed.

In the coup's aftermath, the US government vehemently denied widespread suspicions in the region that they had been involved. But classified documents that emerged at the end of that decade revealed the CIA's role, and Washington was forced to publicly admit its backing of Goulart's removal.

At first, State Department officials tried to minimize their involvement, casting the US role as one of mere communication with, and limited logistical aid for, the coup leaders. But as the years progressed and more and more documents from both countries emerged, US officials were forced to acknowledge a far greater role. As Vincent Bevins wrote in the *New York Review of Books* in 2018, "As part of Operation Brother Sam, Washington secretly made tankers, ammunition, and aircraft carriers available to the coup-plotters." A mountain of other documents from both countries has subsequently been published—including diplomatic cables from the US ambassador in Brazil to the CIA, urging the provision of arms to the coup leaders, as well as Pentagon orders for deployments of US military assets to support them—that establish the central role of the United States as undisputed historical fact.

The Brazilian press, controlled at the time (as it is still) by a handful of oligarchical families, led by the burgeoning *Globo* media empire, celebrated the coup on its front pages as a noble "revolution" against a corrupt communist regime. As Bevins explains, "A huge part of Brazil's political and economic elite supported the [coup] at the time," including "all the major Brazilian newspapers except one." Employing the standard, yet still bizarre, distortion pioneered by the US State Department, they heralded the forced removal of the elected president and imposition of military tyranny as a "restoration of democracy."

The US media was equally effusive in praising the violent overthrow of President Goulart. Echoing the position of the State Department, the most influential US news outlets unflinchingly described the coup as a "pro-democracy revolution" against corruption, repression, and communism. Particularly supportive of the military generals was publisher Henry Luce's then highly influential *Time* magazine, which assumed its traditional role of propagandizing for US foreign policy under the guise of journalism.

The Orwellian rhetorical framework used to depict the overthrow of democracy as a "restoration of democracy" is one that has been applied—before the 1964 coup in Brazil and since—in multiple countries to justify US intervention as a safeguarding of freedom, no matter how repressive the pro-US regime might be. In Cold War terms, because communism is the ultimate expression of repression, any attempts to combat it—no matter how despotic, contrary to popular will, or violent—are inherently noble and democratic.

In the post-Soviet era, Islam has replaced communism in this role. Current US alliances with the tyrannies of Saudi Arabia's Crown Prince Mohammed bin Salman and Egypt's coup general Abdel Fattah al-Sisi are cast as unfortunate yet benign acts, designed to stave off worse (i.e., anti-American) elements from assuming power.

Crucial to this formula is the maintenance of illusory democracy—or symbolic gestures toward political liberalization—as a means to provide plausible deniability against accusations of despotism. When confronted with proof of repression, these regimes and their US patrons hype these "reforms" or nods to democracy as proof that the despots are moving, with the best of intentions, toward democratization, even if the progress is so gradual as to be undetectable. That was the tactic used by US media luminaries, led by *New York Times* columnist Thomas Friedman and *Washington Post* columnist David Ignatius, to create a myth of bin Salman as a crusading pro-democracy reformer—efforts that came crashing down on them only when the Saudi crown prince was caught ordering the murder and chopping up of Ignatius's *Post* colleague Jamal Khashoggi. Similarly, al-Sisi came to power in Egypt after a violent military coup that overthrew the country's first democratically elected president, Mohammed Morsi. Even as al-Sisi brutally cracked down on all dissent following the 2014 putsch, US officials, including then secretary of state John Kerry, praised the coup leaders for "restoring democracy."

This same framework was used to justify and celebrate the Brazil coup as a pro-democracy revolution. Within the State Department and in the US press, President Goulart was imaginatively transformed from an incrementalist, center-left reformist who had, one year earlier, received an overwhelming democratic mandate (even while infuriating the actual left with accommodations to capitalism and oligarchy), into a communist tyrant whose removal was imperative for the salvage of Brazilian freedom and democracy.

— — — — — — — — — —

After forcing President Goulart to flee and installing themselves in power, Brazil's military coup leaders quickly complied with a key condition of US support for the coup: the "opening up" of Brazilian markets to international capital. Within two years of the 1964 coup, roughly half of Brazil's major industries were owned by foreign interests.

Domestically, what followed was a predictable and familiar nightmare. The military regime's first act was a decree entitled First Institutional Act (AI-1), which suspended most of the rights guaranteed by the 1946 constitution, paving the way for increasingly violent and repressive tactics. Supported, trained, and armed by both the United States and the United Kingdom, the dictatorship imprisoned dissidents without trial, murdered leftist journalists, rounded up university students, tortured critics and activists, summarily removed disobedient senators and members of congress, indefinitely suspended basic civil liberties, and proclaimed the right to ignore judicial orders. In just a few years, the coup generals had consolidated their stranglehold over political and cultural life.

In 1968, with the regime's Fifth Institutional Act (AI-5), its leaders arrogated unto themselves virtually absolute control, rendering all other democratic institutions—the courts, Congress, and the media—little more than facades whose real function was unquestioning fealty to the generals. Following the well-established Cold War formula for masking repression, the military dictatorship continued to adhere to empty legalities to provide plausible deniability. The ruling Brazilian general assumed the presidency only after being "elected" by Congress (which the generals controlled on account of their power, aggressively invoked, to summarily remove any noncompliant members). They also avoided having one identifiable strongman, such as Chile's Augusto Pinochet or Paraguay's Alfredo Stroessner (both later praised by President Jair Bolsonaro), serve as the symbol of repression; instead, every few years they passed power from one banal, faceless general to the next.

In order to create cover for their autocratic rule, Brazil's government also followed the well-worn script of allowing a controlled opposition. A decree enacted shortly after the coup established two parties: one was the ruling party, the National Renewal Alliance (ARENA), while the other was the supposed opposition, the Brazilian Democratic Movement Party (PMDB). But allowing an opposition party while maintaining the power to prevent it from taking office, as ARENA did, is fraud.

Once it became apparent that the regime had no intention of returning power to civilian democratic control, a vibrant—and sometimes violent—left-wing resistance arose. This resistance spanned the spectrum, from armed communist guerillas who carried out high-profile kidnappings in order to free imprisoned comrades (such as the 1969 abduction of US ambassador Charles Burke Elbrick), to peaceful socialist activists who sought to use whatever minimal freedoms they possessed to agitate for the return of free and direct elections.

But each minimal advance of the resistance—whether peaceful or armed—was met with increasing violence. Anyone suspected of having ties to, or even harboring sympathy for, the armed resistance was abducted, imprisoned without charges, routinely subjected to brutal methods of torture (which the United States, United Kingdom, and France trained Brazilian interrogators to use), and often killed. Famous artists, writers, and musicians who were critics of the military rulers were arbitrarily imprisoned and then forced into exile. Newspapers that exceeded the bounds of permitted dissent were summarily closed, and their journalists and editors imprisoned or killed.

Among those who took up arms against the military dictatorship was a young student and newspaper editor named Dilma Rousseff. In 1970, at the age of twenty-three, she was kidnapped from a São Paulo restaurant where she had gone to meet a friend, imprisoned without charges, and tortured for twenty-one days, using standard regime interrogation methods such as beating her palms and soles with paddles, punching her, placing her in stress positions, and using electric shocks. Without anything resembling a fair trial, she was imprisoned for more than two years. Thirty-eight years later, in 2010, Dilma, by then a sixty-three-year-old center-left pragmatist, economist, and technocrat in the Workers' Party, was elected as Brazil's first-ever female president.

Despite how widely despised the military dictatorship became, its powers of censorship made successful challenge to its authority virtually impossible. Media loyal to the regime disseminated an endless stream of propaganda that helped render the population largely submissive—especially *Globo*, whose founder, João Roberto Marinho, built one of the most dominant media outlets in the world through his servitude to the regime, in the process becoming one of the world's richest men. (Marinho's three sons—all billionaires—continue to enjoy the fruits of their family's service to the dictatorship through their ongoing control over *Globo*.)

Only in the mid-1970s, when multiple horror stories broke through the regime's wall of censorship and reached the general population, did Brazilians' demands for restoration of their civic rights and democratic freedoms finally become too powerful to suppress. Throughout the late 1970s and into the early 1980s, as street protests grew, the military regime began to realize that it could no longer maintain its control. Finally, in 1985, pro-democracy citizen movements forced the formal process of redemocratization, when indirect elections were held that brought a civilian into the presidency for the first time since 1964. A new constitution, enacted in 1988, reinstated core civil liberties that are the hallmark of any democracy, including robust protections for free speech and a free press that exceed even those offered by the First Amendment to the US Constitution. And in 1989, Brazilians directly elected their first president since the 1961 election, marking the return of democracy.

Many historians identify the tipping point that led to the toppling of the regime as the 1975 murder of Vladimir Herzog, a leftist Jewish journalist who had fled to Brazil in the 1940s after German fascists seized power in his Croatian homeland in Yugoslavia. Herzog was one of the most vocal, prominent, and influential critics of the dictatorship in Brazil. As I myself am a Jewish journalist and immigrant to Brazil—albeit one who began living in the country twenty years after its return to democracy— Herzog's murder, motivated by his dissenting journalism, always struck a chord with me.

On October 24, 1975, Herzog—then the editor in chief of a popular semipublic outlet called *Culture TV* and a journalism professor in São Paulo—received a summons to appear before the most notorious interrogation unit of the military regime, the Department of Information Operations—Center for Internal Defense Operations (DOI-CODI). Though he had been a member of the Brazilian Communist Party (PCB), Herzog had no involvement in the armed resistance. He thus appeared the next day, assuming he would be questioned and released. Instead, he was detained on the spot. By the next morning, he was dead. The regime issued a press release claiming Herzog had committed suicide in his prison cell.

Because it was so common for the military to stage suicides to cover up their murder-by-torture of dissidents, and because Herzog, a husband and father of two small children, had voluntarily appeared after receiving a summons, public skepticism was widespread. Journalists and activists sardonically described Herzog has having "committed suicide by dictatorship." To placate the public doubts, the military released a photograph of Herzog hanging by a belt in his cell.

Photo released by Brazilian military showing Vladimir Herzog hanged in his cell, October 25, 1975. Photo by Silvado Leung Vieira.

Citing the Jewish tradition of burying the dead quickly, the government transferred Herzog's body to the custody of his rabbi. Upon examining Herzog's body, Rabbi Henry Sobel went public with his findings: "There was no doubt that he had been tortured and murdered." Herzog's synagogue, in an act of brave defiance, pointedly buried Herzog in their standard cemetery, rather than in a separate plot for those who committed suicide, thus directly repudiating the military regime's account of his death.

Though the military staunchly denied the allegations, the Brazilian public, by then increasingly distrustful of the regime, largely believed that Herzog had been murdered by his own government. In 1978, in a remarkable development, a federal judge ruled that the military regime bore direct responsibility for his death. However, only in 2012 did Brazil, in a newly issued obituary, officially acknowledge that Herzog's "suicide" had been staged in order to conceal the fact that he had been tortured to death.

Herzog's murder mobilized protests against the military regime that were as large as any since the 1968 enactment of the dictatorial AI-5 decree. Despite significant efforts by the regime to block their transit, more than eight thousand protesters gathered outside the São Paulo cemetery where Herzog was being buried. Among them were numerous public figures, including the French philosopher Michel Foucault.

Years later, Rabbi Sobel remarked that the "murder of Herzog was the catalyst for the return of democracy." Indeed, within eighteen months of Herzog's murder, as similar stories of torture, censorship, and murder emerged, massive streets demonstrations had become commonplace in the nation's largest cities. Brazilians had had enough of the military regime.

— — — — — — — — — —

That Brazil's 1985 redemocratization improved political life is beyond dispute, but it was far from a panacea. Even with the establishment of moderately healthy democratic institutions since then, the country's politics have been unstable, rough, driven by systemic corruption, and not infrequently plagued by violence and nostalgia for authoritarian rule.

Unlike other countries haunted by past dictatorships, where repression is a distant memory, roughly half of the current population of Brazil lived through some part of the dictatorship. As memories of its horrors become more distant, and the failures of democracy more vivid and more present, more and more Brazilians remember that era with fondness rather than terror.

Since the first direct presidential election in 1989, two of the country's first four elected presidents have been impeached, including Dilma in 2016. The country has also never fully escaped its colonial relationship with the United States, which still regards Latin America as its "backyard" to control. I learned that lesson firsthand during my reporting on NSA whistleblower Edward Snowden, when I received a call in late 2013 from one of the most well-known and accomplished national security journalists in the United States. He told me that, even three decades after the end of the military dictatorship, Brazil remained the country with the largest CIA presence in the hemisphere, and that some sectors of the Brazilian military and intelligence services remained highly subservient to the US and UK governments—a result of bonds formed during the military regime.

He also confirmed what had been widely suspected: that email and telephone communications of mine and my husband were being monitored by Washington and London. He suggested that this was likely happening as a result of friendly factions within the Brazilian Intelligence Agency (ABIN), a domestic counterpart to the CIA. That our phones and emails were indeed subject to electronic surveillance was confirmed when David successfully sued the UK government, forcing it to provide an explanation for why he was detained for twelve hours in London's Heathrow Airport in August 2013, as he was traveling back home after meeting the journalist Laura Poitras in Berlin: their response justifying his detention was based on our private communications, which they had obviously monitored. It is unlikely, given the precautions we were taking, that this could have been accomplished without cooperation from rogue factions in Brazilian intelligence.

Despite such security cooperation, Brazil has made great strides in forging its own independent foreign policy and identity. Particularly under the 2003–2011 presidency of Luiz Inácio Lula da Silva, Brazil moved away—sometimes quite radically—from US control. For years under Lula, as Brazil experienced an economic and cultural resurgence, there was talk of a new and powerful alliance that would finally offer a counterweight to US hegemony, composed of the "emerging nations" of Brazil, Russia, India, China, and South Africa (the so-called BRICS).

Still traumatized by the way it was abused and exploited during the Cold War, Brazil adopted a policy of steadfast neutrality, prioritizing the maintenance of amiable commercial relations. Under this rubric, it built a diplomatic corps that developed a reputation as one of the best and most sophisticated in the world.

In the early months of 2010, Lula infuriated the administration of President Barack Obama, which was working to isolate Iran and force it to accept a lopsided nuclear agreement. Behind the back of the United States, Lula's government worked with President Recep Tayyip Erdoğan of Turkey to offer Iran a much more favorable deal.

When Lula and Erdoğan appeared with President Mahmoud Ahmadinejad of Iran to announce their agreement on a peace plan that May, US officials strongly denounced them. "We have very serious disagreements with Brazil's diplomacy vis-à-vis Iran," said Secretary of State Hillary Clinton. To the United States and establishment media outlets, the audacity of Turkey and especially Brazil forging their own foreign policy in a way that diverged from US dictates was intolerable. "Shameful," said *New York Times* columnist Thomas Friedman in an op-ed that reserved its most virulent rage for Lula, adding about the joint agreement with Iran, "That's about as ugly as it gets." Friedman quoted Moisés Naím, then editor in chief of the establishment journal *Foreign Policy* (and a former official in a right-wing Venezuelan government) to proclaim: "Lula is a political giant, but morally he has been a deep disappointment."

In Friedman's column, Naím denounced Lula on the grounds that he "has supported the thwarting of democracy across Latin America." What proof was cited in support of this accusation? As Friedman put it: "He regularly praises Venezuela's strongmen Hugo Chávez and Fidel Castro, the Cuban dictator—and now Ahmadinejad—while denouncing Colombia, one of the great democratic success stories, because it let U.S. planes use Colombian airfields to fight narco-traffickers." In other words, Lula was somehow guilty of "thwarting democracy across Latin America" because he supported the democratically elected and unquestionably popular president of Venezuela (Chávez), while also criticizing Colombia for being too subservient to the United States and enabling an American military presence in Latin America. It was this modest disobedience to US interests that earned Lula such grave denunciation in the West's most influential newspaper by its star foreign policy columnist.

Other US media stars were even more scathing in their denunciation of Lula for his crime of forging an independent course. *Washington Post* editorialist Jackson Diehl—writing under the headline "Has Brazil's Lula Become Iran's Useful Idiot?"—wrote, "Lula is providing Iran with valuable time to delay sanctions, even as it presses ahead with enrichment and prepares a new generation of centrifuges to do it more efficiently." Illustrating the fury that US journalists feel whenever a country acts in defiance of Washington, Diehl insisted that Lula's motives were selfish and egotistical: a desire to demonstrate independence from the United States, as if that were a sin:

> So why would Lula jump in? For the same reason as Turkish Prime Minister Recep Tayyip Erdogan: to prove that his country is an emerg-

ing world power that is capable of acting independently—and defying the United States. It doesn't matter to Lula that his diplomacy has no chance of succeeding. What matters are the wire service stories describing Brazil as "an emerging world player" and Lula himself as one of the globe's most influential leaders.

Diehl complained bitterly that the Obama administration appeared unwilling to impose "consequences for Lula"—as if he were a child in need of punishment by a stern parent—and said the failure by the United States was sending a clear message: "In other words: Lula, go ahead and grandstand." That Brazil and Turkey may have genuinely different views than the United States about how to achieve peace with Iran, and different national interests to pursue, was unthinkable to Diehl.

To elite Western institutions, any display by Brazil of an independent foreign policy aimed at averting global conflict was proof of recklessness. But to tens of millions of Brazilians, this agreement struck by Lula in cooperation with Erdoğan signified the arrival of Brazil on the world stage—and perhaps even more importantly, the emancipation of Brazil from US control.

Whatever the achievements it made in projecting itself internally, the process of democratization in Brazil never made a major dent in the country's notorious and brutal wealth disparity. Even Lula's presidency only scratched the surface of those inequities. And the country's oligarchical class, which thrived by serving the military regime, remains as dominant as ever.

Two competing national slogans highlight Brazil's aspirations and its seeming inability to escape the problems of its past. "God is Brazilian" expresses the unique gifts the country and its people possess, while "Brazil: Always the Country of the Future" laments its seemingly eternal failure to fulfill its potential.

━ ━ ━ ━ ━ ━ ━ ━ ━ ━

Brazil's size, unique diversity and culture, natural resources, wealth, and political influence have always made the country impossible to write off, no matter how intractable its problems seem.

To begin with, the country's massive oil reserves, including much of the planet's so-called pre-salt reserves, are of particular geostrategic and environmental importance. "Pre-salt" is a geological designation for oil that is extremely old and thus buried far deeper in the earth than standard petroleum. That makes its extraction more difficult and expensive, but it also provides far more potential in terms of volume than most of the world's remaining reserves. Brazil's Petrobras first discovered the massive pre-salt reserves in 2006, but it is still unknown just how large they are. What is beyond doubt is that the oil is of immense value to a world still dependent on fossil fuels, yet whose reserves are dwindling.

Beyond the sprawling, untapped pre-salt petroleum, the country controls the vast majority of the environmental asset scientists around the world agree is the single most important, by far, for averting global catastrophic climate scenarios: the Amazon. In recent years, the centrality of the Amazon for the planet's future survival has been catapulted from the realm of obscure technical knowledge of climate scientists into that of mainstream global concern.

The Amazon's primary value lies in its capacity to absorb carbon dioxide, a key catalyst for global warming. As a comprehensive Associated Press article about the region explained, "Currently, the world is emitting around 40 billion tons of CO_2 into the atmosphere every year. The Amazon absorbs 2 billion tons of CO_2 per year (or 5 percent of annual emissions), making it a vital part of preventing climate change."

The context for that AP article—and literally thousands more like it from around the world—was that in mid-2019, the world was watching in horror as the Brazilian Amazon burned. French president Emmanuel Macron spoke for much of the world when he posted the following tweet:

Emmanuel Macron ✓
@EmmanuelMacron

Our house is burning. Literally. The Amazon rain forest –
the lungs which produces 20% of our planet's oxygen – is
on fire. It is an international crisis. Members of the G7
Summit, let's discuss this emergency first order in two
days! #ActForTheAmazon

These Amazon fires, largely the result of ranchers and farmers illegally clearing the land, were so globally alarming because they signified serious regression in the fight against climate deterioration at a time when
radical progress is most sorely needed. As the AP article detailed, "Fires
in the Amazon not only mean the carbon-absorbing forest is disappear-
ing, but the flames themselves are emitting millions of tons of carbon
every day." It cited the Brazilian climate scientist Carlos Nobre, who
warned that "we're close to a 'tipping point' that would turn the thick
jungle into a tropical savannah."

The fires rapidly elevated Brazil's importance to the world, largely
because so many realized that these fires had ignited not spontaneously
or due to natural causes, but as a direct result of policy and ideology. Specifically, the policies and ideology of one man: Jair Bolsonaro, who, after
serving for almost thirty years on the fringes of political life, shocked the
country, the continent, and the world by winning the 2018 presidential
election, thereby becoming one of the most fanatical and unstable far-
right extremists to govern any large democracy in quite some time.

Bolsonaro has long railed against the protections accorded to the
indigenous tribes of Brazil and to the Amazon territory where they have

lived for centuries. Along with his defense of all forms of military and police violence, the aggressive exploitation of the Amazon is one of the few core beliefs Bolsonaro has championed consistently throughout his decades as a politician. For that reason, his presidential candidacy was supported by the nation's extremely powerful, and very rich, agricultural and logging industries, long before it was viewed as viable. Indeed, they were eager to find a president who would unleash commercial interests without the slightest regard for the environmental value of the Amazon or the survival of the indigenous tribes.

In fact, nobody paying close attention to Brazil was surprised by the Amazon fires, caused by the very industries that now compose such a vital part of his base of support. The increase in their number, as Nobre explained in the AP report, is because the cattle ranchers and farmers that set them "think law enforcement won't punish them." The report continued, "President Jair Bolsonaro has decreased the power and autonomy of forest protection agencies, which he says get in the way of licensing for developing land and accuses of being 'fines industries.'"

Bolsonaro all but made deforestation an explicit goal, and his choice for environment minister, the previously obscure Ricardo Salles, touted rifle bullets as the "solution" for indigenous tribes, environmental and homeless activists, and "the left" generally. In his short stint as a local environmental official in the state of São Paulo, Salles was convicted of administrative improprieties for forged environmental studies published by his office and was barred from seeking elective office for three years—two weeks before he was appointed environment minister by Bolsonaro in December 2018. That a resource as vital as the Amazon is now in the hands of these two fanatics is alone reason that the world must pay attention to Brazil; the horrific fires that have raged in Brazil are directly attributable to their actions, and will only continue and worsen if they remain unconstrained.

Even in his support for the Amazon's destruction, Bolsonaro is following the ethos of the military dictatorship that he admires. Thousands of indigenous citizens were killed during that era by a regime intent on developing and exploiting the Amazon, regardless of the human, cultural, environmental, or other costs. Indeed, the leaders of the 1964 coup frequently spoke of Brazil's indigenous with a level of contempt only slightly less explicit than Bolsonaro's.

But an eagerness to destroy the Amazon for short-term profit is just one of the attributes that makes Bolsonaro so dangerous. He is as unhinged in his comportment as he is neofascistic in his ideology. Far more chilling than Bolsonaro's adolescent and reckless behavior—such as his mockery of the physical appearance of Macron's wife in response to the French president's viral tweet—are his core beliefs, which had for years relegated him to the role of clownish sideshow rather than that of a legislator of any significance.

After Brazil's 1985 redemocratization, it was taboo in any mainstream precinct to speak favorably about the military dictatorship. It had, after all, dismantled basic liberties and ruled with violence, torture, and savagery that terrorized the population for two decades. But Bolsonaro violated this taboo repeatedly, vocally, and gleefully. An army captain during the years of the dictatorship, he was expelled in 1988 for planning to detonate small bombs on military installations in protest of what he regarded as the unjustly low salary received by soldiers. He had previously been disciplined by the military for publishing an article in the widely circulated *Veja* magazine that denounced soldiers' pay, an act that also turned him into a minor celebrity among supportive soldiers. He launched his political career that year with a successful run for city council of Rio de Janeiro, on a pro-military platform.

Despite his eventual expulsion from the military, he remained an ardent and explicit fan of the regime, defending the 1964 coup as a "democratic and popular revolution," calling the era of dictatorship "glorious," and insisting for three decades that Brazil was better off under despotism than under democracy. He went out of his way to justify the use of torture against domestic dissidents, praising the military regime's most notorious torturers. In 1999, he said he would "without doubt" close Congress if he became president.

Indeed, Bolsonaro has often said that his only criticism of the military dictatorship is that it did not go far enough—specifically, that it did not kill enough people. In a now-iconic 1999 television appearance, Bolsonaro said, "Voting won't change anything in this country. Nothing! Things will only change, unfortunately, after starting a civil war here, and doing the work the dictatorship didn't do. Killing some 30,000 people, and starting with FHC [Fernando Henrique Cardoso, the center-right president at the time]. If some innocents die, that's just fine." Similarly, in 2015, Bolsonaro responded to an Amnesty International report that Brazil's police kills more people than any other country by saying, "I think what the Military Police has to do is kill more." As journalist Vincent Bevins wrote in the *New York Review of Books* in 2018: "Bolsonaro is not merely nostalgic for that era; he would reintroduce the dictatorship's political ethos, preserved and intact, into modern Brazil. . . . What Bolsonaro offers is an explicit return to the values that underpinned Brazil's brutal dictatorship."

As Bolsonaro's presidential candidacy strengthened through 2018, the Western press—which has never paid much attention to Brazil—struggled to convey who he was. They called him the "Trump of the Tropics," which they believed was an insulting nickname; in reality, it was far too cute, provincial, and ethnocentric to be anything other than wildly misleading. That nickname also had the unintended effect of normalizing Bolsonaro in Brazil. After decades of being told Brazil is a "developing country" or part of the "Third World" and "global South," many Brazilians felt, not unreasonably, that if Bolsonaro were similar to the president of the richest and most powerful country on the planet, he must be doing something right.

Yet for so many reasons—from Bolsonaro's explicit admiration for torture and killing to his unique mix of militarism, religious fervor, anti-gay fixation, and anti-communist obsession—Bolsonaro is unlike other modern far-right leaders such as Trump, Marine Le Pen, or the Brexit leaders in the United Kingdom. He's far darker and more menacing; indeed, in mentality, disposition, ideology, and ultimate vision, he is more like President Rodrigo Duterte of the Philippines or even General al-Sisi of Egypt.

Whatever else one might say about him, Bolsonaro is a charismatic figure and talented demagogue who knows how to attract attention and manipulate people's worst, most primal drives. He has built a political dynasty. Three of his sons are prominent elected officials in Brazil: the oldest, Flavio, was a state legislator representing Rio de Janeiro for a decade and was elected with an overwhelming vote total to the Federal Senate in the same 2018 election that brought his father to the presidency; his youngest political son, Eduardo, is a federal representative from São Paulo who was reelected in 2018 with the largest vote total for a member of Congress in the history of Brazilian democracy; and the middle political son, Carlos, is a longtime member of Rio de Janeiro's city council and the mastermind of his father's online network of fake news and hate-driven attacks against the family's critics.

Conjuring the image of deposed Iraqi dictator Saddam Hussein's sons Uday and Qusay, Bolsonaro's sons are all very similar to him, yet somehow even worse. Shortly before Bolsonaro's election as president, Eduardo spoke openly about how easy it would be to close the Supreme Court (STF) if it ruled that his father's campaign had violated election laws: "Dude, if you want to shut down the [Supreme Court], do you know what you do? You don't even send a jeep. Send a soldier and a corporal." He then added, even more menacingly: "What is the STF? It takes its power from the pen of an STF minister. If you arrest an STF minister, do you think there will be a popular demonstration in favor of the STF minister, millions on the streets?"

In 2019, as approval of the president's administration plunged, Eduardo—whom his father had tried and failed to appoint as Brazil's ambassador to the United States—issued a public threat. He said that if political street protests against his father took place in Brazil, the way street protesters in Chile were demanding an end to harsh austerity measures at the time, there would be a restoration of AI-5—the terrifying decree that Brazil's military dictatorship issued to summarily abolish any residual democratic rights and establish Brazil as an absolute tyranny.

Meanwhile, almost immediately after his father's election as president, Senator Flavio Bolsonaro became engulfed in a scandal that is still unfolding, involving close connections on the part of the whole family to violent paramilitary gangs. These militias, composed of rogue current and former members of the Military Police, rule Rio de Janeiro with tactics that make the Italian mafia seem like pacifists.

One of the Bolsonaros' most potent and reliable political weapons is religious fanaticism—a variant that mixes ostensible Catholicism with Latin American evangelical fervor—which the entire family uses to stimulate widespread hatred against Brazil's LGBT population. Indeed, anti-LGBT fervor has become one of their signature issues: President Bolsonaro infamously told *Playboy* that he'd rather learn that his son were dead than gay; one of his only proposed laws in Congress was a bill to ban same-sex couples from adopting children, despite the tens of thousands of Brazilian children who linger in shelters and orphanages without parents; and, he ran his 2018 presidential campaign on a claim that gay men were trying to infiltrate schools, using a fictitious tool he called a "gay kit," which he told parents across the country was being used by gay people and their teacher allies to indoctrinate youth and turn their children gay.

What made Bolsonaro's election particularly jarring was that it was such a radical shift from Brazil's recent political history. Brazil has never been anything close to a far-right country. To the contrary, the prior four presidential elections before Bolsonaro's 2018 victory were all won by the center-left Workers' Party (PT). Bolsonaro was preceded by that party's founder, Lula—a factory worker born to extreme poverty who was illiterate until the age of ten—and his anointed successor, Dilma—a former Marxist guerilla and the first female president of the country.

How did Brazil leap from being a center-left country that fit comfortably into the mainstream ideological wing of the Western neoliberal order to one ruled by a figure as extreme as Bolsonaro? Here, and only here, is the comparison to Trump helpful, since a similar question can be asked, and a similar answer provided, about the United States: How did a country that twice elected Barack Obama suddenly empower Donald Trump in the White House? Or, how did a country as integrated into Europe as the United Kingdom suddenly opt for "Brexit," despite all the clear evidence of the harm that would result, especially for the members of the working classes who voted for it?

As has happened in so many countries, the failure of Brazil's establishment—and particularly its prevailing neoliberal ideology—had left so many people so angry with the political system that they were willing to gamble on anyone who could successfully portray themselves as an enemy of the political class the population (rightly) blames for so much of their suffering and deprivation.

Prior to Bolsonaro's rise, a convergence of crises had engulfed Brazil: an economic crisis that was due at least in part to the 2008 financial collapse caused by Wall Street; a crisis in public security that came with skyrocketing poverty and unemployment; a murder rate that was comparable to Baghdad at the height of the US occupation of Iraq; and a massive corruption scandal, driven by the probe known as Operation Car Wash, that implicated almost every major political party (including the long-governing Workers' Party), as well as the country's richest oligarchs and its most powerful companies (with the state-owned Petrobras, once Brazil's national pride, at the center of it all).

The widespread popular rage toward the political establishment that propelled Bolsonaro's victory was many years in the making. And the evidence for it could be heard by anyone listening to the Brazilian people.

Perhaps one of the first signs of the intensity and ubiquity of the disgust with the political process were the sustained and rancorous street protests of 2013. The protests began with a narrow and provincial cause: an increase in bus and subway fares of twenty Brazilian cents (equivalent to five US cents) across the country, which hurt those who could least afford to pay: the country's poorest laborers and the lower-middle-classes, who exclusively used public transit to commute to work, often crammed into buses and trains for hours during their commute from the cities' impoverished peripheries to their upper-middle-class neighborhoods and corporatized downtowns.

At first, the specificity of the issue that provoked the protests meant that relatively few people attended. But soon, the grievances expressed at the protests expanded, and so, too, did the crowd sizes. Within weeks, the protests became the largest demonstrations Brazil had seen since millions took to the streets in 1992 to successfully demand the impeachment of President Fernando Collor de Mello, who was part of a grave corruption scandal.

The protests quickly became a general vehicle for the registration of anger: with Dilma's government, corruption, and unemployment; with rising violent crime, profiteering associated with the approaching 2014 FIFA World Cup, and the *Globo* broadcasting empire; and with the political class generally. Throughout June and July 2013, two million Brazilians from across the political spectrum ended up in the streets at various points. Even as Brazil's largest media outlets—led by *Globo*—vehemently denounced the protesters as vandals and idle malcontents, in the process becoming main targets of their anger, polls showed that more than 80 percent of the population were sympathetic to the protesters and their various causes, however ill-defined.

The protests defied easy ideological categories, and virtually no power center or mainstream institution was spared. Shortly after the protests began unfolding around the country, President Dilma Rousseff herself became one of their primary targets—a bitter irony for a party that claimed to represent the very working-class people who were the victims of the bus fare increase. Ugly and thuggish governmental attempts to repress the protests with police violence only fueled their growth.

Efforts by Dilma and by the Congress to appease the protesters—including the rescindment of the fare increase that originally sparked the demonstrations, as well as the withdrawal of a series of measures designed to make it more difficult to prosecute corrupt politicians—did little to assuage the unbottled rage. Though the protests gradually reduced in size, the reverberations extended far beyond the marches.

The rapid transformation of the 2013 protests was an early sign that Brazilians were deeply angry. More importantly, the protests showed that their anger was not reserved for any one party or any single ideology, but for anyone and everyone who wielded power in Brazil.

In this critical regard, Bolsonaro's ascension to power was driven not so much by agreement with his ideology, but rather by a pervasive and justified disgust with ruling institutions and their prevailing orthodoxies. That Bolsonaro had been ejected from the mainstream precincts of "decency," and that he was so clearly feared and despised by mainstream institutions, became one of his most powerful political assets. Bolsonaro is a gifted demagogue who succeeded in channeling the hatred that elite institutions harbored against him to his own advantage.

Anyone who is hated by the political system that we despise and the elites who control it, and who promises to burn it and them down to the ground, is on our side. This mentality explains the otherwise-inexplicable phenomenon of so many people in the United States voting for Barack Obama in 2008 as he promised to usher in substantial "change," and then for Donald Trump in 2016 when he promised to "drain the swamp." Both these "outsiders," despite their obvious ideological differences, shared the much more important quality of appearing to be adversarial to the hated establishment. Indeed, the notion of Trump the billionaire real estate mogul and NBC star as an "outsider" is only slightly more ridiculous than the outsider image of Obama, who went from Columbia University to Harvard Law School to the US Senate before running against the establishment.

Bolsonaro, while not a billionaire or Harvard Law graduate, is no more an outsider than Trump or Obama. After all, Bolsonaro spent three decades in politics, representing the most corrupt state in the country—Rio de Janeiro—as a member of eight different political parties, several of which were implicated in the Operation Car Wash anti-corruption probe. And, during his 2018 presidential campaign, he vowed to empower Paulo Guedes as his economics minister, touting him as a University of Chicago–trained academic who would follow the Pinochet model of privatizing industry and slashing social benefits—not exactly an antiestablishment icon.

Like Obama and Trump, though, Bolsonaro was far enough outside of elite political circles that he could convincingly depict himself as their adversary. And all three successfully spoke to the anger and sense of betrayal of tens of millions of people.

Many Brazilians voted for Bolsonaro—including many of David's and my friends, some of whom are black, some of whom are working-class or favela residents, and some of whom are LGBT or close friends of the LGBT community. They did so not because of his history of hateful and extremist comments, bigotry, and support for tyranny, but despite them. They did so from desperation: when you can't find work that provides a living wage, when your children have no access to health care or drinkable water, when you have reasonable grounds to worry each day as your children leave for school that they will not come home alive because of indiscriminate street violence, and when you watch a tiny portion of the population prosper from a political system that seems to care only for their own interests while harboring contemptuous indifference to your plight, it's not irrational to send in an agent of chaos to disrupt and even destroy the political system—even if you don't believe that he's actually competent to fix it or well intentioned enough to try.

At the very least, people confronting such deprivation will be highly susceptible to angry scapegoating and easy solutions: kill all criminals, restore public morality through religion, wipe out corruption. That's the formula used by countless right-wing demagogues for the last century to seize power, and that's what worked so effectively for Bolsonaro in 2018.

The more the perceived enemies of the popular classes, or at least those who seemed contemptuously indifferent to their deprivations (perfectly coiffed *Globo* stars in glittery Rio and São Paulo studios, or "well-respected" political luminaries), expressed their horror at Bolsonaro's latest pronouncements and issued pompous decrees about his unsuitability to occupy the presidency, the more his backers delighted in the suffering and upset that Bolsonaro caused them. That's a dynamic that should sound familiar to US voters, where the candidate who was endorsed by fifty-seven of the nation's leading newspapers lost the 2016 election to the candidate who so horrified them that he received the endorsement of only two. It's a dynamic that is also increasingly familiar to Western Europeans as they watch Brexit and the rise of once-unthinkable far-right parties.

As the celebrated scholar and activist Noam Chomsky has noted on many occasions, popular contempt for elite institutions and political insiders is driving election results across the democratic world. While no elite institution in Brazil was spared this scorn, the Workers' Party generated unusually high levels of animosity—not unexpected for the party that occupied the presidency from 2002 until Dilma's impeachment in 2016, and that for all those years was one of the largest parties in Congress, when it was not in the majority.

Just as Trump in 2016 successfully channeled widespread distrust and contempt for Hillary Clinton, Bolsonaro was able to tap into not just generalized anger, but specific anti-PT sentiment to defeat Fernando Haddad, the Workers' Party candidate backed by Lula. Even many on the left were angry that Lula, despite knowing how widespread anti-PT anger was, insisted on anointing a highly competent but little-known one-term mayor from his own party, rather than throwing his support behind the viable center-left candidate and former governor Ciro Gomes—who, as the leader of a different party, was free of the anti-PT sentiment that had been building for years.

But that criticism of Lula, valid though it may be, relies on the dubious assumption that Bolsonaro would have lost to a non-PT center-left candidate. One can never know the outcome of this counterfactual with certainty, but it's highly likely that 2018 was simply Bolsonaro's moment, and that nobody, perhaps not even Lula, could have stopped him. So pervasive and deep was the antiestablishment rage in Brazil that, as has happened in so many other countries, only the candidate who appeared most adversarial to ruling elites could win a majority of votes.

In Brazil, the 2018 ascension of Bolsonaro to the presidential palace was accompanied by a far-right tidal wave that swept into various halls of power a herd of previously obscure figures. Bolsonaro's party—which barely existed prior to 2018—elected the second-highest number of members to the National Congress, just one seat behind the long-dominant Workers' Party. Seemingly without warning, Brazil had been transformed from a standard center-left country into the latest addition to the global axis of repressive, authoritarian, far-right regimes. But this did not happen overnight. Instead, it was the by-product of trends that had grown over decades, rendering the population ready to explode the political system that they held responsible for the nation's many crises.

Whatever the causes, the 2018 election installed a government guided by a far-right ideology more violent, hate-driven, and archaic in its bigotries than can be seen in any other large democracy. One went to sleep in Brazil before the 2018 election in a seemingly stable and steadfastly democratic country, yet woke up the next day in a country where democratic values are threatened and the viability of core civic liberties is very much in doubt.

That remains the political climate in my adopted country, where my husband and I live with our two Brazilian children. And it was in this climate that I spent most of 2019 publishing leaked documents and doing highly controversial reporting that shook the Bolsonaro government to its core.

Chapter 2

— — — — — — — — —

THE JUDGE WHO PAVED BOLSONARO'S PATH TO POWER

I regard my journalistic exposés on corruption in Bolsonaro's Brazil as comparable, in several key aspects, to my reporting on NSA spying enabled by whistleblower Edward Snowden—and arguably more consequential. Though the two stories, journalistically speaking, were radically different in subject matter, they began in strikingly similar ways. In each case, an anonymous source emerged who made convincing claims to having a massive archive of secret information regarding powerful political figures and institutions.

In early May 2019, my new source told me that he had hacked into the telephones of some of Brazil's most powerful officials. He had spent weeks downloading years' worth of secret conversations, documents, videos, audio files, and other content sent and received by them using the encrypted Telegram app, the preferred platform of high-level Brazilian authorities for communicating in what they believed was a secure environment.

But my initial feeling that this Brazil leak would be similar to the Snowden story was quickly dispelled when I began talking with my husband, David Miranda. David, who was famously involved in the Snowden story when he was detained by British authorities at Heathrow Airport in 2013, is now a member of Brazil's National Congress, after serving two years on the city council of Rio de Janeiro. He felt this archive would be an entirely different animal.

To begin with, David pointed out, Bolsonaro had been in office barely five months when I was given this explosive material, much of which implicated key figures in the Bolsonaro government. That meant he was still enjoying the tail end of his honeymoon period, where his popularity was high and his movement still riding the adrenaline wave from such a resounding electoral victory. There had been no real Bolsonaro-era press freedom challenges yet, but he had repeatedly threatened the media during the campaign. Given Bolsonaro's overt admiration for the military dictatorship and his obvious desire to resuscitate at least some of its most repressive measures, it was just a matter of time before Brazil's basic civil liberties and the strength of its democratic institutions would be tested. Nobody knew what Bolsonaro was capable of, and it seemed clear that doing this reporting was going to provoke the first significant conflict of his presidency. But there was something that made the Brazil archive more dangerous still. The primary official whose corruption this archive exposed was, depending on how one looked at it, either the second-most powerful person in Brazil, or the most powerful person (which is how I saw it): Justice Minister Sérgio Moro.

Beginning in 2014, from his position as a low-level federal judge in the midsize city of Curitiba, Moro oversaw what began as a routine case involving a currency trader who was laundering money through a local gas station car wash. Following his arrest, the money launderer made an extraordinary claim: he said he had been involved in serious crimes with the nation's most powerful politicians and business leaders, and that he was willing to spill everything he knew about their corruption in exchange for leniency.

As it turned out, the man, Alberto Youssef, was not bluffing. He had indeed been involved as a fixer in complex corruption schemes involving the richest and most powerful people in the country—including an elaborate kickback and bribery scheme relating to Brazil's state-owned oil company, Petrobras. And with that, the most sweeping anti-corruption probe in the country's history had essentially fallen into Judge Moro's lap, and Moro made the most of it. Over the next four years, he presided over the trials and convictions of dozens of high-profile figures, including billionaires and famous political officials, which ultimately became known as Operation Car Wash, a nod to the probe's humble beginnings. Judge

Moro imposed harsh sentences, was famously intolerant of any calls for leniency, and used innovative, controversial, and repressive legal practices to secure convictions.

Brazilians across the political spectrum came to view Moro as a symbol of hope, integrity, and probity in a country whose population had impotently endured systemic corruption for as long as most Brazilians could remember. After a year or so of blockbuster revelations and convictions, polls showed that nobody even came close to Moro's level of popularity and approval.

Along with his appearance on the *Time* 100 list, the *Financial Times*, in December 2019, named Moro one of the decade's "fifty most influential figures" in the world—the only Brazilian to appear on the list—along with Barack Obama, Angela Merkel, Vladimir Putin, Donald Trump, Mark Zuckerberg, and Saudi crown prince Mohammed bin Salman. So great was Moro's popular support that no politicians or even superior courts were willing to challenge or question him. Brazil's largest media outlets—never bastions of plurality of opinion under the best of circumstances—became his biggest fans, featuring close to unanimous reverence and praise.

Moro's popular support made him virtually invulnerable, even when he acted with seeming lawlessness. Everyone feared him, including the judges ostensibly above him whose duty was to overturn his rulings when they exceeded the limits of the Constitution or other legal doctrines. But no matter how dubious and reckless Moro's legal doctrines became, his rulings were upheld and affirmed almost as a matter of course, with a few rare and ultimately harmless exceptions.

As Judge Moro's popularity grew, so did his ambitions. In 2017, he finally secured what had long been regarded as the greatest catch of the Car Wash probe: the imprisonment of former president Luiz Inácio Lula da Silva. Lula had previously attained his own folk hero status in Brazil. One of eight children who grew up dirt poor in Brazil's most impoverished region, the Northeast, he suffered numerous tragedies, including the death from hepatitis of his first wife while she was eight months pregnant (along with the child). By the mid-1970s, while Brazil was still under military rule, Lula had become president of the metalworkers union and an outspoken advocate of a burgeoning left-wing ideology in Latin America.

By the early 1980s, when pro-democratization sentiments were growing, Lula's singular charisma established him as the left's most rousing and exciting figure. He parlayed his growing influence by cofounding the Workers' Party (PT), which rose in popularity among the Brazilian poor throughout the decade. Shortly after the party's founding, Lula was arrested and jailed for one month for leading what the military regime regarded as an illegal strike under its amorphous but potent National Security Law.

The Workers' Party soon began placing increasing numbers of its members in elected office. Lula himself was a candidate early on, including an unsuccessful run for governor of São Paulo. But in 1986, as redemocratization was underway, he was elected to the National Congress to represent São Paulo with a record-breaking number of votes, which established him as a powerful national force.

The first direct presidential election to be decided by popular vote since the 1964 coup took place in 1989, and twenty-two people announced their candidacy. Once Lula announced his, the socialist left consolidated behind him, while more mainstream liberal and even some left-wing factions supported a rival candidate. Outside of his strong base of supporters, few took Lula's candidacy seriously. In a country shaped by extreme wealth and income inequality, where the rich wielded unchallenged power, Lula was regarded with contempt and condescension by mainstream political and media forces, who saw him as an uneducated radical and crypto-communist.

In the first round of voting, though, Lula shocked the Brazilian establishment by placing second and making the runoff election. With 17 percent of the vote, he was the underdog against the consummate centrist candidate Fernando Collor de Mello, who had garnered 30 percent. The aristocratic Mello was not only the pure antithesis of the unkempt, working-class Lula; as the handsome son of a governor, husband to the heiress of an industrial family, and a former governor, he was the prototype of dynastic, plutocratic Brazilian politics.

The second-round runoff was a far closer contest than anyone had anticipated. Lula's charismatic, lively speeches were inspiring the country's long-suffering poor. As the prospect of a Lula presidency started to become a reality, the establishment center did what establishment centers do: parlayed all their resources and power to destroy Lula's candidacy without the slightest regard for truth or ethics.

Despite Lula's professed support for some form of social democracy, they relentlessly depicted him as a communist—a difficult label at the time of the fall of the Berlin Wall and collapse of the Soviet Union. Television ads bombarded the country, warning of the communist evils and isolation that awaited Brazil if Lula won. Perhaps most significantly, and notoriously, the country's overwhelmingly dominant *Globo* television network—just a few years away from its two-decade role as prime dictatorship supporter—did everything possible to sink Lula's candidacy, featuring a highly distorted and manipulative video of the final presidential debate on its flagship television program, *Jornal Nacional*, that made it appear Lula had been lost, confused, and humiliated.

The establishment tactics were sufficient to impede Lula's ascension to the presidency. Mello won by 54 to 46 percent. Still, Lula's vote total of thirty-one million, compared to Mello's thirty-five million, left no doubt that the forty-four-year-old Workers' Party leader would be a force to be reckoned with for years to come. When President Mello was impeached after a sprawling corruption scandal in 1992, less than two years into his term, it seemed only a matter of time before Brazil was governed by Lula.

It took longer than many expected for that to happen. After his narrow 1989 loss, Lula ran for president in the next two elections, in 1994 and 1998. Both times, Lula again came in second place to the center-right candidate, losing each time to the paradigmatic establishment figure Fernando Henrique Cardoso. Though he came in second, Lula failed in both of those elections to make the runoff, with Cardoso earning more than half of the vote in the first round.

To many, it seemed that Lula was going backward. Based on the emerging consensus in the Workers' Party that it would be impossible for any left-wing candidate—even Lula—to overcome the immensely powerful forces of the establishment determined to sabotage a PT candidacy, Lula and the party shifted tactics, endeavoring to make themselves more palatable to economic elites. With President Cardoso limited to two terms in office, Lula decided to do everything possible to finally win in 2002. He chose as his vice president a respected oligarch from the banking world, José Alencar, and wrote his iconic "Letter to the Brazilian

People," which repudiated any radical socialist aspirations, pledging to adhere to a moderate course that respected the free market—a pledge that would appease both domestic oligarchs and international capital.

Lula's moderating tactics were successful. On his fourth attempt, he was elected to the presidency in 2002. In the first round, he fell short of the 50 percent needed to avoid a runoff against Cardoso's hand-picked center-right successor, but in the second round, with the support of both the third- and fourth-place candidates, Lula was unstoppable. He cruised to victory, winning by twenty-three points with close to fifty-eight million votes.

Lula's presidency was almost immediately beset by problems: lingering economic woes from the Cardoso years, along with a sprawling corruption scandal known as "Mensalão," in which the Workers' Party was caught, along with other parties, buying and selling votes in Congress. But after weathering those early crises, Lula's presidency became a success beyond all expectations. Innovative social programs, including a guaranteed monthly payment to parents from the government in exchange for proof of school attendance and health care for children, lifted millions out of poverty for the first time. A steadily improving economy, an aversion to radical changes, and Brazil's rise in international prominence through its developing BRICS alliance with Russia, India, China, and South Africa appeased the opposition and even engendered some comfort with Lula's governance among the Brazilian elite. Rejecting the left's desire to democratize the media through legislative reform, Lula, for better or worse, even succeeded in placating the *Globo* empire by making clear he would not threaten its hegemony.

All of this led to a stunningly easy reelection victory in 2006. Although the first round of voting was somewhat close—Lula received just short of the 50 percent needed (48.6 percent), while his nearest competitor, center-right São Paulo governor Geraldo Alckmin, received 41.6 percent—Lula won easily in the second round with 60.8 percent of the vote.

It was in Lula's second term that his status as an iconic political leader was cemented. Having lifted tens of millions of Brazilians out of poverty with pioneering social programs praised even by Western think tanks and some capitalist media outlets, Lula was widely regarded as the planet's most successful political leader. When Barack Obama met Lula in 2009 at the G20 summit in London, the newly elected US president said, "That's my man right there. The most popular politician on earth." Lula's popularity ratings soared as the country experienced unprecedented economic growth. And Brazil's standing on the world stage rose with his political strength. Under Lula's presidency, Brazil became the first-ever Latin American country to be awarded the Summer Olympics with the successful bid to organize the 2016 games, and Lula also succeeded in securing Brazil as host to the 2014 FIFA World Cup. Domestically, as well, it seemed that everything Lula touched turned to gold. When he was term-limited out of office in 2010, his approval rating hovered near 90 percent.

So beloved was Lula that he was able to anoint his successor, the previously unknown and uncharismatic Dilma Rousseff. Though Dilma had in her youth been a Marxist guerilla fighter, she had in the subsequent decades become a competent but unglamorous technocrat. Through sheer force of will and personality, Lula convinced Brazilians to elect Dilma—a woman in a deeply patriarchal country—as their president.

Dilma's presidency, after a promising beginning, ran into every conceivable problem. Though she was very narrowly reelected against a center-right candidate in 2014 in a bitterly contested campaign, a convergence of crises and epidemics—including economic problems, street violence, and the Car Wash probe—doomed her presidency. Though Dilma was never charged with any crimes by the Car Wash operation, during the Lula years, she had been the president of Petrobras, the epicenter of the corruption scandal; therefore, most believed that she was at best responsible through negligence and indifference, while others held that she had deliberately ignored the corruption around her.

With approval ratings near single digits, Dilma was impeached in 2016 on the ground that she had committed so-called crimes of responsibility (the Brazilian equivalent of "high crimes and misdemeanors," the standard in the United States for impeaching a president). The principal accusation, obviously a pretext, was that she had invoked an obscure and highly technical budgetary maneuver called *pedaladas* ("peddling" in Portuguese, as on a bicycle) that enabled the government to borrow more credit from the state bank and for longer periods of time than the law allowed, thus making it appear that the deficit was lower than it really was.

What made Dilma's impeachment so preposterous was not the debate over whether she did or did not use this budgetary maneuver (an official study, issued after she was already removed, concluded that she had not). It was that in Brazilian politics—which has operated for decades on massive bribes to key officials in exchange for governmental favors—it was ludicrous to invoke an obscure budgetary infraction (often used by other Western leaders) as a basis for the impeachment of a sitting president. The farce of Dilma's impeachment became even more obvious when one considered who was leading the effort to remove her: a cast of characters composed almost entirely of career criminals and gangsters, politicians notorious for having bulging Swiss bank accounts and taking millions of dollars in bribes.

For the first year after her reelection in 2014, while longtime opponents of the Workers' Party never really overcame their seething anger over her narrow election win (the fourth consecutive PT presidential victory since 2002), Dilma's impeachment was little more than the pipe dream of *Globo* and the Brazilian far right. The Workers' Party had built a dominant coalition over the preceding one and a half decades in power, one that seemingly precluded the formation of any majority in support of her removal. But overnight, impeachment was transformed into a virtually inevitable reality when the then omnipotent speaker of the house, the evangelical fanatic Eduardo Cunha, decided to support it. Cunha, despite his hardcore social conservatism, had been a crucial coalition ally from the start of Dilma's presidency. In fact, Cunha's turn against her was in retaliation for the Workers Party's refusal to block an ethics probe into allegations that he had received millions of dollars, perhaps tens of millions, in bribes that he had stashed away in Swiss bank accounts. In other words, Dilma's impeachment—ostensibly necessitated by the need to combat corruption—was enabled by one of the region's most corrupt politicians, as vengeance for Dilma's refusal to protect him from corruption investigations.

Cunha became the face of Dilma's impeachment—and appropriately so. Unlike Dilma, whom nobody had ever accused of accepting an improper penny for personal wealth during her decades in politics, it was common knowledge that Cunha had become unimaginably wealthy by selling political favors for large bribes. Shortly after he presided over

Dilma's impeachment proceedings as the speaker of the lower house, Cunha—having served his purpose—was arrested and convicted for corruption, money laundering, and tax evasion. He is currently serving a fifteen-year prison term and has numerous other criminal cases against him pending.

The impeachment leaders—the men who surrounded Dilma and wanted her head on a pike—were almost all hardened criminals like Cunha. Once the lower house had impeached Dilma and sent her case to the Senate to be tried, one of the key leaders advocating for her conviction and removal was the center-right senator she narrowly defeated in the 2014 election, Aécio Neves. Like Cunha, Neves currently faces more than a dozen criminal cases, including charges that he plotted to kill his own cousin in order to silence him—a plan caught on tape and played to the nation after his leading role in the feigned outrage over Dilma's transgressions was concluded and Dilma removed from office.

These were the politicians who role-played righteous anger and moral indignation over Dilma's use of pedaladas to artificially reduce government debt. As the *Guardian* reported the evening of April 17, 2016, following the daylong lower house vote to impeach Dilma:

> Deputies were called one by one to the microphone by the instigator of the impeachment process, Cunha—an evangelical conservative who is himself accused of perjury and corruption—and one by one they condemned the president.
>
> Yes, voted Paulo Maluf, who is on Interpol's red list for conspiracy. Yes, voted Nilton Capixiba, who is accused of money laundering. "For the love of God, yes!" declared Silas Camara, who is under investigation for forging documents and misappropriating public funds.
>
> And yes, voted the vast majority of the more than 150 deputies who are implicated in crimes but protected by their status as parliamentarians.

Among the members of Congress flamboyantly waving the anti-corruption flag that boisterous day were Jair Bolsonaro and his son Eduardo. Both delivered particularly radical one-minute speeches when explaining their support for impeachment, with Jair paying homage to the military regime as he voted yes, while his son specifically heralded the nobility of the regime's most notorious torturer, Colonel Carlos Alberto Brilhante Ustra. With that, the Bolsonaros, with the entire nation watching, grafted themselves onto the anti-corruption movement driven by Moro and his Car Wash prosecutors.

None of this is to say that the Workers' Party is free of corruption: far from it. As Lula himself acknowledged in my first interview with him in 2016, the party was plagued by "grave" and systemic corruption. But concern with corruption was clearly not the motive for this group of gangsters in the capital to remove Dilma. This pretext revealed how easily the anti-corruption script could be cynically exploited to achieve political change outside of the ballot box and the democratic process.

Indeed, the anti-corruption fervor generated by Judge Moro and the Car Wash prosecutors became something akin to a state religion, or at least the only ideology that most of the population came to trust. With that anti-corruption weapon now aimed directly at Dilma and the Workers' Party, the same electorate that had just elected her eighteen months earlier overwhelmingly supported Dilma's removal from office in 2016.

However mendacious, Dilma's impeachment finally achieved what the enemies of the Workers' Party had for almost two decades failed to accomplish at the ballot box: the removal of the party from the presidency. Her impeachment resulted in the installation of her vice president, the little-known seventy-five-year-old career politician Michel Temer of the centrist Brazilian Democratic Movement Party (PMDB) to which lower house Speaker Eduardo Cunha also belonged.

The PMDB was a somewhat-noble historical political brand, as the successor to the "opposition" party that the military regime had allowed in order to maintain a democratic facade. Because its principal plank had been a restoration of democracy, it had long claimed a place in the hearts of many pro-democracy Brazilians. But by the time of Dilma's impeachment, the party had little to do with anything virtuous in its past. It was a purely transactional, nonideological party in the worst senses of those terms. The PMDB existed to empower whichever faction bestowed it with favors, influence, and wealth. Though it had few popular politicians, the party nonetheless elected huge numbers of officials across the country by systematically paying off drug traffickers and militias that controlled large neighborhoods representing tens or hundreds of thousands of votes. The idea that this party would be installed in the name of anti-corruption was laughable—akin to empowering Dick Cheney for the sake of pacifism. But that's precisely what Dilma's removal did.

Like Cunha and Aécio, Temer was an unreconstructed criminal, and everyone who worked to remove Dilma and install him as president—including the *Globo* stars who had united behind impeachment—knew it. While occupying the presidency for the two and a half remaining years of Dilma's term, Temer was caught on tape with a police informant plotting to pay bribes to various criminals, including his party compatriot Cunha, in order to silence them about corruption.

Even after Congress, along with the rest of the nation, had heard the bribery recordings, the very politicians that had impeached Dilma refused to impeach Temer. Nevertheless, within a short time, Temer's unpopularity drastically exceeded Dilma's. Illustrating the severity of the political crises plaguing the country prior to Bolsonaro's victory, his approval rating fell to *4 percent* in most polls.

Now that he, too, has served his purpose, Temer faces the same fate as Cunha. In 2019, he was twice arrested and jailed, only to be ordered freed by a court pending his various criminal trials. As of this writing, he is battling a multitude of criminal charges.

Dilma's impeachment taught Bolsonaro that waving the anti-corruption banner represented by Moro and Operation Car Wash would trump any other political considerations. And it taught much of the country that democratic elections were not all they were cracked up to be, that majorities make bad decisions at the ballot box that sometimes need to be reversed, that the outcome of the democratic process is far from sacrosanct, and that democracy, as Bolsonaro had spent three decades insisting, may not be the best way to choose leaders.

Chapter 3

— — — — — — — — — — —

THE SOURCE AND HIS ARCHIVE

On Mother's Day, May 12, 2019, I was at home in Rio de Janeiro with my husband David and our two sons when, at roughly noon, I received a call from a number I did not recognize. As is my custom with unknown callers, I didn't answer.

Less than a minute later, I received a message on WhatsApp from Manuela d'Ávila, one of Brazil's most popular and influential left-wing politicians. She said she needed to speak with me about what she described as an "URGENT" matter. That definitely caught my attention.

Manuela is from the city of Porto Alegre, in the southern state of Rio Grande do Sul. She graduated university with a journalism degree in 2003 and then, the following year, was elected to the city council at the age of twenty-three, making her the youngest-ever elected official in that city. At only twenty-six, she was elected to the National Congress representing Rio Grande do Sul, and then reelected with a massive vote total four years later.

From the start of her career, Manuela has been a member of the Communist Party of Brazil (PCdoB), which, despite its name, has become a pragmatic member of Brazil's long-governing center-left ruling coalition led by the Workers' Party. As a result, some of the more doctrinal Communist parties in Latin America view the party as unworthy of its title.

41

In 2014, Manuela gave up her seat in Congress to run for the state assembly in Rio Grande do Sul, arguing that she could have more of an impact working on local issues. She won easily, with a record vote for a candidate seeking that seat, but allies and friends told her they thought this "regression" back to local office would mean the end of what had seemed to be a skyrocketing national political career. In 2018, Manuela proved those prognostications wrong, taking center stage during that year's extremely contentious and highly consequential presidential election. After Lula was imprisoned in 2017 on a corruption conviction and then barred from seeking elective office, he endeavored, from his prison cell, to transfer his popularity to his chosen successor, former São Paulo mayor Fernando Haddad.

Once Haddad had secured his position as the 2018 presidential candidate for the Workers' Party, Haddad chose Manuela, at the age of thirty-seven, to be his vice presidential running mate. After a brutal first round of voting, which weeded out all of the other contenders except for two, Lula was able to sway enough votes to the Haddad/Manuela ticket to enable them to obtain a second-place finish and earn the right to face Jair Bolsonaro and his running mate, General Hamilton Mourão, in the second-round runoff.

In the three weeks between the first-round vote and the runoff, Haddad and Manuela traveled the country tirelessly, trying to warn the nation of the threat to democracy posed by Bolsonaro. But Bolsonaro's self-styled outsider, antiestablishment posture prevailed, and he won the election by twelve points. Despite the defeat, the consensus was that Manuela had performed with remarkable charisma and poise, and had reestablished herself as a future political star with national aspirations.

Prior to her message on Mother's Day 2019, I'd had only passing interactions with Manuela. In my capacity as a journalist for the Intercept, I had interviewed Manuela during the 2018 election. But when she called that day, I did not regard Manuela as a friend, which is why I initially regarded her Sunday message as so unusual. Moreover, Manuela is herself a mother, and as a longtime feminist, has made her efforts to balance that role with her career a public cause. That also made a call from her that Mother's Day altogether unexpected.

I quickly replied that I would call her back imminently, but asked if she was comfortable if I included David on the call. As a politician from the left-wing Socialism and Liberty Party (PSOL), David had his own acquaintance with Manuela, and while I speak Portuguese fluently, I wanted to make certain that I did not miss or misunderstand anything Manuela had to say. Most of all, as with anything of importance David and I do in our lives, we wanted to do it together.

David and I called Manuela from our bedroom, putting her on speaker phone. She then told us an extraordinary story—one that would change my life, David's life, and our family's life, as well as Brazilian politics, the Bolsonaro government, the reputations of some of the nation's most revered figures, the country's criminal justice system, and the fates of countless high-profile prisoners and accused criminals.

Earlier that day, Manuela explained, she had received a message from Brazilian senator Cid Gomes on the Telegram encrypted communications app. Founded by two Russian brothers, the app touts itself as being highly secure, and many high-profile Brazilians at the time used Telegram to avoid surveillance of their communication. But there have long been doubts raised by experts about its security, including most famously by Edward Snowden, the former NSA whistleblower. Snowden, echoed by many other information security experts, asserted, with strong evidence, that other apps such as Signal were far safer than Telegram, but it was the latter, for reasons nobody quite understands, that remained the choice for Brazilian authorities when it came to securing their communications.

Manuela told us that her first thought when seeing that Senator Gomes was messaging her "urgently" was that something terrible had happened to his brother Ciro—a very famous former governor and senator who had also run for president in 2018, coming in third behind Bolsonaro and the Haddad/Manuela ticket. But soon after replying to the message, Manuela realized that the person messaging her under his name was not Gomes. Instead, he was a hacker who had taken over the senator's Telegram account in order to speak with Manuela and to prove how serious his abilities were.

The hacker then told Manuela that he had the power to hack into *any* Telegram account. Indeed, he said, prior to hacking into Senator Gomes's account, he had also hacked into her own. To prove this, he sent Manuela copies of her private conversations with some of her closest friends and associates, including several famous politicians, that she had had on the app.

Manuela told us that her initial reaction was, understandably, fear that the hacker wanted to harm or blackmail her. But the hacker quickly assured Manuela that she was not his target and that she had nothing to worry about. To the contrary, he wanted to work with her on highly explosive materials he claimed to possess.

But if Manuela was not the hacker's target, who was? The hacker told her that he had hacked and downloaded, and then spent months reviewing, the Telegram accounts of Brazil's most powerful judges and prosecutors—including, most importantly, the Operation Car Wash anti-corruption task force. He had collected vast amounts of data: private chats with dozens of political, business, and media figures; drafts of documents; photos, audio files, videos—every conceivable type of communication. He said he had downloaded years' worth of their private communications, and that the archive of material he had gathered was gigantic.

That the primary subject, if not target, of this hack was Operation Car Wash made its incomparable importance immediately clear. The hacker told Manuela that he had found "mountains" of evidence showing serious, systemic wrongdoing and even illegalities on the part of the prosecutors.

He said he had contacted Manuela because he knew that, prior to entering politics, she had graduated from journalism school and worked as a journalist. "I want to give all of this information to you," he explained.

Manuela quickly interrupted the hacker to tell him that she could not receive any of the material. In order to run for vice president, she had given up her ability to seek reelection to her seat in the state assembly, which meant that she had none of the various legal immunities from prosecution enjoyed by Brazilian officials for acts in connection with their work. Moreover, she explained, she had not worked as a journalist for many years, had no team of journalists or editors to assist her, and would also likely lack the protections of immunity afforded to journalists by the Brazilian Constitution.

Manuela told the hacker that he needed to provide the material to a working journalist who had experience with leaks of this sort and who would have the legal protections and the professional ability to protect and report the material. "I'm thinking of Glenn Greenwald, who did the

Snowden case," the hacker told Manuela, asking what she thought and if she knew me. In response, Manuela told him she thought I would be the ideal reporter to work with, believing that the source saw Snowden as the model he wanted to replicate. She told him she would call me and see if I would speak to him.

Manuela asked whether I would be willing to speak to the source and, without hesitation—indeed, trying to stifle my excitement—I said I would. Manuela remained concerned about what the hacker might do with the access he had to her Telegram account, but she believed that he seemed genuine about his intentions as expressed to her: to expose corruption on the part of many of Brazil's most powerful political officials, beginning with President Bolsonaro's justice minister, Sérgio Moro.

The hacker told Manuela that he had no politics or ideology, and was adamant that no politician or party be protected from any of the incriminating information that might be contained in the archive. He repeatedly told her, she said, that he did not want any payment. "I only want justice," he stressed to her.

"I told him that he should work with you because you would treat the material journalistically, be judicious and careful with its contents," she said, "but not spare anyone whose bad acts could be demonstrated by the archive."

Manuela said the source requested that I contact him on Telegram, and she passed me his contact information. In light of the concerns voiced by Snowden and others, I had never even installed Telegram and so asked Manuela if he would use Signal. That the source had just proven Telegram's vulnerability made me even more eager to avoid using it for such a sensitive conversation. But Manuela said the source was adamant that we use that app.

It took roughly three minutes to install Telegram. The first thing I did was search for the name Manuela had provided me: "Brazil Baronil," which, roughly translated, means "Brazilian Baron." The hacker's name quickly appeared in my contact list.

At 1:18 p.m., I typed: "Hi, this is Glenn Greenwald." Almost instantly, the source replied: "Hi."

After a quick exchange of nervous joking, the source asked whether I preferred to speak in Portuguese or English (adding an LOL at the end).

When I replied that either was fine, he said, "I prefer Portuguese." We got down to business quickly. In response to his first question to me—"What can we do with all of this?"—I replied in the most neutral way possible. I told him that my first question, naturally, was what he had in his possession.

He then sent lines of rapid-fire responses, written one after the next, without any need for me to say anything. The words had a breathless quality to them, and weren't always completely clear in their meaning.

"Exactly everything," he said, summarizing what he had. "I accessed the bank information of the [Car Wash] task force in Curitiba," the city in which the prosecutors and then judge Moro were based. "Those to which nobody has had access. I got all of their conversations over the last five years," he continued. "All of the archives."

He then added, "I haven't even been able to read 10 percent of it. But I found audios of agreements made outside of Brazil: directly with defendants. I studied everything about collaboration [between prosecutors and defendants]. It was a tactic to manipulate the public. They were giving preventative prison to people who had not been convicted of anything, where imprisonment cannot be justified."

— — — — — — — — —

That Brazil has been governed through systemic corruption for decades is one of the best-known facts about the country's political culture. Brazilians so readily assume the corruption of all politicians that they popularized a slogan to justify voting for conspicuous criminals who at least occasionally provide for their constituents: "He steals but he gets things done" (*Ele rouba mas faz*).

To take one of countless examples, Paulo Maluf served as governor of São Paulo state, twice as mayor of São Paulo, and four terms in the National Congress, and even once ran for president, despite being repeatedly indicted as a criminal and spending years on the Interpol red list for international crimes at the request of the US government. He was convicted in France and other countries of money laundering. In 2017, while serving in Congress, Maluf was convicted by the Brazilian Supreme Court of having pilfered close to one billion dollars in bribes as mayor of São Paulo, which he had stashed away in Swiss bank accounts.

Despite this chronic and well-known criminality, Maluf continued to be elected to high governmental offices with large vote totals, and he enjoyed record popularity as mayor because of his constant introduction of new construction and renovation projects. That he was stealing from those projects did not undermine the appreciation they had for his work, particularly since they believed—often with good reason—that most politicians stole. (In 2018, less than two years after supporting the impeachment of Dilma, Maluf, at the age of eighty-seven, was finally convicted of election-related crimes in Brazil and sentenced to eight years in prison.)

But such jaded acceptance of systemic corruption as a political reality does not mean that Brazilians are at peace with it, which is why anti-corruption has always been a potent political currency. Anyone who can credibly promise to clean up corruption, and punish the corrupt, can appeal to a large swath of the populace regardless of their ideology.

What enabled Operation Car Wash to claim such a hold on the hopes and loyalties of Brazilians was that it appeared to be the first-ever genuine attempt to cleanse the nation's political system of the crooks and gangsters who have plagued the country for decades by leveraging their influence over governance into personal wealth at the expense of most of the population. As the Car Wash task force imprisoned more and more of the country's once-untouchable elites, the judges, prosecutors, and Federal Police officers involved gained iconic status, becoming the hope of the population for a better future.

As previously discussed, Operation Car Wash eventually grew into the largest anti-corruption probe in the history of any country, but its origins were unexceptional. Beginning in 2008, Federal Police were investigating what appeared to be a relatively low-level and limited scheme by Federal Police officers and a member of Congress. One of the witnesses who turned informant identified a ring of money launderers who specialized in running small businesses to disguise the sources of illicit funds. The investigation led to a money launderer who appeared to be involved in many illegal schemes, Alberto Youssef. To uncover this ring, the Federal Police monitored the telephone conversations of his close associate Carlos Habib Chater, the owner of a small gas station and car wash in Brasilia used to launder money.

Among the corrupt transactions discovered by investigators while monitoring their conversations was Youssef's gift of a new Land Rover as a bribe to an official of Petrobras, on behalf of a corrupt large construction company for whom Youssef was acting, in exchange for lucrative contracts. That Petrobras official, Paulo Roberto Costa, ultimately confessed to moving more than one billion dollars in bribes received by Petrobras executives and high-level government officials who oversaw the company—senators, powerful members of Congress, government ministers—in exchange for contracts.

As investigators focused more on Youssef, they realized he was no ordinary money launderer. He was instead a central cog in an apparatus of corrupt transactions at the highest crossroads of business and politics, serving as a fixer in every sense: he not only facilitated the transport (via private plane) of suitcases full of cash to foreign bank accounts, but mediated disputes over payment amounts and promised favors. Investigators did not know everything Youssef was involved in, but it became increasingly clear that it was far more than they had originally understood.

Ultimately, it was the connection of the corruption schemes to Petrobras that significantly elevated the importance of this investigation. Indeed, it is difficult to overstate the centrality of Petrobras to Brazilian politics, finance, culture, and national identity. The magnitude of its revenue alone makes it a crucial driver of economic growth, but the fact that it's state-owned means that it has long financed social programs designed to uplift the country's poor—its majority—and give them hope for a better future. It is also a potent symbol in the Brazilian imagination of the country's readiness to be a major player on the world stage.

That a company this vital was snared at its core in dirty bribery and kickbacks was a huge blow. Even for a population as jaded as Brazil's, learning that public assets were being stashed away by the hundreds of millions, or even billions, in the Swiss bank accounts of powerful politicians infuriated a public that, just a year after the raucous 2013 protests, was already outraged toward the political class.

When the Operation Car Wash task force was unveiled in 2014, in the wake of the discovery of the Petrobras connection, it was notably composed of, and even led by, very young prosecutors. Almost all of them were in their thirties, including the task force's coordinating prosecutor, Deltan Dallagnol. The thirty-four-year-old had under his command a large team of prosecutors and agents from the Federal Police, all of whom possessed subpoena power and the authority to offer leniency in exchange for confessions that implicated more powerful actors of corruption. The primary judge assigned to these cases, Sérgio Moro, was also young for a judge: forty-two years old at the time the nation was introduced to him.

Their youth had both symbolic value and substantive importance. These prosecutors grew up not under the military dictatorship, but under democracy, and were thus inculcated with the ideals of equality and the rule of law—principles incompatible with the long-standing Brazilian reality that powerful politicians were all but entitled to enrich themselves through corruption, and then to enjoy impunity, even when caught.

It also appeared, probably accurately, that the youth of the task force members, and the idealism and fanaticism that often accompany it, made them righteously intolerant of the type of systemic corruption that veteran operatives in Brasilia, even ones who were not themselves corrupt, had come to accept as so entrenched that it was immune to any real reform.

The public viewed these fresh faces as new, swaggering sheriffs riding into town to rid the crime-ridden community of a corrupt old guard. It was an imagery that held great theatrical value for the Brazilian media, which from the start depicted the Car Wash prosecutors and Judge Moro in the most adoring, deferential, and even reverential terms. They were youthful heroes and warriors single-mindedly devoted to integrity and ethics. The fact that they were state agents armed with immense powers of investigation, surveillance, and imprisonment, who had the potential to abuse their power or even to err, was excluded from the prevailing script. As a result, the public popularity of the Car Wash stars was far greater than that of the subjects of their investigations, or of any other political or legal institution that might challenge, question, or limit them.

The key event that transformed Operation Car Wash from a significant but contained investigation into a sprawling, transformative, and unprecedented one was the decision by Youssef to fully cooperate with investigators in exchange for leniency in his sentence. Youssef knew where every body was buried, where every Swiss bank account was stashed, and made clear early on that he was prepared to disclose everything in order to save himself. He told investigators that he had more dirt on the most powerful people in Brazil than they could possibly imagine. Though skeptical of him at the start—he was, after all, a career grifter and criminal with an incentive to lie—they gradually began to believe him, particularly when their search and seizure and electronic surveillance operations began to confirm his testimony.

Within a relatively short period of time, Youssef's cooperation led the Car Wash investigators to some of the country's richest and most powerful figures. By far the most significant early captures were the presidents of the two largest construction companies, Marcelo Odebrecht and Otávio Marques Azevedo, both of whom were arrested in 2015.

The imprisonment of Odebrecht was particularly stunning. The scion of one of Brazil's richest and most powerful families—his father, Emilio Odebrecht, is a billionaire with long-standing influence in almost every sector of Brasilia—he seemed untouchable under unwritten rules long governing how Brazil functioned. Thus, to see a powerful billionaire imprisoned for corruption was an uplifting and inspiring event for a population that had long accepted that rich and powerful people suffer no consequences for their crimes.

As adoration for the Car Wash probe soared, so too did the task force's willingness to use aggressive, and even radical, tactics. Under Brazilian law, the imprisonment of a defendant prior to their conviction had been permitted only in the rarest and narrowest of circumstances: when the prosecutors presented concrete and definitive evidence that the accused presented a danger to witnesses or to the investigation, were they to remain free pending their trial. But the Car Wash prosecutors began demanding "preventative imprisonment" of suspects almost as a matter of course, and Judge Moro radically expanded the grounds on which those requests could be granted. More than 120 people were preventatively imprisoned as part of Operation Car Wash—most of them for many months, and some more than a year, without having been convicted of anything. Brazil's prison system segregates those who hold college degrees from those who do not, and while conditions for the former are mildly better, all Brazilian prisons are notorious for their harshness.

Once preventatively imprisoned, Car Wash prosecutors made clear that the only path the suspects had to leave prison was to accuse other, more powerful, people of crimes. Sometimes that coercive tactic provoked accurate disclosures, but very often it induced false confessions and baseless accusations against others. To be sure, in the United States and Europe, prosecutors similarly attempt to induce defendants to turn on higher-ups in exchange for leniency. But the power to indefinitely imprison people whose guilt has not even been proven vests the judge and prosecutor with virtually unlimited power over their lives. It also renders the imprisoned suspects willing to do virtually anything—including endorse false accusations against others—to secure a ticket out of their jail cell.

Even worse, Car Wash prosecutors used aggressive public campaigns and illegal media leaks to demonize, threaten, and destroy the reputations of suspects who hadn't been convicted of anything. In dozens of instances where people who were preventatively imprisoned signed confessions that contained accusations against others, Car Wash officials leaked the news of those accusations to the media—most frequently to *Globo*—which trumpeted the explosive accusations as if they were proven fact, in the process destroying the reputation of the accused.

In many instances, those accused and vilified by these media leaks never had charges brought against them, because the prosecutors were unable to find evidence to substantiate the coerced confessions. But the media outlets that trumpeted the leaked accusations at the start of their news broadcast or in their headlines rarely informed their audience that the accusations turned out to be unproven or false. People were thus found guilty by media leak, with no opportunity to defend themselves. Aside from generating massive profit for these news outlets with virtually no money spent—Brazilians tuned in by the millions to hear who was the latest powerful politician accused of corruption—the leaks also vested enormous power in the task force: the power to destroy someone's reputation overnight.

Largely because of these dubious methods, there was no stopping the Car Wash train. From 2015 to 2017, the task force and Judge Moro prosecuted, convicted, and imprisoned senators, powerful members of the lower house, key government ministers, captains of industry, billionaires, and the largest players in the construction and petroleum sectors. Whatever else one wants to say about this investigation, it clearly signaled an end to full-scale impunity for powerful criminals—at least some of them.

For the first two years of the Car Wash probe, it seemed the prosecutors could do no wrong. And clearly, many of the powerful people they were imprisoning were deeply corrupt and deserved punishment. Indeed, the early stages of Operation Car Wash appeared genuinely healthy and cleansing for the Brazilian body politic. But serious causes for concern and doubt about the integrity of the probe began to emerge after that first stage. Perhaps the most serious early warning was in 2016, when Moro secretly tape-recorded the telephone conversation of President Dilma Rousseff without obtaining Supreme Court authorization as required by law, precisely when the impeachment movement against her was picking up steam.

The target of Moro's wiretap order was Lula. Among the conversations Moro taped of the former president and his successor, Dilma, was a discussion over the possibility of his joining her government as a minister. Lula and Dilma claimed that they hoped to use Lula's political skills and connections in Brasilia to help her navigate the impeachment crises she was facing. But critics claimed their true motive was to protect Lula from possible prosecution, given that ministers—along with senators and members of Congress—enjoy protection from prosecution in any court other than the Supreme Court. That protection, called *foro privilegiado*, was introduced during redemocratization to counter the military dictatorship's tactic of summarily removing any members of Congress who opposed or impeded their will through sham trials. But in practice, this privilege became a form of effective immunity. So many members of Congress and ministers were implicated in corruption allegations that it would take years, if not decades, for the Supreme Court to adjudicate them all.

Judge Moro not only wiretapped Lula's telephone conversations, including with the sitting president of the country. He also purposely ensured that they leaked to the media, along with a slew of Lula's personal calls in which the former president made embarrassing comments about women and various luminaries—clearly released with the intention to further undermine his reputation.

The leaked conversation between Lula and Dilma became one of the most significant political events of the decade. It first appeared on *Globo's* flagship nightly news show, *Jornal Nacional*, which has by far the biggest audience of any news program in Brazil. That program devoted its entire show to the topic, with its two hosts—one male and one female—reenacting the conversations verbatim, as if they were soap opera actors.

The effect was explosive. With virtual unanimity, the Brazilian media treated the taped conversation as proof of the corruption of both the Workers' Party leaders. That the Supreme Court justice overseeing the Car Wash probe subsequently ruled that Judge Moro acted illegally in wiretapping Dilma's conversations made little difference. *Globo* and the other large media outlets relentlessly trumpeted and dramatized the plan to make Lula a minister as proof of corruption, the effect of which was to drown out any concerns about whether Moro abused his power to obtain it.

The leak by Judge Moro of her call with Lula was the key driver of Dilma's impeachment. Indeed, in 2019 the center-right speaker of the lower house, Rodrigo Maia, said that the idea of impeaching Dilma had been "dead" until Moro released that wiretapped call.

Through abuse of his judicial power, Judge Moro not only took down one president through impeachment, but severely crippled the political influence of her predecessor. Ultimately, Moro found Lula guilty on highly dubious charges, sentenced him to a decade in prison, and ensured he would be ineligible to run for the presidency, at a time when all polls showed that he was the overwhelming favorite in 2018 against Bolsonaro.

At the same time, the leak was the incident that for the first time provoked significant doubts about Moro's integrity. Even many of his most ardent fans in judicial and legal circles criticized him. Some started to question whether Moro was truly an apolitical figure, devoted to fighting corruption, or whether—like so many before him—he was exploiting anti-corruption themes to destroy center-left and left-wing political factions and empower the Brazilian right.

Operation Car Wash was not merely the most significant legal event in Brazil, but by far the most influential and consequential *political* process. Brazilian politics was being driven much more by Judge Moro's rulings and the public and legal accusations of the Car Wash task force than it was by politics, electioneering, and democratic outcomes. An unelected low-level federal judge had somehow become the prime author of Brazilian democracy.

The first time I publicly criticized Judge Moro was in 2016, after the Dilma/Lula leaks. My prior work as a journalist in revealing and denouncing illegal state surveillance clearly shaped my perceptions, but my suspicions that Moro was really a right-wing operative exploiting his judicial power for political ends continued to grow. I was still not on board, however, with the critique of Moro and Operation Car Wash that it was a plot to destroy the Workers' Party. I still believed, notwithstanding serious flaws, that the crux of Car Wash was positive.

In fact, eighteen months before I was contacted by my source with evidence that incriminated Moro and his colleagues, I had defended Operation Car Wash in a very public setting. In 2017, I was invited to deliver the keynote speech at an event in Vancouver, Canada, to honor anti-corruption crusaders with an award called the Allard Prize for International Integrity, along with a $100,000 payment. Each year, the Allard Prize chooses three finalists and then announces the winner on the night of the event. Only after I had accepted the invitation to speak were the finalists announced: a journalist from Egypt under house arrest, another in Azerbaijan who was forbidden to leave her country, and the Car Wash task force. The choice provoked significant anger among the Brazilian left; Lula had been found guilty by Judge Moro only weeks earlier, and a consensus was growing on the Brazilian left that Moro and the prosecutors were abusing the force of law to achieve the destruction of the Workers' Party.

Loyalists of Lula and Dilma's party initiated a campaign demanding that the Allard Prize rescind the task force's nomination. When that failed, they directed their activism toward me, demanding I boycott the event. I refused to do so and defended my position that anti-corruption activism is important for any democracy.

On the night of the ceremony in Vancouver, I attended a pre-event cocktail party for the sponsors, the Allard Prize judges, and the finalists themselves. When I entered the room, I immediately recognized the chief prosecutor who had led the Car Wash probe, Deltan Dallagnol. Accompanying him were three other senior prosecutors.

They approached me, clearly nervous. Dallagnol's hands were visibly shaking as he held his glass. I had vocally criticized actions of the Car Wash task force in the past—including for illegal leaks by Judge Moro, as well as the prosecutors' abusive use of "preventative imprisonment"—

and they were worried about what I might say in my keynote speech. After all, they had traveled all the way from Curitiba to Vancouver to be heralded and praised, not to be attacked as power-hungry prosecutors who had politicized their office.

But once I ascended the stage, I spoke positively about all of the finalists, including the Car Wash prosecutors. I noted that while I did have criticisms of their work, some quite serious, I viewed the imprisonment of numerous Brazilian billionaires and powerful political officials as something, on balance, to be admired. I noted that I viewed the work of the task force through the prism of being a citizen of a country—the United States—where I had watched for years as political and economic elites were immunized from legal consequences for the most egregious crimes: torture, illegal domestic spying, the fraud that triggered the 2008 financial crisis. I even wrote a book in 2011, entitled *With Liberty and Justice for Some*, lamenting this two-tiered justice system in which such elite immunity is paired with unforgiving and limitlessly harsh punishment for society's ordinary citizens, to the point that the United States has become the most prolific prison state on the planet. "Notwithstanding the errors I think they've made and the very valid critiques that have occasionally been voiced against them," I said in that speech, the task force's work "is something I consider extraordinarily brave and worthy of being honored."

After my speech, Dallagnol and his prosecutorial team appeared far more relaxed—giddy, even. The notoriously reserved, austere prosecutor practically hugged me as he gushed praise and gratitude for my speech. We spent roughly an hour talking—including debating my criticisms of their work—and exchanged telephone numbers, agreeing to continue chatting.

A couple of weeks after that event in Canada, Dallagnol posted to his personal Facebook page—with more than a million followers—a video with the excerpt of the speech about their work (from "the renowned journalist Glenn Greenwald," he wrote), with Portuguese subtitles. Over 180,000 have watched that video excerpt on Dallagnol's page alone. (One of the chat archives provided to me by my source showed Dallagnol speaking to his colleagues about my speech, telling them how vital it was to translate it and post it as soon as possible with the expectation that it could bolster their standing with the left).

Over the next eighteen months, Dallagnol and I exchanged some messages and discussed the possibility that I might interview him. Then in mid-2019, just a few weeks prior to being contacted by Manuela d'Ávila and the source, I learned that a petition I had submitted during the 2018 election to the Supreme Court to interview Lula had finally been approved, and that I was authorized to travel to Curitiba—the home base of Operation Car Wash, where Lula was imprisoned—to interview the former president for the second time.

When I learned that I would be visiting Curitiba to interview Lula, I sent Dallagnol a message asking if he would be in town and whether he'd be available for an interview. He said he might be, but then claimed he'd be out of town on those dates. We agreed to try again.

In other words, just a couple of weeks before receiving years' worth of Dallagnol's secret and highly incriminating conversations, he and I were casually chatting by WhatsApp about the possibility of scheduling what he almost certainly assumed would be a friendly interview. So when I received the archive filled with secret Car Wash chats and documents, I was skeptical of some of their work, but not filled with entrenched hostility toward the probe or a belief, outside of a few isolated instances, that it had been either politicized or systematically corrupt.

— — — — — — — — —

The conversation I had on Mother's Day with the source was awkward, stilted, and nervous. As a journalist, an endless array of considerations, concerns, and questions pass through your head when you begin speaking for the first time with an unknown source who may be able to provide significant information. When the interaction is online, the process is even more challenging. As typed words appear on your screen, you have no idea who the person is—or the people who may be behind them. At first, you have no way of knowing whether any of what they have claimed about themselves is true, or whether the material they claim to have is real. The fear that one wrong word can scare off the source, or create a climate of distrust, is acute. The concern that the person has been sent to entrap or otherwise incriminate you increases your caution even further, as does the concern that they may be monitored by authorities as they speak to you.

The best course is to say as little as possible while still manifesting serious interest in the source and his material, and hope that the source does most of the talking, allowing you time to develop a basic understanding of their mindset. This is something I learned most vividly when I began speaking to Edward Snowden in late 2012. When he appeared on my screen—first via emails and then through real-time chats—I knew nothing about him other than the fact that he had a huge number of extremely sensitive and newsworthy top secret documents from the most secretive agency within the world's most powerful government, and that he wanted to give them to me to report on their contents.

In that case, it was at least two weeks before I felt comfortable doing more than just uttering neutral phrases such as "I understand" and "That makes sense." Since my interaction with Snowden eventually blossomed into a productive journalist–source relationship based on trust and confidence (and later a friendship that endures to this day), I attempted to replicate a similar strategy when speaking with my new Brazilian source.

After the source and I shared our awkward preliminary greetings, he began describing the task force's use of "preventative imprisonment" and the coercive confessions and recoupment of monies the tactic induced, claiming: "They used this collaboration to get money. And nobody knows where it is going to." Unprompted, he then began describing the international repercussions of what he had seen in the archive: "They were expanding the 'Car Wash' ideology to be the biggest operation in history, expanding it to other countries that collaborated with them. And they are even investigating Venezuelans with billions in Swiss bank accounts."

He continued, "I have a lot of archives, and I just need to understand them now. Do you have the capacity to fully process archives?"

He quickly started showing me what he had, wanting to prove that his claims were credible. "Have you heard the audio of Orlando? LOL." I wasn't sure what he meant. I knew there was a high-level Car Wash prosecutor named Orlando Martello Júnior. But, trying to say as little as possible until I had a better sense of my source, I typed, "I haven't."

He then uploaded to our chat an audio message that Telegram indicated was one minute and fifty seconds in length, then proceeded to instruct me: "Listen to this first. Orlando, in his own voice, saying that Renato Duque, the ex-president of Petrobras, already entered into an agreement outside of Brazil, in which they are giving some form of immunity to them. And to reduce their punishment. But this is nothing compared to what I have here."

Before listening to the audio that he sent, I typed: "This is already a good start." I was seeking to provide some encouragement and also simply to let him know I was paying close attention to his manic typing.

I downloaded the file and clicked play. A man's voice described in some detail a call he had just had with Petrobras lawyers. The call concerned part of an agreement the Brazilian oil giant was attempting to close with the US Department of Justice and Brazilian prosecutors to settle various criminal charges relating to bribery allegations and kickback schemes.

Without any context, it was difficult to assess the significance of this audio. But, by all appearances, I was listening to a private message in the voice of one of the most senior Car Wash prosecutors as he discussed a sensitive matter, which significantly increased my trust in this source's claims about what he had obtained.

From there, the source began to describe, somewhat frantically but cogently, a long list of improprieties he believed the archive revealed: the task force had fabricated a medical certification to publicly explain the removal of a prominent prosecutor who was in reality removed for corruption; it had fraudulently altered statements from defendants before leaking them to the press; and it had abused the power of preventative imprisonment to coerce defendants to sign statements of accusations against other defendants that the prosecutors knew were likely false.

My source's list of allegations against Moro and the task force—all of which he insisted were proven by the archive—was long and dire. I quickly realized that if even a small fraction of his assertions were true, it would be one of the biggest, most important, and most dangerous stories to report in Brazilian politics in some time.

Then the source made an extremely unexpected request: "Can I call you?"

Among other things, this was the first sign that I was most definitely not speaking with someone like Edward Snowden. When Snowden first contacted me in December 2012, he was obsessive about the security of our communications and the protection of his anonymity until we met in

Hong Kong five months later. He had always planned to publicly identify himself as the source once we had met him, received the archive, and begun our reporting, but he demanded constant vigilance about communication security until then, fearing he would be caught before he could meet us and share these documents. He insisted that I install sophisticated encryption programs and that we use numerous covert tactics that he learned in his years with the CIA and NSA. He told me nothing about himself: I didn't know his name, age, or where he worked. During the weeks Snowden and I spent speaking over the Internet, a phone call was unthinkable.

But that's exactly what this Brazilian source requested, soon after our first online interaction. This concerned me for several reasons. By confining himself to online chats, he would make it more difficult for authorities to identify him and prove he was the source; his voice, however, would be the best and easiest evidence law enforcement agents could wish for. Why was he so nonchalant about using a far less secure means of communication?

This made me wonder how serious and/or careful he was. It made me question his sophistication, which in turn could be a factor in assessing the reliability of the material he was providing or the likelihood that he had already attracted the attention of law enforcement. Could someone this reckless really have managed to hack the most powerful people in Brazil without being noticed?

I was also concerned for myself. I knew US and European law extremely well when it came to press freedom protections, having been a constitutional lawyer in the United States for more than a decade and having worked on the Snowden story in multiple countries in the West, where the threat of prosecution and imprisonment always lurked. But in the United States and most of Europe, journalists who receive information that a source obtains illegally—whether by hacking it, stealing it, or acting as a whistleblowing insider who leaks it—cannot be criminally prosecuted simply for receiving and then reporting that material. As long as journalists do not themselves participate in criminal acts enabling the acquisition of the information, they have strong protections from prosecution—not absolute protections, as the US government's ongoing attempts to extradite and prosecute WikiLeaks founder Julian Assange demonstrate, but strong ones.

All the same, I had never had occasion to study closely Brazilian press freedom law. As I talked to Manuela and then the source for the first time, I assumed that it was likely similar to US law, but that was just a guess. Could it be that, under Brazilian law, journalists are deemed part of a criminal conspiracy merely by receiving stolen information? I thought that was unlikely but possible. More importantly, even if Brazilian law provided protections to journalists similar to those in the United States, I was very uncertain, to put it mildly, whether those rights would be upheld in the new Bolsonaro era. I had serious doubts about both the willingness and ability of Brazilian institutions, including the courts, to stand up to this new, powerful, and highly repressive movement—indeed, one that was still enjoying the surge of a massive electoral victory.

Beyond all those considerations, speaking exclusively by text provided an important measure of security for me: everything the source and I were typing was being stored (by me and, presumably, by Telegram), so that nobody in the future could claim I had conspired with, encouraged, or directed the source in any way—that is, crossed the line into conspiracy and criminality. But speaking by voice to the source meant that I would have no record of our conversation, unless I recorded the call. When the source asked to speak by voice, I very quickly tried to analyze the ethics, as well as the logistics and legalities, of the possibility of recording the call. Did I have the obligation to inform him that I would record him? I lacked the time needed to resolve these quandaries. And, as a strategic matter, telling him I wanted to tape the call—before we had established any basis of trust—risked alienating him. After all, his voice could allow law enforcement agents to prove who he was.

I decided the risk of requesting to tape the call—and losing this story by scaring him away—outweighed the risk of talking to him without having a record. (I made these calculations in less than a minute. I did not want to arouse suspicion by delaying in responding to his request.) So I told him I'd be happy to talk by phone.

At 1:33 p.m., the source called me. Though the call was short—just under three minutes—I received a great deal of information. And I did not have to do much work to obtain it. Once again, I said very little, while he offered up rapid-fire information. He told me that he had only read through a small portion of the archive, even though he had been reading it for weeks, but had already found what he called "stunning corruption" on the part of Moro as well as his team of anti-corruption prosecutors.

The source then began talking about his motives, in terms that were, at least on the surface, similar to what Snowden told me about his. They also tracked what Manuela had told me he had said to her. "I have no interest in financial gain," he said, "nor do I have any party or ideology. I want you to expose whatever corruption you find in this material regardless of the party or the ideology. I just want to help clean up my country."

As I deliberately muttered banalities such as "right" and "understood," he then purported to tell me about himself. He said he had studied computer science at Harvard, where he had met someone who he said was friendly with one of the two Russian-born brothers, Pavel and Nikolai Durov, who founded Telegram in 2013. He told me that this connection allowed him full and unfettered access to Telegram's communications. "I can get the conversations of anyone you want," he said.

"If you want, I can hack your phone to prove to you that I have this capability. You can create a new Telegram account . . . and I can hack that," he explained. Having my phone hacked—by him or anyone else—was most definitely not something I was interested in, so I said, "That won't be necessary. You've already sufficiently demonstrated with Manuela that you have this capability."

Although I had heard from Manuela about his hacking powers, I was nonetheless stunned. His claim that this extraordinary access to all of Telegram came from his connections with the founders seemed quite difficult to believe. The Durov brothers had become billionaires not from Telegram but by founding, in 2006, a Facebook-type social media platform, VK, that quickly became the most influential online communications medium and social media network in Russia. Within a few years of the platform's founding, tens of millions of Russians were using VK.

The Durov brothers frequently clashed with the Russian government, often over their refusal to honor censorship or surveillance demands made by Moscow authorities against Russian dissidents. As a result, both brothers left Russia under duress in 2014 after being forced out of their own company, ultimately settling in Dubai as their primary home.

Influenced both by the Snowden revelations and Russian government spying, the Durov brothers built Telegram with the promise that it would be invulnerable to hacking and spying. Though the app was being developed prior to the first Snowden revelation, it was first released on August 14, 2013—just over two months after I published the first Snowden story about NSA spying in the *Guardian*—and by October of that year, it had one hundred thousand active users. By December 2014, Telegram had spread to numerous large countries where surveillance fears and privacy concerns were driven by the Snowden revelations, and fairly quickly skyrocketed to fifty million active users.

Why would Nikolai and Pavel Durov, longtime privacy advocates, risk the credibility of their hugely successful app by providing access to the private conversations of Brazilian judges and prosecutors? If that became known, it would be disastrous for a company that centrally relies on promises of security and privacy. But the source had clearly demonstrated that he was able to access multiple Telegram accounts, seemingly at will.

However dubious I was of his claims about the Durov brothers, I saw the irony that Snowden, on several occasions, had publicly clashed with Telegram founders over his repeated insistence that their app was unsafe and unreliable—something my new source had just rather convincingly demonstrated.

I was also skeptical of the source's claim that he had studied at Harvard. I'm no expert in identifying Brazil's seemingly countless regional accents, but I can identify the most common ones. The source's accent seemed to be from the interior of São Paulo state, which is largely impoverished. His speech was rather pedestrian, even crude. He sounded like someone with a very basic Brazilian public education. The severe and suffocating inequality that has long plagued Brazil means that only those lucky to be born to privileged families have any real chance of attending college of any kind, let alone leaving Brazil to study at an Ivy League university. In a country of 213 million people, there are of course exceptions—some people born into poverty manage to fight their way to the top with a combination of skill, determination, and luck—but it's very rare.

Beyond all that, the source quickly said he wanted to speak Portuguese rather than English, but to study at Harvard would obviously require a mastery of English.

Whatever my doubts, I was eager to terminate the call and return to the safer channel of the Telegram chat. So I said, "Well, it's great to hear your voice. Let's keep chatting online," to which he agreed. Before we hung up, I said to him, "I'm sure you already know this, but you need to be very careful. It's very easy for sources to be found in this world of pervasive surveillance, and you'd obviously be in a great deal of trouble if you got caught." I viewed that warning, that advice, as a part of my journalistic duty to protect my sources, but also as the by-product of years of learning that even technologically sophisticated people can be careless or even reckless, whether from excess confidence or even a subliminal desire to be caught.

One of the original missions of the Intercept was to provide the most advanced tools possible to protect the ability of sources to leak newsworthy information in the safest and most anonymous manner possible. We featured a dedicated article on our site by our information specialist, Micah Lee, in both English and Portuguese, with tips on how sources can communicate securely. But as we made clear, ironclad guarantees of safety are illusory, and complete secrecy does not exist. Any source who engages in unauthorized or illegal leaks runs a risk of getting caught, no matter how careful they are.

In very stark contrast to Snowden, this source seemed decisively indifferent to, even contemptuous of, such concerns. In a boastful manner that bordered on mischievous arrogance, he quickly replied, "Oh, you don't need to worry about that. I'm in the US and I'm never stepping foot in Brazil again." I reminded him that the Trump administration had formed a very close and friendly bond with the new Bolsonaro government (largely due to Bolsonaro's obsequious praise for the US president) and that it would be easy for the Brazilian government to secure his extradition. "That's never going to happen," he said, laughing. "I am using so many proxies and so many levels of encryption that they will never find me no matter how long they look." Multiple times as we chatted, he repeated the same claims:

In reply to this message

Eu moro no EUA há 3 anos kkkk

Nunca mais piso no Brasil

BA 2.odt
Not included, change data exporting settings to
download.
9.0 MB

Glenn Greenwald

sim, mas vc precisa tomar cuidado

BB: "I've lived in the US for 3 years now hahaha."
"I will never set foot in Brazil again."
GG: "Yes, but you need to be careful."

At the end of the call, he promised to begin sending documents from the archive. And he instantly made good on his pledge: as soon as we hung up, documents began appearing on my telephone, one after the next, far more rapidly than I could open and read them. For the next seven days, one secret document after the next involving the communications of the Car Wash prosecutors and Judge Moro materialized on my phone, forming an increasingly huge archive in my Telegram app.

As I opened and read some of the files, I became increasingly convinced of the authenticity of this archive and, consequently, of the source. Many of the documents were complex legal drafts. Others were elaborate technical discussions on prosecutorial strategy. Still others were years' worth of chats between key judges and prosecutors on the Operation Car Wash task force.

Just as I had thought when I first worked to determine the authenticity of the Snowden archive almost exactly six years earlier, it seemed impossible for anyone to fabricate or forge an archive this extensive, detailed, sophisticated, and complex.

Chapter 4

— — — — — — — — —

TAKING THE PLUNGE TO REPORT

Massive leaked archives are becoming increasingly prominent in journalism. The visionary genius of WikiLeaks was that it recognized this trend before anyone else did, and then made use of Julian Assange's hacking skills to construct a system to allow for massive digital leaks in a way that would provide the most security possible to sources.

Since WikiLeaks created its submission system in 2006, it has published troves of secret documents—including the Iraq and Afghanistan War logs, the US State Department diplomatic cables, and the Democratic National Committee and Hillary Clinton emails that shaped much of the 2016 US presidential election—that have shown the world the journalistic power and value of leaks of this sort.

Since then, leaks of comparable size to other media organizations—such as the Panama Papers, the Sony archive, the Snowden files, a massive FBI leak, and the Drone Papers (the last two to the Intercept—have bolstered the recognition that in the digital age, the ability to leak huge amounts of information at once is a major vulnerability for power centers and a unique opportunity for journalists.

As a result, many of the most influential and mainstream news outlets in the world—including the *New York Times* and the *Washington Post*—now use and promote secure file submission systems of the kind first pioneered by WikiLeaks. One leading example is SecureDrop, used by both of those papers and dozens of other large media outlets. SecureDrop, developed by the young digital privacy activist Aaron Swartz—who committed suicide while being prosecuted by the government—is administered by the Freedom of the Press Foundation, a group cofounded by myself, documentary film producer Laura Poitras, Pentagon Papers whistleblower Daniel Ellsberg, digital freedom activist Trevor Timm, actor John Cusack, and others. It is now run by Timm and Edward Snowden.

What was once fringe and radical—to not merely use, but to facilitate and enable large-scale, often-illegal leaks—is now mainstream. As the world's most powerful institutions increasingly store their secrets in digital form, there is little doubt that leaks of the kind my Brazilian source provided will be vital for journalism in the years ahead.

But what many people overlook about this sort of journalism—and about most kinds of journalism—is that there is no such thing as 100 percent certainty. It's not a science. When you receive a gigantic cache of secret information, or even if you receive more traditional leaks from a source who wants to remain anonymous, you can work to obtain high confidence in the authenticity of the material. This is what every responsible journalist devotes themselves to doing before publishing any reporting based on such sources. But you can never prove the negative: that nothing has been altered, fabricated, or forged. That was the lesson learned by the *New York Times* throughout 2003 and 2004, when it became clear that much of the leaked information they were publishing about Saddam Hussein's weapons program was false.

When we received the Snowden archive, my colleagues and I were able to determine that many of the nonpublic documents were real. But how could we know for sure that nothing in the massive archive of secret documents was not altered or otherwise inauthentic as a result of the source's manipulation? How could the *New York Times* and the *Guardian* know for certain that hundreds of thousands of Iraq War logs and diplomatic cables they received from WikiLeaks were all authentic down to the last comma? They couldn't and didn't. But they still reported on and published a number of the documents because they were able to confirm enough to give them a high degree of confidence in the integrity of the material.

As is true of all journalism, we had to do the best we could to obtain the truth about the Brazil archive, using a combination of research, reliance on other sources, and intuition. With the Snowden reporting, every time we published new documents and there was no claim that a document was falsified, our confidence grew that the entire archive was real. The same proved true in the case of this Brazilian source. As I talked more with him, and especially as I reviewed more documents, my confidence in the authenticity of this archive grew. But before publishing, we would need far more than my intuitive assessment. We would need to extensively examine the archive journalistically and technologically to test its authenticity.

My gut, which is crucial in journalism, was telling me that it was all real, if for no other reason than that it would be virtually impossible to fabricate an archive of this size and complexity. But the source periodically said things that made me uncomfortable. He was fond of touting his hacking prowess, and at several points, he asked if there were any specific people whose Telegram accounts I wanted hacked—exactly the kind of direction and encouragement that I knew, for legal reasons, I had to avoid providing lest I become his coconspirator. That he was virtually inviting me to do that raised my guard.

Both in our voice conversations and in the written chats, the source's tone was often playful and facetious. Despite the gravity of what we were doing, he often made remarks in jest and frequently added some version of "LOL" to what he was saying. He boasted about unrelated hacking achievements. He was clearly reveling in the joy of what he had achieved and in his power.

I've reported on the hacker community for years, and this posture is common. Often embedded in the hacker personality is a defiance of authority that can sometimes manifest as adolescent rebellion. Many hackers are motivated by serious political objectives—as this hacker clearly was—but have a type of arrested development that derives from the transgression of boundaries, limits, and rules for its own sake. My source was engaged in behavior for which, if he were caught, he would almost certainly suffer severe punishment, including a lengthy prison sentence. Most people would not frivolously joke in such a situation, except to disguise their anxiety. But there's a rush that comes from successfully breaking into the computers and phones of powerful institutions and people, and hacking culture encourages people to view this kind of transgression as fun.

Despite the periodic frivolity, my source was quite serious when discussing what he had done and why. In between jokes, and in a way that reflected perceptive thinking, he frequently invoked high-minded ideas about democracy, transparency, anti-corruption, and the importance of independent and fearless journalism. Most of all, he repeatedly emphasized to me that he loved Brazil and was acting with the overarching motive of improving his country. This earnest paean to the importance of journalism, early in our communication, was typical of many of his statements to me: "The journalistic community is the only one that will be able to provide limits" to the judicial and prosecutorial abuses that concerned him.

As our conversation progressed and he shared more documents, I became more convinced that he was genuinely who he claimed to be. And, even as we were both vividly aware of the dangers in what we were doing, we both became more comfortable with one another. With that in mind, I told the source about two notable ironies about our situation. The first was that I was scheduled to interview Lula in his prison cell in Curitiba a week from the day the source and I first began speaking.

When I had first interviewed Lula three years earlier, in 2016, at his charitable institute in São Paulo, most of what he had to say was geared toward the denunciation of Judge Sérgio Moro and the Car Wash prosecutorial team as deceitful and ideologically motivated. Something Lula said about Moro struck me as highly insightful and really stayed with me. In response to my question about the crusading-judge-turned-national-hero, Lula said he thought that Moro began his legal career and even Operation Car Wash with good intentions, but that the onslaught of reverential press depictions made Moro believe so unquestioningly in his own goodness that he came to believe that anything he did, no matter how legally dubious or unethical, was justified.

"I think anyone with a lot of power is vulnerable. However, not every human being is able to handle the popularity," Lula told me, obviously speaking from experience. He himself had also enjoyed years of adoring press coverage and glorifying magazine covers both in Brazil and internationally, as he acknowledged: "I know how good it can feel to be on the front page of a newspaper, to be on the television every day. But if you're not careful and responsible, you can go down a totally wrong path." Of Moro, he said, "The media, the photographs, can do a lot of damage. I've seen a lot of people, from baseball, soccer and snooker players to judges, senators, state representatives and even presidents succumb to it."

When I asked whether he had also fallen victim to this dynamic, Lula denied it. "Ever since I was a union leader, I was conscious that I had to be very careful not to allow myself to be influenced by media adoration." A major critique of Lula, though, including on the left, was that his original leftist passion had been replaced by a calculating quest for power. Either way, Lula's diagnosis of Moro's trajectory—from well-intentioned corruption fighter to amoral megalomaniac—struck me as perceptive even back then.

For obvious reasons, that anger Lula expressed toward Moro and his prosecutors back in 2016 escalated after he was imprisoned by them. In the years since, Lula intensified his rhetoric against Moro and Car Wash, constantly insisting that they, not he, were the genuinely corrupt actors.

Now I was receiving over my phone one document after the next that appeared to corroborate Lula's accusations. I knew that there was no way this archive would be ready for publication by the time of my scheduled interview with Lula, so I would have to listen to him rail against his accusers and Moro, but not disclose that I had this archive, either to Lula or the broader public.

There was a second irony I noted to the source. I recounted to him my 2017 speech in Canada defending the Car Wash probe as a necessary tonic to the impunity enjoyed for decades by Brazilian elites, and how that had led its chief prosecutor, Deltan Dallagnol, who was in the audience, to post and praise my speech on his social media accounts, and to develop a friendly association with me. Before being contacted by the source, I had chatted briefly with Dallagnol about the possibility of interviewing him when I traveled to Curitiba to interview Lula, but Dallagnol had been evasive.

Now, however, I had the private chats over the last five years of Dallagnol and his colleagues. With this archive, I could know vastly more about Dallagnol's work than he could possibly tell me in any interview.

I briefly thought that perhaps I should still try to interview him, and use the archive to show how willing he was to lie. But I vastly preferred to spend my time digging through this archive and reporting what he had actually done, rather than listening to him recite his scripted rebuttals to questions and criticisms.

After I told the source about my scheduled interview with Lula the next week and my ongoing conversations with Dallagnol about the possibility of interviewing him during the same trip, the source was amazed. "SURREAL!," he wrote. By now feeling more comfortable with him and wanting to make our interaction more friendly, I replied with an "LOL."

As the documents continued to stream in, I began opening them randomly. I had no system in place yet to review them. A lot of the documents were in highly technical and legalistic Portuguese that took a long time to read and digest, particularly with no context. But the explosiveness of others was immediately apparent. Most immediately striking, and shocking, were the clear signs of secret, sustained collaboration between Judge Moro and the prosecutors.

"I believe it will take ten hours to upload the full archive," the source told me. It took far, far longer than that.

On the day the source first contacted me, I went to bed at roughly 2:00 a.m., after having spent the day reading through huge batches of private communications between Moro and the nation's top prosecutors about the highest-profile prosecutions. When I woke up, I checked my phone. The documents were still appearing, fast and furious.

The same was true when I checked my phone again that night before going to sleep, when I woke up the next day, and when I went to bed the night after that. In fact, every day for the next six days, the documents never stopped appearing, with one materializing every ten seconds or so, depending upon its size. I had installed my Telegram account on a new computer to ensure that the documents were stored somewhere other than my phone, but I still largely avoided using my phone for the entire week. I was afraid I would interrupt the flow of documents or, worse, inadvertently alert authorities.

Once I began to realize the true size of the archive this source was sending me—I did not yet know it would be bigger than the Snowden archive, but began to suspect it would be in that same vicinity—my focus turned to securing the documents. That meant finding a place to store them outside of the reach of the Bolsonaro government, Justice Minister Moro, and Brazilian authorities.

I began to fear that the source was not nearly as careful as he claimed or that perhaps my own communications security—first learned six years earlier under the tutelage of Edward Snowden and since fortified by the Intercept's team of technologists—had already been breached by some combination of US and Brazilian surveillance agencies. As a journalist, when you start working with a source who is providing you documents, you constantly fear it will be taken out of your hands before you have a chance to report it. Fortunately, my experience reporting on the Snowden archive had taught me critical lessons about the indispensability of digital security for journalists in the Internet age, and I knew it was vital to enable sources to pass on information with the utmost security possible. For that reason, when Laura Poitras, investigative journalist Jeremy Scahill, and I cofounded the Intercept in 2013, the first thing we did was hire not editors and journalists, but technology specialists.

One of those technology specialists was Micah Lee, who was instrumental in enabling me and Laura to talk to Snowden and then to safely travel to Hong Kong to receive the NSA archive. Micah was the first person I called as I watched these Brazilian documents pouring in. In a conversation over Signal—the competitor to Telegram that Snowden and other experts, including Micah, believe is the most secure app—I told him about my new source. I stressed the urgent need to get this material out of Brazil and secured in another country as soon as possible. I asked him to tell nobody about these documents yet, and to share them with nobody, including Intercept editors, unless and until I explicitly requested that he do so. He agreed, and told me he'd get to work on this immediately, which I passed on to the source.

A full week after the source and I first began talking, the documents continued to pour in over my telephone—as I ate, as I worked, as I slept.

I spent as many hours as I could reading them, and began to discover that while there were many powerful figures implicated by these documents, the principal target of the reporting would be Justice Minister Moro.

Moro's powerful position in the Bolsonaro government gave him full control over the country's surveillance, investigative, and law enforcement operations. Because I was the founding editor of an anti-Bolsonaro media outlet and my husband is a leftist member of the National Congress, I presumed there was a significant chance that we were already being monitored. I was not confident that an archive this explosive and this large could be first hacked, then sent into my cell phone for days without pause, without that highly unusual activity being detected by an intelligence agency. So I was deeply relieved when Micah told me that he had created a system to transfer the files safely to the United States as we received them.

My journalism assistant, Victor Pougy, who is highly skilled when it comes to questions of technology and online security, worked with Micah on this file transfer. On May 19, a full week after I first began talking to the source, Victor told me, "The files are now with Micah. And as they come in, I'll automatically transfer each new batch to him."

Now that the files were in a secured location in the United States, they were beyond the reach of Brazilian authorities, and the Bolsonaro government couldn't stop our reporting, no matter what they did. That assurance freed me to dive into the content without that nagging concern.

As the days continued to pass, we realized that the archive was so massive that even our carefully constructed system was no longer workable. By now it was clear that the Brazil archive was even larger than the Snowden files, which had been, in terms of sheer size, the largest leak in the history of journalism.

Therefore, Micah created a new system through which the source could upload the whole archive at once to the Intercept's secured servers in New York. After instructing the source how to use it, I received a reassuring message from Micah the following day: "We now have possession of the entire archive."

Throughout this time, I continued speaking with the source by text and, occasionally, when he insisted, by phone.

At the end of the first day of my communications with the source, David had strongly suggested that we film our work. He pointed to the documentary Laura directed about the work we did with Snowden in Hong Kong, and the fallout that ensued from our reporting. That film, *Citizenfour*, won the Academy Award for Best Documentary Feature in 2015. I had stood next to Laura and Snowden's fiancée (now wife) Lindsay Mills as the Oscar statues were handed out by the actors Jennifer

Aniston and David Oyelowo.

David reminded me that the key to that film's power was that it did not rely on retroactive interviews about dramatic events but featured real-time footage of how it all unfolded, thanks to Laura's decision (with Snowden's consent) to begin taping as soon as we began working together in the now-famous room at the Mira Hotel in Hong Kong.

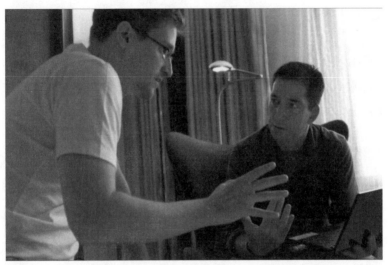

Edward Snowden, left, and Glenn Greenwald at the Mira Hotel in Hong Kong, June 2013. Photo courtesy Laura Poitras, director of Citizenfour.

David insisted that we do the same here—not only because it was clear from the first day, when Manuela had called me and I had talked to the source, that this archive would rock Brazil and our lives in all sorts of unpredictable ways, but also because it would provide crucial protection to me if I had a record of all of my communications with the source, even ones by phone. A photojournalist with whom I had worked and whom I fully trusted recommended a young videographer from São Paulo, and we had him fly to Rio de Janeiro the next day to begin filming. For the next two weeks, he followed me everywhere, filming my work on this story.

Once the archive was fully in our possession, the source began to express the same impatience I had begun to feel myself: *When are you going to start publishing?* He repeatedly insisted that the archive revealed massive corruption far beyond what he was able to find:

PR-PR-00020968.2019.pdf
Not included, change data exporting settings to download.
11.6 MB

14:02

PR-PR-00020968.2019.pdf
Not included, change data exporting settings to download.
11.6 MB

Você vão demorar 1 semana para ler tudo kkkkkk   14:02

E as conversas!   14:02

E com a experiência de vocês, vão encontrar mais inúmeros   14:02
indicios kkkk que eu não encontrei

14:02

PR-PR-00020968.2019 (1).pdf
Not included, change data exporting settings to download.
11.6 MB

14:03

DENUNCIA.circus-maximus.revisado.sara.odt
Not included, change data exporting settings to download.
10.6 MB

14:03

Sentença_sitio.pdf
Not included, change data exporting settings to download.
10.1 MB

14:04

Sentença_sitio.pdf
Not included, change data exporting settings to download.

"It will take you a week to read everything LOL"
"And the chats!"
"And with the experience that all of you have, you'll find innumerable more indicators that I didn't find."

While the source was still uploading the files to my phone, he identified, seemingly without realizing it, the part of the archive that would end up being the most explosive, rock Brazilian politics, and dominate headlines for months: a huge file called "chats" that contained all the different Telegram groups that the prosecutors used to communicate with one another and, most importantly, with Judge Moro:

E mandaram o Moro protocolar, tem tudo na conversa   14:37

14:37

Of. 3257-2017-resposta - solicitação adv.pdf
Not included, change data exporting settings to
download.
2.1 MB

14:37

1_INIC1.pdf
Not included, change data exporting settings to
download.
2.1 MB

Glenn Greenwald   14:37
ta enviando essas conversas?

BRAZIL BARONIL   14:37

102219.pdf
Not included, change data exporting settings to
download.
2.1 MB

14:37

132937.pdf
Not included, change data exporting settings to
download.
2.1 MB

Ainda não, elas tem o nome de chat_ no começo   14:38

Glenn Greenwald   14:38
ok

BRAZIL BARONIL   14:38
Mas vou enviar assim que parar esses

14:38

**Denúncia ELETRONUCLEAR 30_08_2015VERSAO
FINAL.pdf**
Not included, change data exporting settings to
download.
2.1 MB

BB: "And they sent the protocol to Moro, everything is in their conversations."

GG: "Are you sending these conversations?"

BB: "Not yet, they have the name 'chat' at the beginning."

GG: "OK."

BB: "But I'll send it as it is when these stop."

I soon realized I would need the help of trustworthy native Portuguese speakers to navigate the archive and communicate with the source. I called my journalism assistant, Victor, and he came over to my house as I chatted with the source. Needing his help beyond just the work of an assistant, I told Victor, "The job you started with was journalism assistant, but I now need you to immediately upgrade to 'journalist, period': no more 'assistant' anything." He excitedly agreed, and more than rose to the occasion over the difficult months of the reporting.

Later that afternoon, I called Leandro Demori, the dynamic, aggressive young editor in chief we had hired in late 2017 to oversee the Intercept Brasil, and though he was preparing to leave on a weeklong vacation, he came over as well.

I told the source that Victor and Leandro were going to work with me and would be at my side as we spoke and received the files. That's when he sent the "chats" file, which contained five years' worth of conversations among the key players in Operation Car Wash, and contained multiple smoking guns:

47B_Ronaldo_Queiroz_Alterações_na (2).docx
Not included, change data exporting settings to
download.
19.7 KB

Agora vou mandar as conversas!   15:18

Esse dialogs.zip é um compress das conversas, se já quiser ir   15:19
lendo, vai ajudar bastante para entender os arquivos

Já separa ele dos demais!   15:21

                                                                   15:22

dialogs.zip
Not included, change data exporting settings to
download.
61.3 MB

Seus amigos já chegaram?   15:22

GG   **Glenn Greenwald**   15:22
        Sim

BB   **BRAZIL BARONIL**   15:22
        Perfeito kkkk

Eles gostaram do que está acontecendo?   15:22

                                                                   15:23

47B_Ronaldo_Queiroz_Alterações_na (3).docx
Not included, change data exporting settings to
download.
19.7 KB

                                                                   15:23

47B_Ronaldo_Queiroz_Alterações_na.docx
Not included, change data exporting settings to
download

BB: Now I'll send the chats!

-This dialogs.zip is a compression of all the chats, if you already want to start
reading, it will help a huge amount to understand the archive.

-Have your friends arrived yet?

GG: Yes

BB: Perfect LOL

-Do they like what's happening?

With the archive stored in full in the United States, and having confirmed that it contained at least some truly explosive materials, the time came to devise a strategy for how we would report this material. A whole slew of problems and risks were immediately apparent, but I knew I had no choice on the question of whether I would do this reporting. Indeed, it was precisely to report stories like this that I left law and began doing journalism. The Intercept itself, born in the midst of the NSA reporting, was created to enable leaks and reporting that shake power centers at their foundation, and are therefore dangerous. And my work as a journalist and my husband's work as a political official are meant precisely for such moments, when each of us can use the assets and platform we have constructed to enable critical confrontations with power.

Chapter 5

LIFE IN BOLSONARO'S BRAZIL

The overarching context for the reporting we were about to do was the life David and I had built over the prior fifteen years in Brazil, a country now ruled by the Bolsonaro movement. Since we met, everything we have done in our lives we have done together, including preparing to report this story. But the public platform we now occupied both separately and together—I as a journalist, he as an elected official, and we as an openly gay couple in an increasingly antigay political climate—was vital in shaping the events that would follow.

Just as we did prior to beginning our work with Edward Snowden, David and I spent many hours together—before speaking with my colleagues at the Intercept or anyone else—trying to anticipate the risks we were likely to face, the dangers not only to us but to our newly adopted children, and the retaliation we could expect.

"Why is it you who always has to get these huge, dangerous archives?" David said to me only half-jokingly. "Isn't there anyone else they can leak them to?" We both laughed nervously. Yet again, we had no real choice but to forge ahead with reporting an enormous leak, with all that meant for us personally.

Even before I boarded the plane in June 2013 to travel to Hong Kong to meet Snowden, David and I knew this reporting would be very difficult, and we worried we would face serious reprisals. You don't publish thousands of top secret national security documents from the world's sole superpower without expecting to face serious reprisals. We made it through that experience more or less unscathed, although we had some very close calls—including David's now-notorious twelve-hour detention in London's Heathrow Airport in August 2013. David's detention *under a terrorism law* was accompanied by repeated threats to arrest and imprison him on espionage charges, as well as continuous threats from the US government, private and public, that I would be arrested if I tried to leave Brazil.

As a result, it took almost a full year after I returned to Brazil from Hong Kong to feel safe leaving the country. But in May 2014, I did finally return to the United States to receive the George Polk Award for national security reporting, and to learn, the following day, that my NSA reporting for the *Guardian* had been awarded, along with my *Guardian* colleagues and the team at the *Washington Post*, the Pulitzer Prize for public service. So, weighed against the worst-case scenarios that at times seemed probable, it had a largely happy ending for us.

David and I believed the widespread recognition of our work on the Snowden archive gave us some degree of public protection. Indeed, between *Citizenfour*, the acclaimed documentary about the work we had done with Snowden; *No Place to Hide*, the book I wrote chronicling that work, which had been published in more than a dozen languages and spent weeks on the *New York Times* best-seller list; and the feature film by Oliver Stone, in which Snowden was played by Joseph Gordon-Levitt and I was played (flatteringly) by Zachary Quinto, we knew we had developed a substantial public platform that we reasoned would provide at least some measure of protection for these new exposés.

It was this swell of global interest in the Snowden story that enabled Laura, myself, and the investigative journalist Jeremy Scahill, in February 2014, to found a new media outlet—the Intercept, which today employs close to a hundred journalists, editors, and support staff around the world. Then, in 2016, I was able to create the Intercept Brasil, to bring the type of adversarial journalism we had used in the NSA case to a country we believed was sorely lacking in independent reporting.

Still, those ultimate successes of the Snowden journalism sometimes obscure how uncertain our fate was for most of the time we were undertaking it. Our source was charged with multiple felony counts of espionage and remains wanted by the US government. Asylum from the Russian government is all that stands between Snowden and a prison cell in the United States. We were vilified by media outlets around the world, with major newspapers digging deep into the secrets of my past personal life, while other mainstream US journalists explicitly called for my arrest. British agents physically invaded the *Guardian*'s newsroom in London and, under threat of prosecution, forced them to destroy the computers on which they kept their files. I spent almost a full year carrying a backpack wherever I went, filled with encrypted thumb drives containing hundreds of thousands of top secret documents, to ensure that a copy of the archive was always in my possession. Even at home, we were highly guarded in how we spoke, knowing that we were being electronically surveilled.

One daunting lesson David and I learned from the Snowden experience was that however careful you are, it is impossible to anticipate all the threats that you will face when confronting powerful governments.

As stressful and difficult as the Snowden reporting was, we both quickly realized that the dangers from reporting this Brazil archive were going to be entirely different. Navigating the threats posed by the NSA reporting—as grave as they often were—felt more like playing chess than it did some violent contact sport. That was due, in large part, to the fact that the majority of the governments angered most by the NSA reporting (the United States, the United Kingdom, Canada, Australia, and NATO-member intelligence agencies) were thousands of miles away from our Brazil home.

One of the greatest assets I had in reporting on the Snowden archive was that at the time, the Brazilian government viewed that work very favorably, in part because I published a number of stories with the largest Brazilian media outlets revealing how the US, British, and Canadian governments were infiltrating the communications networks of Brazil, spying on Brazilian institutions such as Petrobras and the Ministry of Mines and Energy, monitoring the personal cell phones of Brazilian politicians including President Dilma Rousseff, and collecting massive communications data about the Brazilian population more broadly. The revelations so incensed the Brazilian government that Rousseff canceled a long-planned state dinner at the White House—which would have been the first state dinner for a Brazilian president since the era of the dictatorship—in protest of breaches by the US and its allies of the sanctity of their communications, a transgression that many Brazilians viewed as a new form of colonialism and imperialism. I worked in partnership with the most powerful Brazilian media outlets, principally *Globo*, to do the Snowden reporting, and we received many awards, including the Esso prize, the equivalent of the Pulitzer in Brazilian journalism. Indeed, while the Snowden reporting provoked rage and contempt thousands of miles away in the halls of Washington, it produced support and praise in Brazil.

David and I realized that this time, the dynamic would be exactly the opposite. The Brazilian government, rather than being a key ally, would be our principal adversary, and the interaction would likely be far more acrimonious and threatening.

It is not unusual for journalists to have an adversarial relationship with the governments on which they report. But we knew that we were about to go far beyond standard journalist–politician tensions. Our precarious status—me as a journalist and David as the only LGBT member of the lower house of Congress, in a country with one openly gay senator—hovered over everything we were about to do. Moreover, as I wrote in the first chapter, Brazil is a relatively new democracy, and its politics are often unstable and violent.

Prior to his detention in London, David largely avoided politics. I still vividly recall arguments we had in the first few years after I began my journalism career. When a dinner would be organized for a well-known politician or journalist visiting Brazil, or when we would be invited to similar gatherings during visits to New York or Washington, David would want to stay home, protesting, "You're just going to end up discussing politics all night, and it's going to be sooo boring."

Until 2005, I had worked for a decade as a constitutional lawyer in Manhattan. I had enjoyed litigating, but after ten years, I started to find living and working in New York tiresome. More importantly, the post-9/11 changes in the United States and my perception that rapid erosions in civil liberties were being ignored by the mainstream press compelled me to desire a more public voice in political debates, though I had no idea how to accomplish that. What I knew was that, at the age of thirty-seven, having just ended an eleven-year relationship and working in a profession that was disconnected from what I most wanted to do, I was seeking radical changes in my life.

To figure things out, I cleared my calendar in early 2005 and rented an apartment for seven weeks in Rio, a city I had often visited for vacation and had viscerally loved from the first day I arrived. My infatuation with Rio had grown so much that a couple years earlier, I had begun studying Portuguese with a tutor who came to my law office three times a week. I reasoned that the natural beauty of the city's beaches and mountains, and the natural tendency of its people to find the good in life, would be the ideal setting for thinking clearly about my future. I flew there, with my dog, arriving at night, and checked into the apartment I had rented.

The next morning, I went to the famous Ipanema Beach, only a few blocks from where I was staying. I was there for a couple of hours when a volleyball rolled up to me and knocked over the drink I had ordered. A young, very good-looking Brazilian came to retrieve his ball and, in broken English, apologized for spilling my drink.

We began talking. He introduced himself as David. He abandoned his volleyball game, and we spent the next several hours speaking, alternating from his broken English to my more advanced, but not yet fluent, Portuguese. I had never experienced love at first sight—I didn't believe it even existed—but that all changed as we spent the day on the beach talking, and then had dinner that evening.

We made plans to meet the next day for lunch, and spent virtually every minute of the next week together. We moved in together shortly thereafter, and have been inseparable ever since.

At the time, a law called the Defense of Marriage Act (DOMA)—signed by Bill Clinton in 1994 with vast bipartisan support—expressly prohibited the federal government from recognizing the validity of same-sex marriage and thus from granting any spousal rights to same-sex couples. That was the era of the Newt Gingrich–led Congress, when the social conservative movement had successfully elevated opposition to same-sex marriage to the top of the political agenda. The Democrats had gone along.

DOMA meant that the right automatically enjoyed by US citizens who marry a foreign national of the opposite sex—to have their spouse receive a Green Card and then citizenship, enabling them to live together in the United States—was unavailable to us, as well as numerous other Americans who had fallen in love with a foreign national of the same sex.

To return to live in the United States would mean abandoning the person with whom I knew I wanted to spend the rest of my life. Amazingly, though, Brazil—the largest Catholic country in the world, one that had not yet legalized same-sex marriage, and that, despite its socially permissive reputation, has long been socially conservative—allowed, by virtue of a judicial ruling, Brazilian citizens to obtain permanent residency rights for their same-sex partners. That judicial ruling was based on the principle that it was cruel and inhumane, and a violation of basic human rights, to force Brazilian citizens who fall in love with a same-sex foreigner to choose between departure from their country to live illegally in the country of their same-sex partner, and separation from the person they love.

We used that judicial right to obtain permanent residency status for me, the Brazilian equivalent of a Green Card. Roughly six months later, in October 2005, I created a blog using the free publishing service Blogspot. I had no real plans other than to find a way to express my views and ideas about US politics and law—primarily concerning the War on Terror's assault on civil liberties—that I felt were important but excluded from mainstream US discourse.

Several weeks after I wrote my first post, in December 2005, the *New York Times* reported that the Bush administration was spying on the telephone calls of US citizens without the warrants required by law (namely, the 1978 Foreign Intelligence Surveillance Act, established in the wake of spying abuses uncovered by the Watergate-era Church Committee). The ensuing controversy was the perfect topic for me, given my expertise as a constitutional lawyer, my civil libertarianism and political passions at the time, and my driving belief that core US freedoms were being eroded in the name of the War on Terror. I wrote in depth about that spying scandal almost daily—arguing that the Bush/Cheney administration had engaged in criminal conduct through this illegal domestic spying—and my readership grew very quickly.

At the time, just a few years after the 9/11 attacks and the invasion of Iraq, there were very few voices aggressively challenging the War on Terror as an abusive and even illegal attack on the US Constitution. There was a significant, unfulfilled appetite for the acerbic yet technical daily screeds I was writing about abuses of executive power, which I had not anticipated.

Within six months, I was asked to write a paperback book about the NSA scandal, which I wrote in three months and became a *New York Times* best-seller. A year later, I was invited by the online news site Salon, one of the earliest and most influential online political magazines, to become a columnist and contributing writer. With no real plan, I had stumbled into a new career as a journalist, which enabled me to give up my law practice in the United States and live full-time in Brazil with David.

David was instrumental in shaping my career. He constantly pushed me to believe that I could achieve far more than I thought possible. With an innate interest in and talent for marketing, he negotiated my contracts and created career opportunities for me. And he did all this without any formal education, and without any interest in politics—yet.

An orphan from the age of five, David grew up in Rio's North Zone in one of the city's most deprived and violent slums, Jacarezinho. Rio is famous for beautiful and glamorous beaches such as Ipanema and Copacabana, where rich tourists stay in chic hotels and enjoy perfect weather, glorious sunlight shining down on a picturesque mountain landscape, and glitzy nightlife. But all of that is in the chic South Zone of the city.

The North Zone has no tourists and no beaches. It is composed overwhelmingly of sprawling slums, known as favelas, that were illegally constructed by the city's poor—its majority—using cheap and unreliable construction materials, often only bricks. The favelas hang precariously on the city's hillsides, and it is not uncommon for houses to be washed away during heavy rain and mudslides. Because most favelas remain technically illegal, all services—such as light, water, and cable—were collectively stolen for decades. Though some efforts have been made to legalize them in order to integrate their residents, favelas are still basically gigantic squatting communities.

The favelas are law-free zones, ungoverned by any official municipal or state government. Instead, drug gangs typically rule each community, providing their own form of law and order. While some drug lords are indiscriminately violent and totalitarian, many end up providing more benevolent rule than most city governments. Stealing and other forms of criminality are strictly prohibited inside the favelas, and offenders are subject to summary punishment determined at the sole discretion of the drug gangs, including beating, amputation, and sometimes execution.

Despite all of those deprivations, or perhaps because of them, favelas foster a strong sense of community and an extremely rich and abundant culture. Indeed, most of Brazil's innovative music and art comes from those communities. During my first trips to Rio, I often met people whose stable work and income would allow them to move out of the favela, but who chose to remain; they explained that everything they knew and loved—family, culture, friends—resided there. People in favelas confront horrific deprivation from birth, yet maintain great pride in and love for their communities.

The favelas are nonetheless plagued by horrific violence—typically when the police enter and engage in often-indiscriminate shootouts with the drug gangs, or when rival drug gangs battle for control over territory. Police gun battles with drug gangs are so reckless that children routinely die from stray bullets. In 2019 alone, sixteen Rio de Janeiro children were killed in favelas by bullets, while 1,546 police officers died. In fact, the violence in Rio's slums is so epidemic that the chance someone will be murdered in the city, which really means in the favelas, is higher than in Baghdad at the height of the US war in Iraq.

To grow up in a favela such as Jacarezinho is indescribably difficult, even with family support, and under the best of circumstances. But David grew up there as an orphan. He never knew his father, and his mother, who worked as a prostitute to support him, died from a sexually transmitted disease that turned into ovarian cancer when he was five. Nominally raised by one of his mother's sisters, who worked as a housekeeper and had four children of her own, David had to stop attending school at the age of thirteen to eke out a living by working menial jobs. Eager to be self-sufficient and forge a path in the world, he left home and spent many days sleeping on the street. Beyond all those hardships, he is gay and black in a country where both remain massive social barriers. His intellect and work ethic miraculously enabled him to find stable work in offices by the time we had met.

After we met, David finished the equivalent of junior high, then high school, then graduated one of Rio's most prestigious colleges with a marketing degree. He had a dream to work on the design and promotion of video games for a technology company such as Sony. Like so many people of his generation around the world, it was through video games that David had learned, as a teenager, to speak English, along with much else about the world. (My playful mockery of his love of video games ended with David's vindication when Snowden, in 2013, told me of the key role they had played in forming his childhood conceptions of duty, morality, and purpose.)

But his work with me, and especially his unjust detention in 2013 by British authorities, politicized and radicalized David. His detention in London made worldwide headlines, as it was viewed, rightfully so, as an attempt to threaten and intimidate my husband as a means of punishing me for my journalism.

David was particularly indignant that the UK government had allowed numerous journalists who worked closely on the Snowden story—including Laura Poitras—to pass through Heathrow without any problems, but chose to detain him, someone viewed as ancillary to the journalism controversy. He became convinced that British authorities chose him because he is Brazilian rather than American or British, because he is black rather than white, and because he is from a Third World country perceived as weak rather than a "developed" Western country, and was thus more vulnerable to having his rights deprived.

After this incident, David was reluctantly thrust into the public spotlight. While at first he was somewhat shell-shocked under the media limelight, particularly when giving television interviews in English, his confidence began to grow as he appeared on outlets around the world—CNN, BBC, CBC, and virtually every TV outlet in Brazil. He discussed with growing indignation the threats and manipulation he had endured from British authorities, all with the advance knowledge and tacit approval of the Obama White House.

David's anger over what he regarded as the US government's punitive and unjust treatment of Edward Snowden, whom he had befriended online and then in person when visiting Russia with me, further fueled his politicization. That sense of injustice led David to lead a campaign in Brazil and internationally to secure asylum for Snowden in a country other than Russia. And the opposition he experienced—including from governments that directly benefited from Snowden's revelations, such as

Brazil and Germany—only further cemented his determination to pursue political battles.

Ultimately, David's successful lawsuit against the UK government—in which he obtained a 2016 judicial ruling from a British appeals court that the use of the British terrorism law to detain journalists was an abridgment of the guarantee of a free press under the European Convention on Human Rights—convinced him that politics offered a meaningful and fulfilling path for changing and improving the world. Most of all, David often says, these experiences made him realize that while one may want to avoid politics, politics may not want to avoid you.

After spearheading the effort to secure asylum for Snowden, and organizing a separate campaign for a "Snowden treaty" to create an international convention to establish whistleblower rights, David became active in Brazil's left-wing Socialism and Liberty Party (PSOL). David's involvement with the party began in 2014, in the midst of the presidential campaign of one of PSOL's founders, Luciana Genro. David met with Genro to discuss the campaign, following which she vowed to offer asylum to Snowden if she were elected. Subsequently, she and I held a joint press conference in Rio about her proposal.

Throughout 2014 and 2015, David spent his time building an infrastructure within PSOL for young black, brown, and LGBT people, many of whom were raised in favelas, and all of whom had been largely excluded from politics. He rented a space that he called the House of the Youth, where he hosted political events for these marginalized community members.

That work, along with David's innate charisma and political talent, earned him a devoted and increasingly large pool of young supporters. There were very few political activists in Brazil like David—someone who had been raised as an orphan, in the slums, was both black and LGBT, and faced multiple levels of oppression, with a family who still lived in the favela—and he felt a growing obligation to use the privileges and visibility he had developed to speak out and organize.

In 2016, at the age of thirty-one, David decided to launch his first political campaign, for a seat on the city council of Rio de Janeiro. Like everything in Brazilian politics, municipal elections are brutal: more than fifteen hundred candidates run for fifty-one seats, meaning that less than

5 percent of candidates emerge victorious. There are no districts; all candidates run citywide. A complicated formula determines how many of the fifty-one seats each party receives, and then those parties' seats are filled according to where the candidates' vote totals rank them within the party.

Elections in Brazil are subsumed by systemic corruption. Political parties that have no organic or popular support pay off the chiefs of drug gangs in the favelas, or paramilitary gangs composed of police and military officers, to ensure that the neighborhoods they control deliver all their votes. Many neighborhoods remain off-limits for campaigning unless permission is secured from militia chiefs. Few candidates actually win by grassroots campaigning, and thus very few political experts gave David—a first-time candidate, with no machine support, in a city that had *never* elected any LGBT member to its city council—any real chance of winning.

But David devoted himself day and night to his campaign. He had an army of highly energetic volunteers—students, LGBTs, favela residents, human rights and privacy activists—who worked as hard as he did to find voters to support him. On election night—October 2, 2016—I decided to stay at home to watch the results, too nervous to be around David's campaign team. But minutes before the returns were scheduled, the electricity in our house stopped working, so I rushed to check into a hotel room near David's campaign headquarters to watch the results alone. I decided I would go to David's campaign party only once the result, one way or the other, had become clear.

For three hours as the vote count streamed in, I maniacally clicked "refresh" on the election results app on my phone, and watched as David began well behind where he needed to be, steadily rose as his stronger districts were counted, and then, as the finish line approached, hovered near the number he needed in order to win.

With roughly 98 percent of the vote counted, his campaign manager called to assure me that David's victory was now guaranteed. "Are you absolutely sure?" I asked, still refusing to believe David had won. "Yes," he assured me, "it's mathematically impossible for him to lose his lead."

I ran out of the hotel, hopped into a cab, and arrived just moments before David was poised to give his victory speech. My shock and ecstasy made the rest of the evening a blur. The only thing I recall about the rest of that night was the amazement that my once stubbornly apolitical—even anti-political—husband had defied all odds to win a seat on the city council of one of the world's largest and greatest cities, where he had grown up an orphan in a favela. David made Brazilian history, becoming the first-ever openly LGBT citizen of Rio de Janeiro to be elected to that body.

As extraordinary as David's victory was, there was an even more stunning election win that night. Whereas David eked out victory by a small margin, a black LGBT woman from the favela—Marielle Franco, also a first-time candidate—stunned Rio's political establishment by being elected to the city council with a massive vote total. (Though married to a woman at the time of her election, she did not come out as LGBT in any public setting until shortly after her victory.) Running on the same party ticket as David, Marielle compiled such a large vote total that she ended up as the city's fifth-most popular candidate, surpassing incumbents who had served multiple terms over decades and beating almost all of the corrupt machine candidates.

The similarities between Marielle's and David's trajectories were obvious: in addition to their identities and backgrounds, they had very similar political causes, including a devotion to opposing notorious, rampant, and lethal police violence against minorities and the poor in the city's favelas. Marielle had become a single mother at the age of nineteen, but like David, she went back to school and ended up with a master's degree in sociology. They were exactly the kind of people who have long been excluded from positions of power in Brazil, one of the world's most unequal countries.

Marielle had a much longer political presence in the city's political life than David. She had worked for a decade as a top aide to the de facto leader of PSOL in Rio, State Representative Marcelo Freixo. And their work was very dangerous: one of Freixo's primary causes was the defense of the city's poor and black residents from human rights abuses at the hands of the police.

Even more dangerously, Marielle had worked with Freixo on a multiyear investigation into the city's paramilitary gangs. While favela "drug lords" receive the vast bulk of media attention when it comes to discussions of Brazil's crime epidemic—their black faces make compelling media villains for white, middle-class television audiences—it is the country's paramilitary gangs, or militias, that are far more organized, violent, and dangerous. But because they are largely white, from middle-class neighborhoods, and composed of former and current police officers and military members, Rio's militias have long been viewed by the Brazilian bourgeoisie as benign. As data published by the Intercept Brasil shows, they are anything but; indeed, in 2016 and 2017, militia activity was associated with a far higher percentage of criminal occurrences than were drug gangs:

Criminal Occurrences
2016–2017

Drug Gangs	Militias
34.8%	65.2%

Source: Data from Disque-Denúncia.

The investigation ended up successfully identifying hundreds of militia within the police forces, military branches, the state legislature of Rio (where Marielle worked at the time), and the Rio city council. As a result of that investigation, dozens of leading militia members were sent to prison.

Throughout the investigation, and long after, Freixo was deluged by serious and detailed death threats. He could never leave his home without a team of armed guards and armored vehicles. (Now a member of the National Congress, Freixo is still forced to use the same extreme security measures for protection from the city's most violent militia leaders, who continue to want him dead.) And such fears proved well founded: in 2011, the judge who oversaw the trials and convictions of the militia members uncovered by Freixo and Marielle was gunned down by masked assassins at close range with twenty-one bullets as she left her house in broad daylight. Six police officers, including a lieutenant colonel, were ultimately arrested and convicted for the judge's murder.

Marielle's extraordinary 2016 victory meant she was no longer Freixo's aide and protégé. She was now a political force of her own to be reckoned with.

Immediately upon their January 1, 2017, inauguration as members of the city council, Marielle and David decided to sit next to one another in the august chamber. The symbolism of two black, LGBT, favela-raised, young, and highly defiant left-wing activists occupying a traditionally white, wealthy, corrupt, and conservative legislative body was powerful. Marielle and David did not merely sit next to each other, but became best friends, working day and night on their joint causes. Marielle's wife, Mônica Benício, also became a close personal friend of ours. We talked often of how Marielle and David and people like them had to be the future not only of PSOL, but of the left in Brazil—a country in which middle-class and wealthy whites were a minority yet still dominated all institutions of power.

In 2017, David and I adopted two biological brothers, aged ten and eight, from an orphanage in Brazil's Northeast. One of the first things we did was invite Marielle over to our house so that our new sons could meet this extraordinary, charismatic, powerful living testament to the principle that no barrier in life, no prejudice in Brazil, is insurmountable.

Marielle, center left, with her wife, Mônica Benício, center right, and our children, early 2018 at our Rio de Janeiro home. Photo by David Miranda.

Once he was elected to the city council, I knew that David's political future was extremely bright, but as a newcomer David was still relatively little known. So my certainty was not shared by everyone; indeed, at that point, very few people thought of David that way. On the other hand, everyone regarded Marielle as a certain future political star with unlimited potential. Meeting Marielle, you knew you were in the presence of someone truly special. It was impossible to take your eyes off her. Without trying, she dominated every room she was in. Tall and proud in stature, dynamic, beautiful, fearless, and with a universally inspiring biography, it seemed as if Marielle was built in a factory to be the perfect political leader. But what made Marielle such a unique political force was a combination of strength and humility that I had rarely if ever encountered in my life. She would be unfailingly polite, respectful, and courteous to everyone from the waitstaff in the council chamber to the lowest-level aides. The next minute, she would be unbelievably assertive, courageous, and self-possessed in the presence of powerful and intimidating people who treated her as if she did not belong in their halls of power.

Powerful white men in Brazil expect deference, not defiance, from black women from favelas. Ones who are LGBT provoke even more contempt. There are inspiring videos of Marielle in which she chastises long-serving, militia-linked members of the city council who had acted in a disrespectful or abusive manner toward her or others she was there to represent. As Marielle is speaking, you can see the discomfort, the rage, the offense in their body language and face—it is visceral. And she makes clear, without an ounce of fear or intimidation, that she has every right to not just be present in the chamber but to be heard on equal terms. In one particularly contentious and now-iconic exchange, she ascends to the podium on the council floor to denounce a notorious militia-linked city council member for muttering misogynistic and homophobic comments under his breath while in an elevator with her. In her rebuke, she riffed on his comment, asserting that her colleagues would need to learn "how to listen to a woman who was . . . *elected*."

Marielle was an inspiration to me and David, both politically and personally. But she was also a crucial symbol to hundreds of thousands of people in Rio who saw in her, likely for the first time, someone who was not only devoted to speaking and working for them but who was one of them. Her political future was boundless, not only in terms of what she could achieve for herself, but of what she could achieve for Rio and for Brazil.

On March 14, 2018—just over a year after David and Marielle took their seats—I heard David's cell phone ring as we were in bed, preparing to go to sleep: 10:20 p.m., a time of night when one does not expect to receive calls absent bad news. This call brought news that wasn't bad. It was unimaginably horrific.

Within seconds of David answering his phone, I heard sounds coming out of his body that I had never heard in all our years together. He began howling, screaming, sobbing. It was impossible for me to make out any words. It was obvious that something unbearable had happened. After hanging up the telephone, David sobbed for five minutes straight. My attempts to calm him down enough to tell me what happened were futile.

After those moments of all-consuming fear and pain, watching my husband sob and convulse with emotional torment, he finally gathered himself enough to speak a sentence—one that, to this day, horrifies me as much as the first time I heard it. "They killed Marielle."

The person who delivered this devastating news was the manager of David's 2016 campaign, now serving as his chief of staff, Honório Oliveira. Honório told David it was already beyond doubt that this was an execution: a political assassination, not a botched robbery or random killing.

Earlier that night, Marielle had participated in a publicly promoted panel event in downtown Rio entitled "Black Women Moving Political Structures." She left once the event concluded at roughly 9:00 p.m. Along with her press aide, she entered the car where her driver was waiting. Although it was typically Marielle's custom to sit in the front seat next to her driver—part of her egalitarian nature—on this night she atypically sat in the back seat, on the opposite side of her driver, so that she could talk with her press aide, who sat directly behind him.

Within twenty minutes of her leaving the building, a black Chevrolet Cobalt with fully tinted windows pulled up next to Marielle's car, hovering just a few inches behind it. Someone in the back seat of that car opened the window as both cars were moving, pointed a gun at Marielle's car, and fired thirteen bullets into it, aimed at exactly the seat Marielle was occupying in the back. Four of those bullets entered Marielle's skull, killing her instantly. Three of the bullets penetrated the back of her driver, Anderson Gomes, who also died instantly.

The diagonal trajectory of the bullets meant that Marielle's press aide, seated behind the driver, was miraculously spared. As the car came to a stop, the press aide watched the black car speed off. No effort was made to steal any belongings. The only goal was Marielle's assassination.

After hearing this news from my sobbing husband, I watched news of Marielle's murder quickly spread online. A couple of foreign journalists, with good intentions, inaccurately suggested that she was killed as part of a mugging. Knowing the truth, and not knowing what else to do with my shock and pain, I went to Twitter to ensure that the truth about Marielle's death, and her life, was known to Brazil and to the world.

Through tears, I posted in both Portuguese and English that Marielle was executed—not killed as part of a robbery. I then felt a compulsion to tell the world who Marielle was and why her assassination was so devastating. I wrote a series of tweets about Marielle's background, her life, her character, her trajectory, and what she symbolized to a city and country that has suffered so much and had so few causes for hope. I posted photos of Marielle and did my best to convey what the world had lost.

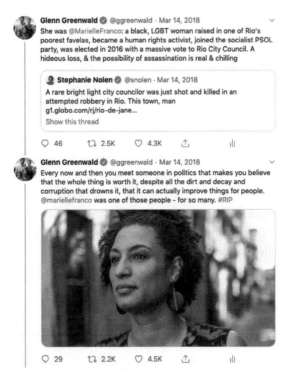

Glenn Greenwald ✓ @ggreenwald · Mar 14, 2018

She was @MarielleFranco: a black, LGBT woman raised in one of Rio's poorest favelas, became a human rights activist, joined the socialist PSOL party, was elected in 2016 with a massive vote to Rio City Council. A hideous loss, & the possibility of assassination is real & chilling

> Stephanie Nolen ✓ @snolen · Mar 14, 2018
> A rare bright light city councilor was just shot and killed in an attempted robbery in Rio. This town, man
> g1.globo.com/rj/rio-de-jane...
> Show this thread

♡ 46   ↩ 2.5K   ♡ 4.3K   ⬆   �ﬞ

Glenn Greenwald ✓ @ggreenwald · Mar 14, 2018

Every now and then you meet someone in politics that makes you believe that the whole thing is worth it, despite all the dirt and decay and corruption that drowns it, that it can actually improve things for people. @mariellefranco was one of those people - for so many. #RIP

♡ 29   ↩ 2.2K   ♡ 4.5K   ⬆   �ﬞ

Glenn Greenwald
@ggreenwald

Marielle was a black, LGBT woman raised in one of Rio's poorest favelas, became a human rights activist, joined the socialist PSOL party, was elected in 2016 with a massive vote to Rio City Council. Among her primary work was police violence & extra-judicial murders. So horrible.

7:35 AM · Mar 15, 2018 · Twitter Web Client

View Tweet activity

1.8K Retweets 3.2K Likes

As I watched those tweets go viral around the world, I felt some small satisfaction that Marielle would influence the world in death as she had in life. But nothing could numb the fundamental horror: one of the most powerful, inspiring, and beautiful forces of life I had ever encountered had been eradicated in an instant, at the age of thirty-eight, in an act of brazen political violence, carried out on the downtown streets of Rio de Janeiro at 9:45 that night.

David's chief of staff called again to say that various PSOL elected officials were headed toward the murder scene, and suggested David should go. But I pleaded with him not to leave the house. We had no idea what the motive was behind this assassination. Was it part of some planned murder spree against PSOL politicians, prominent LGBTs, left-wing officials, city council members who denounced police violence and militias, or favela residents who didn't know their place? Because our kids were sleeping, I couldn't go with David, which meant he'd have to leave the house alone. He agreed to stay with me.

We were then told that Marielle's funeral and wake would be held the next morning, at the city council chamber. Along with Freixo and several members of Marielle's family, David would carry the coffin up the stairs of the chamber where Marielle, along with her driver, Anderson, would lie in wake. We stayed up all night crying in grief, horror, and terror: If they could murder Marielle like this, who was safe?

That night changed everything for Rio politics, David's work, and our sense of physical safety. Brazil has certainly been plagued by shocking political violence in the past, but Marielle's assassination was so close, so personal, so emotionally devastating, unsettling, and terrifying.

As we spent the next several weeks comforting Marielle's grieving, emotionally destroyed widow, Mônica, I often pondered how easily it could have been me grieving the sudden murder of my spouse. David thought often of how easily it could have been him rather than Marielle. Political violence in the abstract is scary. Political violence that comes an inch from your family's life is terrorizing, by design. And that's what it was for us.

Marielle's death attracted international attention. Celebrities from around the world, particularly black ones such as Viola Davis, Naomi Campbell, RuPaul, and Janelle Monáe, publicly expressed their anger over her execution. Katy Perry and Roger Waters both paid homage to her at their concerts in Brazil. International reporters began writing appreciations of the magnitude of her life and death. I was asked by the *Independent* to write her obituary, and poured more energy and thought into that article than almost any I have ever written. While all of that provided some solace—Marielle was a political person, and her death needed to have political meaning—nothing could numb the pain.

The day after Marielle's assassination was perhaps the worst day of my life. We arrived at the city council chamber at roughly 8:00 a.m., and everyone sobbed uncontrollably. Nobody could comfort anyone else.

As the crowd of mourners grew by the thousands, we tried to understand what could have motivated such a barbaric act. Marielle had not been on the verge of uncovering any ring of corruption by powerful actors or of leading any particularly threatening investigation. She had spent the days before her death loudly protesting the killing of a young boy in a favela by an especially notorious police battalion, but that was something that she did with regularity, along with most other left-wing politicians in the city. It was hard to believe that routine condemnations of police killings could have prompted the execution of a city councilwoman.

In what now seemed like dark prescience, on the day before her death, Marielle tweeted, "Another homicide of a young man that can be credited to the police. Matheus Melo was leaving church when he was killed. How many others will have to die for this war to end?"

How many others will have to die for this war to end?

As we struggled to make some sense of this loss, and to alleviate what felt like a complete loss of control, we considered the possibility that this was an attempt to exact vengeance on Marcelo Freixo, Marielle's mentor who led the investigations into militias. Or perhaps it was a political hate crime: the first in a spree against LGBT, leftist, black, or socialist public figures that endangered everyone in those groups, including David, myself, and so many of our friends, colleagues, and associates.

Nobody knew. That somehow made Marielle's murder all the more terrifying and painful.

Marielle's coffin finally arrived at the chamber at roughly 11:00 a.m. I saw the crowd parting as David, holding the front end of the coffin on one end, with Freixo on the other, struggled to hold its weight. Marielle's weeping relatives, behind them, were barely able to stand, let alone offer assistance in carrying the heavy box that held the corpse of their murdered loved one.

I will never forget the sight of David's face—red, sobbing, and strained—as he carried the coffin of his best friend up the majestic staircase of Rio's historic city council building, while thousands of people sobbed together. Nor will I ever forget the first time after Marielle's assassination that I saw Mônica being pushed through the council chamber in a wheelchair, unable to stand, with her face buried in her hands, weeping through the shock.

David Miranda (left) and Marcelo Freixo (right) carry the coffin of Marielle Franco outside the Rio de Janeiro City Council Chamber March 15, 2018. Photo by Ricardo Borges.

Photo by Ricardo Moraes.

Marielle's assassination transformed the political climate in Rio and in Brazil, not just for me and David but for everyone we knew. As the trauma and grief finally began to stabilize, international media attention slowly shifted to other tragedies and injustices, and the weeks of mass daily protests on the streets of Rio finally began to subside, our attention turned to one question: Who killed Marielle Franco and why? By this question, we meant not so much who pulled the trigger—though we obviously wanted to know that—but rather, who ordered and paid for the trigger to be pulled?

Marielle's assassination changed our lives, and the way we lived them. David immediately rented an armored car impenetrable to bullets. His driver took lessons in security. We significantly increased the number of cameras monitoring our home and made other modifications recommended by security specialists. Citing my prominent role as a left-wing journalist in Brazil and cofounder of a very vocal independent media outlet that was increasingly critical of Bolsonaro, David urged me not to walk around Rio any longer without armed security. He insisted that I also obtain an armored car and a similar security protocol.

I wasn't yet ready to live under such a repressive regime. I had rejected Federal Police protection offered to me by the Brazilian Senate during the Snowden reporting because of the confining nature of such a high level of security. It robs you of so much privacy and liberty. But now, the threat of violence had become far more real. I reluctantly started using security teams for publicly announced events.

As the weeks and then the months passed after Marielle's assassination without any arrests, one fact became clear: the killers had executed her murder with an extreme level of precision and professionalism, one possible only with detailed knowledge of how murder investigations are conducted. The skill with which her killing was carried out was virtually perfect. Security cameras showed two cars waiting outside of the event, both with completely impenetrable tinted windows, preventing security cameras from detecting who was inside. They waited for hours for Marielle without getting out of the car, opening the window, or turning on the light. The license plate on each car was fake.

Although there are security cameras placed in most locations on the street Marielle used to travel home, her killers knew to choose exactly the spot where there was none. And somehow, for some still-unexplained reason, the closest cameras to the point where they killed her had been turned off the day before.

In the weeks following Marielle's death, police investigators released snippets and clues that strongly supported the thesis most already believed: that her assassination was linked with, and possibly directly ordered and carried out by, militias composed of military and police officers—former or current armed law enforcement agents of the state.

The weapon of death was a nine-millimeter submachine gun commonly used by the military and police. And the bullets used to kill her and her driver were linked to a batch originally purchased in 2006 by the Federal Police, the same batch used in Brazil's worst-ever *chacina*, or "slaughter"—a chilling term that refers to indiscriminate murder sprees on the part of the Brazilian police against large numbers of people, as revenge or vigilante justice. In that 2015 chacina, seventeen people were murdered on the same night in São Paulo. Three Military Police officers and one officer from the civilian police were convicted of the murders.

David and I struggled to find the balance between processing Marielle's murder as a crucial political event and as the devastating emotional loss of a close friend. We grew even closer to Mônica, who, following Marielle's example, found the internal strength to transform her grief into something she never wanted to be: a political activist, traveling the country and then the world in a search for justice. I felt a particular duty to use my international platform as a journalist to do everything I could to prevent the world from forgetting about Marielle's murder, and to pressure Brazilian authorities to find her killers. David assumed a deep and heavy obligation to redouble his work on the causes to which he and Marielle were devoted.

In mid-2018, several months after Marielle's murder, we began to discuss the possibility that David would run for Congress in that year's federal elections in October. He was serving a four-year term as city councilman, which meant he could keep his seat until 2020, even if he ran for Congress and lost.

There were serious factors mitigating against David's run for Congress: we had two newly adopted children; the campaign, his second in two years, would be exhausting and brutal; if he won the election, David would be required to spend most of the week in Brasilia, the country's depressing capital, a two-hour flight from Rio; there was only one openly LGBT member in the entire 513-seat lower house, Jean Wyllys, but he was also from Rio and in David's party, which meant David would have to compete with him, a two-term incumbent, for LGBT votes; and the campaign, especially if successful, would only further increase our visibility, and therefore our vulnerability.

But ultimately, the course David had chosen for his life by entering politics—and what we both felt was the universe's plan for him—left us with no real choice. The last conversation I had with Marielle, in our home, with her wife, just a couple of weeks before her death, was filled with talk about Marielle's and David's political futures. We spent hours discussing how PSOL, and Brazilian politics generally, urgently needed more voices like theirs—elected officials who could speak from experience about poverty, deprivation, favela life, repression of LGBTs and racial minorities, and wholesale denial of opportunity; who had that understanding in their blood and bones, rather than as abstract theories learned in well-intentioned but still-insulated college courses taught by middle-class or wealthy leftists.

The void left by Marielle made us feel that David's congressional campaign was as much of an obligation as it was a choice. I assured David that I would do everything necessary to make our family life function smoothly if he won and had to spend much of his week away from our Rio home and our two young sons.

And with that, we decided: David would spend 2018 running for a seat in Congress, simultaneous with Jair Bolsonaro's bid for the presidency.

— — — — — — — — — —

After an extremely arduous and difficult year—for our family and for Brazil—election night finally arrived on October 7. Supporters gathered at David's campaign headquarters to watch the results come in. This time, confident in the campaign David had run, I decided I could bear the tension and didn't hide alone in a hotel room nearby.

The initial results looked reasonably good for David. With the first returns from Niterói—a large city located just outside of the Rio precincts where David's was strongest—he was already in seventh place out of more than fifty PSOL candidates, just two spots behind the fifth-place finish we all believed he needed to win. The expectation was that PSOL would win five congressional seats, ensuring that David would win as long he came in fifth or better within his party. Because two of the candidates in front of him were from Niterói, I was confident David would easily pass them as the much-larger Rio precincts started to be counted. Within less than an hour, David moved into the coveted fifth-place spot within his party. I wasn't relaxed about the outcome, but for the first time I felt confident that David would win.

However, as the evening progressed, it started to become clear that the far-right Bolsonaro-led wave that was sweeping the entire country, including Rio, was far more extensive and engulfing than anyone had predicted. At roughly 9:00 p.m.—with only a fraction of the votes in the congressional races counted—the final total for the presidential race was announced. Bolsonaro had come close to a 50 percent majority in the first round of voting, among a crowded field of eight major-party candidates, something that would have been unprecedented in Brazilian democracy. He had received 46.2 percent of the vote, 17 points ahead of the second-place Workers' Party ticket. That margin was overwhelming, and given how many of the eliminated candidates were from the center-right or the right, and thus would almost certainly end up endorsing Bolsonaro, the results left little to no hope that Bolsonaro could be defeated in the runoff. Those early results not only forced all of us to face the reality that it would be highly likely that a figure relegated to the far-right fringes of Brazilian politics for decades would become president, but also that his tiny far-right party would do far better than anyone anticipated.

As we hit the 10:00 p.m. mark, the large majority of the votes in the Rio congressional race had been counted. David continued to remain comfortably in fifth place. But the magnitude of the far-right wave made me question whether his party would in fact get five congressional seats from the state, as the party's political advisers and experts had told us all year was essentially assured. Indeed, going into election night, the only question anyone was asking was whether PSOL would get a sixth seat. But it began to appear that the key assumptions behind this electoral calculus were failing.

With trepidation, I asked Honório, David's campaign manager: "Are we still sure that PSOL is going to win five seats?"

Honório replied carefully: "I'm not sure anymore, to be honest." I could tell by the tone of his voice that, contrary to his words, he was quite close to certain.

Minutes later, one of Brazil's largest media outlets estimated that PSOL would win only four seats from the state of Rio de Janeiro, which meant that David would end up not as a congressman but as first alternate. That grim news was soon accompanied by even worse. The previously obscure far-right candidate for governor of Rio state, Wilson Witzel—an ex-judge who celebrated the destruction of a street sign in Marielle Franco's honor with a raised fist in the air, and whose entire campaign was explicitly based on the implementation of Filipino strongman Rodrigo Duterte's fascist model of widespread extrajudicial killings in slums in the name of fighting crime and drugs—came in first place with 41 percent of the vote, a massive 21 points ahead of Rio's popular former two-term centrist mayor, Eduardo Paes. That meant that not only were we about to have Bolsonaro running the country, but an even more extreme version of Bolsonaro as governor of the state where we lived, overseeing the Military Police.

Shortly thereafter, we learned that Rodrigo Amorim, the former running mate of Bolsonaro's son—who had, in fact, been the one to destroy the Marielle sign—had not only won a seat in the Rio state legislature as a member of Bolsonaro's new party, but had received the highest vote total of any of the winning candidates in the entire city of Rio. Moreover, the Military Police officer from Bolsonaro's party who had helped Amorim break that sign, Daniel Silveira, was elected to the National Congress, also as part of Bolsonaro's new party.

I will never forget the sound of Mônica weeping next to me as she learned that the authoritarian cretins who had cruelly and vindictively destroyed a tribute to her murdered wife were rewarded for that act. Marielle had been assassinated less than seven months earlier, and we had to watch representatives of the faction that rejoiced in her killing ascend to the highest levels of power.

Once this horrible night was finally over, the full extent of the damage became clear. Bolsonaro's crypto-fascist party, which had barely existed a year earlier, had won so many seats in the National Congress—fifty-two—that it would be the second-largest party in Brazil, just four seats behind the Workers' Party. Numerous governors aligned with Bolsonaro had also won, and the country's state houses were now filled with extremists, charlatans, and outright fascists who were swept from total obscurity into political power by associating themselves with Bolsonaro.

Brazil was about to be dominated from top to bottom by the Bolsonaro political machine and an ideology so extreme—one that was pro-dictatorship, fanatically anti-LGBT, and driven by religious zealotry—that it did not even fit on the country's mainstream political spectrum a year earlier.

David and I had had previous personal encounters with Bolsonaro, all of which were uniformly and deeply acrimonious, and reflective of how central anti-LGBT animus has always been to his political identity and worldview. One of them arose from the first time I ever wrote about Bolsonaro, in 2014. Back then, it was unthinkable that he would ever be president. Indeed, I wanted to write about him to convey to the English-speaking world how shocking it was that he could even be a member of the Brazilian Congress. What prompted that article were comments Bolsonaro had made to a left-wing member of congress, Maria do Rosário, after she accused him, accurately, of having defended the torturers and rapists who ruled Brazil's military dictatorship. In response, Bolsonaro told her, in front of a crowd of journalists: "Don't worry, I wouldn't rape you: you don't merit my rape." Bolsonaro later told the newspaper *Zero Hora* that he would not rape do Rosario, because she is "ugly" and "not his type."

As part of the article, we tried to interview Bolsonaro. David, working at the time with me on my journalism, called him to conduct the interview. After asking Bolsonaro about those comments, David also asked about his bill to ban same-sex couples from adopting children, specifically inquiring whether he thought it preferable to leave the nation's fifty thousand unadopted children in orphanages rather than allow them to be with two loving parents. David and I were actively considering adopting children at that time, so this bill was of personal as well as journalistic interest to us.

At that point, Bolsonaro said to David, "You're Glenn Greenwald's husband, right?" After David confirmed he was, Bolsonaro said, "If you want a baby so badly, why don't you go and rent a woman's belly?" He added, "Don't worry, soon homosexuals will be able to have a uterus implanted in them, and then you can have a baby." We included that quote, along with several other of his most horrifying statements—among them his decades-old praise of Brazil's military dictatorship—under this 2014 headline:

THE MOST MISOGYNISTIC, HATEFUL ELECTED OFFICIAL IN THE DEMOCRATIC WORLD: BRAZIL'S JAIR BOLSONARO

Congresswoman doesn't "merit being raped."

started to become apparent that his presidential campaign was far stronger than anyone had anticipated. In a discussion with another journalist about the threat he posed, I called him a "fascist cretin" on Twitter. He saw the tweet, and responded to me by using a crude, homophobic epithet in Portuguese for anal sex—"burning the donut"—which he translated into English using Google Translate:

Jair M. Bolsonaro ✔
@jairbolsonaro   Follow   ˅

"Do you burn the donut?" I don't care! Be happy! Hugs for you!

> Glenn Greenwald ✔ @ggreenwald
> Replying to @Gerson775 @jairbolsonaro
> Bolsonaro is a fascist cretin for reasons having nothing to do with Maia's praise. This reflects poorly on Maia, not Bolsonaro.

7:59 AM - 4 Sep 2017

5,122 Retweets 14,097 Likes

♡ 1.3K   ⇅ 5.1K   ♡ 14K

While journalists from major media outlets condemned his tweet, his followers loved it. The tweet went viral, and for weeks I was inundated with homophobic messages invoking this slur. New memes of my photo along with images of a donut on fire were created by his movement.

Anti-LGBT hatred was a key driver of Bolsonaro's popularity, and with the 2018 election, we had to accept that he, his family, and his party had just become the most powerful players in all of Brazil.

The political dominance of the far-right wave after the first round of voting left much of the country in shock: Bolsonaro's oldest son, Flavio, moved from the Rio state house, where he had served for a decade, to the Federal Senate; his 4.3 million votes virtually doubled the vote total of the second-place candidate. Bolsonaro's youngest son, Eduardo, was reelected to the lower house of Congress from São Paulo with 1.8 million votes, by far the largest vote total ever received by a congressional candidate in the history of Brazilian democracy. And Bolsonaro's middle son, Carlos, remained on the city council of Rio, where David served with him, and was widely credited (or, more accurately, scorned) as the mastermind of his father's online communication strategy of fake news and defamatory lies against his adversaries and critics.

One of the only eventful episodes of the runoff election took place on October 22, just days before the second round of voting. In the weeks leading up to the first round of voting, Bolsonaro had been near-fatally stabbed by a deranged lone actor. He had spent weeks in the hospital, which relieved him of difficult debates and challenging interviews as he cruised to his first-round victory. He had rarely been seen in public since that win, except in sympathy-generating hospital videos featuring his sons affectionately wiping sweat from his forehead as he struggled to speak through the tubes in his throat. In one memorable hospital scene, Bolsonaro warned that "only election fraud by the Workers' Party" could cause him to lose the election, and he urged his "friends in the Armed Forces" to prepare to intervene if he did not win.

But on this date, a huge crowd of his followers gathered in São Paulo, Brazil's largest city, and Bolsonaro spoke to them from his Rio home using his cell phone. He proceeded to deliver one of the most deranged and frightening political speeches I've heard from a major political figure in my lifetime. Though it lasted just ten minutes, he managed to confirm the worst fears of his opponents, providing a virtual checklist of what fascists do once they wield power. All at once, the suspicion that his near-fatal stabbing would radicalize him seemed to be confirmed even further.

The headline of the *Guardian* article about Bolsonaro's speech the next day told much of the story: "Brazil's Jair Bolsonaro Threatens Purge of Leftwing 'Outlaws.'" In what that paper described as "a menacing address that left opponents outraged and unnerved," Bolsonaro bellowed one threat after the next into his cell phone, which in turn were amplified by giant speakers at the venue where his supporters had gathered.

Of his "red" political opponents, Bolsonaro decreed, "Either they go overseas, or they go to jail." Invoking Hitler-like imagery, he added, "These red outlaws will be banished from our homeland. It will be a cleansing the likes of which has never been seen in Brazilian history."

Bolsonaro vowed that he would imprison his runoff opponent,

Fernando Haddad. Referring to Haddad's frequent trips to visit Lula in prison, Bolsonaro said Haddad would no longer have to travel there because he would be sharing a cell with Lula. Addressing Lula, Bolsonaro proclaimed, "You will rot in jail. And soon you'll have Lindbergh Farias [a Workers' Party senator who had been defeated] to play dominoes and chess. Wait, Haddad will get there too. But it won't be to visit you, no: it will be to be with you for a few years."

Adding more threats, Bolsonaro said of his opponents, "You will all be put at the end of the beach. You will no longer have our homeland. There will be no more NGOs to satisfy your hunger for *mortadella*"—a reference to a cheap meat the Brazilian right uses as a symbol for how left-wing parties are paid off. Bolsonaro explicitly threatened to treat Brazil's traditional left-wing homeless advocacy groups, particularly those that occupy abandoned buildings to provide homeless people a place to live, as "terrorists."

In the speech, Bolsonaro also took aim at the country's largest newspaper, promising a Brazil "without lies! Without fake news! And without the *Folha* of São Paulo!" *Folha* had recently published a major exposé on how Bolsonaro's campaign was being driven by illegal financing. In particular, the report showed that several oligarchs were secretly paying for mass messaging campaigns on WhatsApp designed to glorify Bolsonaro and defame Haddad. These revelations were a serious danger to Bolsonaro's candidacy, as they appeared to disclose illegalities at the heart of his campaign. As a result of that reporting, *Folha* became a prime enemy of the Bolsonaro movement. The reporter who broke the story, Patrícia Campos Mello, was the target of a stunningly coordinated online campaign of hatred, threats, and fake news that shocked many in Brazil for how intense, organized, well financed, and sustained it was.

The thousands of supporters gathered to hear Bolsonaro that day swooned in collective delight, exuding a pulsating sense of revenge against the center-left Workers' Party of Lula and the rest of their perceived enemies. Throughout Bolsonaro's speech, and after, they chanted in unison what had become Bolsonaro's hallmark nickname for his most devoted followers: "Mito, Mito, Mito . . ."—meaning "myth" in the sense of "legend." It was a chant of leader adoration.

As much of the country reeled from the extremism and explicit threats of authoritarianism that dominated Bolsonaro's speech, another episode quickly reinforced fears that his presidency could easily result in the end of Brazil's thirty-five-year experiment with democracy. On October 28, 2018, just a couple of hours after the polls closed, the results of the runoff were announced. Bolsonaro had defeated Haddad by eleven points—55 to 44 percent—and received 57.7 million votes, almost 11 million more than his Workers' Party opponent. Notably, Bolsonaro became the first active or former member of the military to assume the presidency since Brazil's last military dictator in 1985. Bolsonaro's vice president was now a reserve general in that same military. A return of the military to power in Brazil had been unthinkable for years, but now it seemed to have happened through the ballot box, by majoritarian sentiment.

Bolsonaro's even more extreme counterpart, gubernatorial candidate Wilson Witzel, destroyed his runoff opponent, winning with almost 60 percent of the vote. In Rio de Janeiro, Bolsonaro won with 65 percent of the vote, which means that two out of every three voters in our home city cast a ballot for him.

After the election, it seemed as if the climate in Brazil could not get any darker—either for us personally or for the country. But it did just that, quickly and radically.

In December, weeks before his January 1 inauguration, news broke that Bolsonaro's eldest son, senator-elect Flavio Bolsonaro, was under investigation for a series of very large deposits made in cash over several years into his bank account. The pattern of the deposits was virtually identical to a long-known corruption scheme in Brazil in which legislators hire "phantom" employees and then receive the bulk of the salary as a kickback.

Flavio had spent the last decade as a state legislator and had a couple of dozen employees. The amounts deposited into his account were made each month, in small increments seemingly designed to avoid detection by keeping the deposits below a threshold that would trigger automatic scrutiny. The total of the deposits into Flavio Bolsonaro's account vastly exceeded his salary as a state legislator, and he had no explanation for the source of those deposits.

That Bolsonaro's eldest son was implicated in a corruption scheme was damaging for a president-elect who rode to victory, in large part, by depicting himself as an outsider sent to "cleanse" Brazil's hated and corrupt political system. But then new facts emerged that transformed Flavio's scandal into something far more disturbing than a garden-variety kickback scheme. First, it was reported that the aide who made the monthly deposits into Flavio's account each month was Fabrício Queiroz, an ex–police officer who served as Flavio's longtime driver. Queiroz was also a personal friend of the president-elect himself. As reporters dug into Queiroz's identity, they found disturbing signs that he was closely linked to the city's most violent militias. That meant that Flavio's close aide and president-elect Bolsonaro's friend—a retired police officer who seemed to have engineered Flavio's corruption scheme—was a member of the paramilitary gangs ruling Rio with barbaric violence and murder.

After the scandal broke, facts emerged that placed the scandal even closer to Jair Bolsonaro's door. One of the mysterious cash payments made by Queiroz was deposited into the account of the president-elect's wife, Michelle, in the amount of seven thousand dollars. When Bolsonaro was asked why Queiroz had deposited cash into his wife's account, he claimed it was repayment for an unspecified loan. How Jair Bolsonaro himself—after thirty years as a politician—had excess cash sufficient to make loans to anyone, and why he would be loaning money specifically to a known militia member, had no rational explanation other than the Bolsonaro family's connections to those militias.

As the scandal unfolded, Queiroz gave only one television interview—an utterly bizarre spectacle in which he attempted to explain how someone with his small income could possibly have deposited so much money into the accounts of Flavio and Michelle Bolsonaro. "I'm a business guy," he said. "I make money, buy, sell, buy, sell, buy cars, renovate cars. I've always been like this. I really like to buy a car, in my spare time, buy a small car, refurbish it, resell, have some security."

After that rambling and incoherent explanation, Queiroz simply disappeared. After he failed to appear for multiple police summonses, reporters discovered a disturbing but now-unsurprising fact: Queiroz was hiding out in a neighborhood called Rio das Pedras, notorious for being completely controlled and shielded by one of the worst paramilitary gangs in Rio, composed almost entirely of ex–police officers and military members (like Queiroz).

It was as if one learned that the militias themselves now occupied the highest offices of political power in the country.

That realization became unavoidable with truly alarming news that emerged in January, just after Bolsonaro assumed the presidency. In a major breakthrough, the Rio police investigating Marielle's assassination raided the homes of top leaders of the so-called Crime Office, a unit of Rio's most violent militia that was notorious for carrying out for-hire executions with extreme professionalism, and that homicide investigators on Marielle's case had concluded was hired to carry out her assassination.

Officers succeeded in apprehending five of its top six leaders, but the one who evaded arrest, and later became a fugitive, was very significant because he was its chief, ex–police captain Adriano Magalhães da Nóbrega, who was already wanted for other murders and subject to an Interpol arrest warrant.

This raid was the first time Brazilians learned the identities of those who ran the terrifying Crime Office murder ring. And the following day, they learned something else that has continued to shape the political climate in Brazil to this very day—and certainly shapes the decisions David and I make in our work and our lives.

Both the mother and the wife of Nóbrega—the chief of Rio's most murderous and notorious militia—were employed in the office of Flavio Bolsonaro for the prior ten years. They were terminated only once he won his Senate election. This means that the Bolsonaro family had deep, long-standing ties to the police and military militias that assassinated Marielle. It does not mean that they were participants in the planning or the execution of the murder itself—it is hard to imagine what motive they would have for wanting Marielle dead—but it does mean that they are closely linked to the militias that so savagely ended her life.

The depth of the links between the Bolsonaro family and Rio's most dangerous paramilitary gangs became even clearer as the Marielle investigation proceeded. In early March 2019, just two days shy of the one-year anniversary of her assassination, the Rio police arrested two men they insisted were inside the car that killed Marielle, including the one who pulled the trigger. Unsurprisingly, both were members of Brazil's Military Police. And they had numerous connections to the Bolsonaros: photos emerged of the shooter with Bolsonaro; his daughter had dated Bolsonaro's son; and the driver lived in Bolsonaro's upscale gated community, an extreme coincidence in a city as sprawling as Rio de Janeiro, a city of six million people.

The impact of the knowledge that the Bolsonaros had such extensive ties to the monsters who assassinated our friend is hard to put into words. It shaped every decision we made, every emotion we felt, in thinking about the new Brazil and our role in it.

— — — — — — — — — —

In early 2019, a few weeks after Bolsonaro's inauguration but just before the new Congress was scheduled to be installed on February 1, political violence in Brazil yet again radically transformed our lives.

In the wake of the revelations of the close ties of the Bolsonaro family to Marielle's killers, LGBT congressman Jean Wyllys announced, out of the blue, that he was fleeing Brazil in fear of his life and would not assume his seat in the lower house, to which he had just been reelected. This was a devastating blow to the LGBT community in Brazil. We had just watched a politician who had spent decades stoking hatred toward LGBTs ascend to the presidency of the country. Now we learned that Jean—who, despite being a controversial figure even on the left, was an icon and pioneer for LGBT visibility in Brazil—was renouncing residence in the only country he had ever known, and was giving up his seat in Congress, due to multiple credible threats on his life.

Because Jean was in David's party, we knew that he had been receiving horrific death threats for years. He was constantly bullied in the Congress itself. Members of right-wing parties would bash Jean with their shoulder when he passed them in congressional corridors and then mutter "faggot" under their breath. It got to the point where he was afraid to use the bathroom without security protection in the very body to which he had been elected.

But in the wake of an emboldened Bolsonaro movement, the threats and contempt toward Jean as a longtime symbol of LGBT visibility in Brazil drastically intensified. He received threatening emails with photos of the license plate on his car, and of the front door of his mother's house, accompanied by vows to murder him and his family members.

He had been one of the country's only prominent openly LGBT figures since 2004, when he became a contestant on, and ultimately won, the reality show *Big Brother Brasil*—at its peak, by the far the most watched television program in the country. He first ran for Congress in 2010, as part of David's left-wing PSOL party, and won. Jean was then reelected in 2014, with a very large vote total: the seventh-highest in Rio state. For years, his status as the only LGBT member of the entire Congress, along with his polarizing personality, made him the target of an endless tidal wave of hatred.

With Bolsonaro in power, Jean decided that these risks were no longer worth it. On the enemy list of the Bolsonaro movement, Jean occupied a special place because he had once spit on Bolsonaro himself when the two were in Congress. Jean had also been a friend of Marielle. With his arch enemy in power, the Bolsonaro family proven to have links to the militias that killed his friend, and the threats intensifying, Jean decided that self-exile was preferable to the escalating risks to his life. "I want to live, not be a martyr," he said.

While Jean's decision had a crushing effect on the LGBT community—it compounded the feeling that gays would not be safe in Bolsonaro's Brazil—it had a very dramatic effect on my and David's life in particular.

In winning reelection, Jean came in fourth, while David came in fifth. That meant that David, as the alternate, would automatically take the congressional seat Jean decided not to assume.

I learned of Jean's decision just one week before the February 1 inauguration, in a car headed back to our home. A friend called and, in a frenzied voice, asked, "Did you see the news about Jean? Is it really true?" When I asked what he meant, he said, "I'll send you the link over WhatsApp. Read it now."

Even though I was only about five minutes from home, I pulled my car over to the side of the road, clicked the link, and read the *Folha* headline, "With Fear of Threats, Jean Wyllys, of PSOL, Gives Up His Term and Leaves Brazil." *Folha* regarded the news as so significant that they translated the interview into English for an international audience. In the interview, Jean said, "I was already thinking about giving up public life since I had to start living under armed guard, which happened after Marielle's execution." He added, "In addition to these death threats from these groups of hit men, militia-related hit men, there was another possibility: an attack by religious fanatics who believe the systematic defamation against me."

I immediately called David—now I was the one in a frenzy—and asked if he had heard the news. He hadn't. "Jean said he's not going to take his seat. He's leaving Brazil because he fears for his life. You're going to Congress."

Neither of us knew how to react. Obviously, David ran for Congress in the first place because we thought he could do immense good by being there. But we did not anticipate that he would enter because the only other LGBT member was fleeing the country on account of death threats and a highly repressive, hateful atmosphere toward leftists, people from favelas, and especially LGBTs.

By the time I got home, President Bolsonaro had already tweeted his glee over Jean's decision, disgustingly but characteristically posting "Great Day!" along with a thumbs-up sign. Though he did not mention Jean's name or explicitly refer to Jean's announcement, nobody had any doubt that he was celebrating Jean's flight from Brazil in fear for his life.

Within minutes, Honório, David's chief of staff, was at our house to discuss how we should handle these obviously shocking events. The first order of business was for David—with all eyes now on him—to respond to Bolsonaro's vindictive and ugly Twitter provocation.

David picked up his cell phone and began crafting his message. Honório and I looked at his draft tweet, and immediately realized it was perfect—the exact right mix of defiance, righteousness, and respect for Jean. David posted it, and it quickly became one of the most viral tweets of the year, catapulting David into the national spotlight.

When Bolsonaro responded to David, it only further elevated David's visibility. This was the Twitter exchange between David and President Bolsonaro:

Jair M. Bolsonaro ✔ @jairbolsonaro · Jan 24, 2019
Grande dia! 👍

  💬 11.9K   🔁 20.5K   ❤️ 77.1K   ⬆️

David Miranda ✔
@davidmirandario

Replying to @jairbolsonaro

Respeite o Jean, Jair, e segura sua empolgação. Sai um LGBT mas entra outro, e que vem do Jacarezinho. Outro que em 2 anos aprovou mais projetos que você em 28. Nos vemos em Brasília.

Translate Tweet

2:27 PM · Jan 24, 2019 · Twitter for Android

19.4K Retweets   **2.9K** Quote Tweets   **73.2K** Likes

  💬   🔁   ❤️   ⬆️

Jair M. Bolsonaro ✔ @jairbolsonaro · Jan 24, 2019
Replying to @davidmirandario
Seja feliz! 👍 Um forte abraço!

  💬 905   🔁 1.4K   ❤️ 13.9K   ⬆️

Great day!
Respect Jean, Jair, and hold your excitement. One LGBT is leaving, but another is entering, this one who is from Jacarezinho. One who, in 2 years, approved more laws than you did in 28. We'll see each other in Brasilia.
Be happy! A big hug!

For at least a week, David became the center of Brazil's media focus. It was truly an extraordinary coincidence that Brazil's only LGBT member of Congress was forced to flee the only country he ever knew, but was being replaced by one of the country's very few other openly LGBT elected officials.

That remarkable fact obviously took on greater significance in the Bolsonaro era. David seized the moment, earning substantial approval from the public and the media with his trademark combination of charm, a defiant posture and street speech that came from being raised as an orphan in a favela, intellectual sophistication, and vows of resistance against the new, repressive forces that ruled Brasilia—the city in which, in just seven days, he would be working and living as Brazil's only openly LGBT member of the lower house of Congress.

On January 31, we traveled with our two sons to Brasilia and stayed in David's temporary, state-provided apartment. The following day, we watched his inauguration as a member of Brazil's Congress, along with his 512 colleagues.

That's how we started 2019: with me and David in the spotlight as one of Brazil's most politicized LGBT couples; with the Intercept Brasil, the outlet I founded, becoming one of the leading voices of independent journalism and anti-Bolsonaro sentiment in the country; with the Bolsonaros, now the most powerful family in Brazil, already deeply hostile toward us; and with an intensely bigoted and fanatical far-right family and movement dominating the country.

And that was the context as David and I began to assess, as best as we could, the consequences of reporting on a massive and anonymous leak of a kind never previously seen in Brazil.

Chapter 6

— — — — — — — — —

CORRUPTION EXPOSED

I n May 2019, as the documents from the source's massive archive poured in, I worked with Victor Pougy, my Brazilian journalism assistant, to decipher what we had.

On the very first day, we discovered multiple explosive stories. The first was a series of chats Victor found, in which the most senior anti-corruption prosecutors—the ones who had prosecuted Lula and countless other leftist politicians—plotted openly about how to use their prosecutorial power to prevent the Workers' Party (PT) from winning the 2018 presidential election.

In one particularly dramatic chat group over Telegram, in which Deltan Dallagnol, the lead Car Wash prosecutor, spoke with a fellow prosecutor just days before the first round of presidential voting in fall 2018, both agreed that they were "praying" the Workers' Party would not return to power. The group plotted extensively, with the explicit goal of preventing a PT election victory.

That Lula's prosecutors appeared to be right-wing ideologues—or at least deeply opposed to the Workers' Party as a political preference—came as no surprise. Indeed, supporters of Lula and Car Wash critics had long expressed those suspicions. But the prosecutors vehemently denied this, publicly insisting they had no ideological preferences and no political agenda. They repeatedly mocked such concerns as defamatory and

baseless conspiracy-mongering. The claim that they were apolitical—
merely applying the law without ideological or partisan objectives—was
central to the legitimacy of their prosecutions.

Now we had proof that they were lying, and that they had been plotting
with one another to defeat the Workers' Party. The publication of those secret chats would alone be a devastating blow to their credibility and the legitimacy of the convictions they obtained. But the deeper we delved into the
archive, the more apparent it became that to report this material properly, I
would need a large team of Brazilian journalists who were both native Portuguese speakers and deeply familiar with the facts of the Car Wash investigation. Unlike the Snowden archive—which was in English and encompassed
topics I had long been studying and reporting: digital surveillance and privacy—this archive was in a foreign language, often highly technical, and depended on expert-level knowledge of the Car Wash prosecutions.

Fortunately, I had relationships with a team of editors and journalists perfect for this journalism—an entire newsroom of them, in fact—at
the Intercept Brasil.

— — — — — — — — — —

In 2016, Brazil was in the midst of the debate over whether to impeach
Lula's successor, President Dilma Rousseff.

I was vehemently opposed—not because I was a fan of Dilma or the
Workers' Party, but because the people leading the effort to impeach her,
and those who would be empowered if she were removed, were far more
corrupt than Dilma was accused of being; and more significantly, they
were intent on implementing a center-right ideology of economic austerity that they could not succeed in having democratically ratified.

As I paid closer attention to the impeachment debate, I began noticing that almost the entire mainstream media of Brazil was united in favor
of Dilma's impeachment and, worse, that it allowed virtually no dissent
to be heard. Brazil's media has long been notorious for being homoge-
nous, corporatized, and monopolistic. It is dominated by a single media
giant, the Globo Group. In 2014, the *Economist* featured a long profile
detailing how *Globo*'s media dominance in Brazil is unmatched by any
other media behemoth in any other large democracy:

Business
Jun 5th 2014 edition ›

Television in Brazil

Globo domination

Brazil's biggest media firm is flourishing with an old-fashioned business model

RIO DE JANEIRO

WHEN the football World Cup begins on June 12th in Brazil, tens of millions of Brazilians will watch the festivities on TV Globo, the country's largest broadcast network. But for Globo it will be just another day of vast audiences. No fewer than 91m people, just under half the population, tune in to it each day: the sort of audience that, in the United States, is to be had only once a year, and only for the one network that has won the rights that year to broadcast American football's Super Bowl championship game.

Globo is surely Brazil's most powerful company, given its reach into so many homes. Its nearest competitor in free-to-air television, Record, has an audience share of only about 13%. America's most popular broadcast network, CBS, has a mere 12% share of audience during prime time, and its main competitors have around 8%.

Beyond *Globo*, Brazil has a few other large media outlets, all of which are also owned by rich industrial families. Press freedom groups have spent years denouncing this state of affairs, noting that the control of information by a few oligarchical interests ensures that there is little to no plurality of opinion or dissent.

Some of this has since begun to improve as a result of the proliferation of online news sources, which has given rise to some significant outlets not controlled by these families. But in 2016, the dominance of these large media outlets was palpable, as was my frustration and anger as I watched virtually all voices of opposition be excluded from debate over the most traumatic and significant decision a democracy can undertake—removal of an elected president.

I began using my platform at the Intercept to report on—and to denounce—the effort to impeach Dilma. With my Brazilian journalism assistant at the time, Erick Dau, and with David, who was working as a journalist and activist before running for office, I published numerous articles that criticized misleading and propagandistic reports in *Globo* and similar outlets. In order to maximize the impact of these articles in Brazil, we began publishing the articles in both English and Portuguese, with Erick providing the translation.

The reaction to the articles was extraordinary. Almost every piece we published in Portuguese went viral, and they quickly became among the most-read articles in the history of the Intercept. We realized we were filling a vital need for independent reporting not captive to the agenda of a small handful of powerful families.

The impact of these articles led to our decision to create a Brazilian branch of the Intercept. While there are some excellent independent sites and bloggers in Brazil, none had the resources to support the large team of editors, lawyers, technologists, and reporters needed to enable sustained, in-depth investigative journalism of the kind the Intercept was founded to support. After securing a significant commitment of resources from First Look Media, the publishing company that funds the Intercept, we began to build the Intercept Brasil.

Throughout 2016 and into 2017, we operated the Intercept Brasil on a fairly small budget. The idea was to get our feet wet and to demonstrate that we were a serious news outlet created to do credible, independent investigative journalism.

One major challenge was that the tiny size of the Brazilian media world meant that there was a culture in which journalists did not criticize other media outlets or report critically on them. When there are only two or three major employers, to express criticisms of any of them can be fatal to one's career. Thus, it was not easy to find young Brazilian journalists who were eager to do the kind of adversarial journalism we expected. But slowly, one by one, we did. Throughout the first eighteen months of the Intercept Brasil, we published numerous solid stories, including several important investigative scoops.

The one key ingredient that was missing for that first year and a half was an editor in chief. Just as was true of the Intercept itself—Jeremy Scahill, Laura Poitras, and I knew from the start that we wanted to focus on our own journalism, not run this new media outlet day to day—I knew we needed a dynamic editorial leader to build and manage the Intercept Brasil.

In late 2017, we found exactly the person I had been envisioning all along. Leandro Demori was relatively young, thirty-six, and had some experience inside the big Brazilian media machine—just enough to decide he wanted no part of it. I interviewed Leandro three times, and then suggested the Intercept's US editor in chief, Betsy Reed, interview him to make sure she was comfortable with him. She was, and we hired him.

My deal with Leandro was that he would have the same autonomy I would want. He wanted to ensure that he would have the power to hire and fire whom he wanted and shape the editorial mission without my control or interference. Subject to his commitment to consult with me and Betsy on matters of great or enduring importance to the Intercept Brasil's brand and reputation, we agreed to give him that freedom.

Leandro proceeded to build an incredibly dynamic newsroom of young, inventive Brazilian journalists, editors, and staff. By the time I started texting my new source in early 2019, the highly motivated, professional, and fearless journalists of the Intercept Brasil had already broken very significant stories that carried considerable risks—including several scoops about the investigation into the assassination of Marielle Franco.

As a result of this hard-hitting journalism—with a loud voice and defiant posture Brazil had never quite seen before in a well-financed news organization—the Intercept Brasil quickly built up a large readership. Some of the articles in Portuguese were among the most read of any at the Intercept, in some months accounting for more than 35 percent of the Intercept's overall traffic, with only roughly 10 percent of the budget. It was a success story by every metric, and I felt very comfortable—and relieved—that, under Leandro's leadership, the Intercept Brasil had built just the kind of journalistic team I had hoped to bring to Brazil.

For all these reasons, once I realized the magnitude of this new leak, I called Leandro. "I have an extremely urgent matter to discuss with you. I need you to come here right away. I can't discuss it over the phone," I told him. He agreed to come over later that day.

— — — — — — — — — — —

On May 13, 2019, Leandro and I sat at my living room table. By now I was in full security mode, aware of the gravity of the situation. I began using the same security protocols I had learned from Edward Snowden. I asked Leandro to give me his cell phone so I could put it in another room; he had seen *Citizenfour* and knew exactly why I had requested this.

With all potential spying devices at a safe distance, I described the archive I had received and explained how it had come into my hands. I showed him parts of the chats I had with Manuela and then with the source.

I could see that Leandro's reaction was similar to mine: concern over the gravity of the material and the risks we would likely face given the targets, but also great excitement over what this reporting could achieve.

"If we do this right, this is going to change your career. It's going to change your life. It's going to change Brazil," I told him. Leandro needed no convincing.

"I know," he told me. "I'm ready to go." I could see by his face that he meant it.

Although I expected this, it was still a relief to see Leandro's reaction. One never knows how another person will respond when faced with a risky situation. Leandro's wife had just given birth, and I wasn't completely sure that he would be eager to be centrally involved in all-consuming reporting that could result in his prosecution, or worse.

But this was just the kind of opportunity Leandro had in mind when he left his well-paying, stable job in journalism to come work with me and run the Intercept Brasil. He knew my history working on the Snowden story and my general views on journalism, and he was clearly on board with those when he agreed to take this job.

I could have found some other journalistic partner to do the work with me. I knew that most media outlets—even the corporatist organizations that formed Brazil's large media—would kill for a scoop like this. But I believed their yearslong closeness to Moro and Car Wash would shape their coverage—just as Snowden avoided news outlets overly friendly to the US government's security state, such as the *New York Times* and *Washington Post*, when seeking journalists to work on his archive. Moreover, I had created the Intercept Brasil to be an outlet for precisely this kind of journalism. It was my clear first choice.

After Leandro confirmed his excitement for the project, we went upstairs to my home office, where Victor was working on reading as much of the archive as he could. Earlier that day, the source had indicated he wanted to speak by phone again. Knowing that Leandro was coming over, I thought it wise to wait so that Leandro could participate and hear his voice. The source agreed that he would wait for my unnamed colleague to arrive.

Victor showed Leandro a few randomly selected parts of the archive, to give him a taste of its format and appearance. Then we called the source, whom I put on speaker phone for all of us to hear.

It was obvious that since the first time we spoke, the source had been frantically reading through the archive. He was eager to rattle off everything he believed he had found that was incriminating and significant.

We listened with interest but also skeptically: he was a hacker, not a journalist, and it was unclear how much of what he claimed to see was really proven by these materials. But we were very interested in what he had to say, and took notes on his potential leads.

After we hung up with the source, I told Leandro that our principal challenge was how to review an archive this massive. For the Snowden archive, we had installed a program called Intella, used by litigation law firms who often have to work with millions of documents. The highly advanced program allows the user to search massive document archives by keywords, so that one isn't consigned to simply opening millions of documents randomly, looking for a needle in the haystack.

It was this system that had enabled me to find the most significant Snowden stories. I still remember, as if it were yesterday, the moments when I entered "Brazil" and "Petrobras" into Intella, and then discovered the documents that proved that the NSA and the Government Communications Headquarters (GCHQ) in the UK were spying on the state-owned oil company whose proceeds fund Brazil's social programs. It was by entering "NSA" and "Dilma" that I found the documents proving that the NSA was spying on the former Brazilian president. Both stories created huge tidal waves in Brazil, and ultimately a rupture of diplomatic relations between the two countries.

For the new archive, however, Micah Lee, the Intercept's technologist, told me that its enormous size meant it would likely take weeks for it to be properly uploaded in the needed format, and for these search functions to become functional. That meant we would have to use cruder and less precise means in the effort to make sense of what we had.

I showed Leandro what we had already found: prosecutors in Telegram chat groups plotting how to use their prosecutorial powers, in their words, "to prevent the return to power of PT."

Those conversations had come from a file the source had flagged: CHATS_TXT. Though just one file in an archive of at least tens of thousands, it was huge. It contained every chat group in which these prosecutors had participated over the course of many years, including the prosecutors' ongoing conversations with Judge Sérgio Moro. Some of those chat groups contained ten or twenty prosecutors or more, while others were just one-on-one conversations. One particularly large and obviously relevant subfile was the years' worth of ongoing conversations between Moro and chief Car Wash prosecutor Deltan Dallagnol.

Although I trusted Leandro and the other editors and reporters at the Intercept Brasil, we had never worked together on a story this sensitive. I didn't even know what was in this archive, so I didn't feel comfortable—from an ethical, journalistic, or legal perspective—simply handing it over to a newsroom, even one that I had founded.

Leandro wanted the full archive, arguing that the newsroom needed it in order to work on the materials. I was not yet convinced, so we settled on an intermediary step: I would give him the full "chats" file and then we would reconvene to see what we found.

Victor copied the chats file onto a thumb drive, encrypted it, and then gave it to Leandro. I was still slightly uncomfortable even with this partial step, given how explosive and legally perilous this entire enterprise was.

Leandro suggested that we include a reporter with extensive experience covering the Car Wash probe, Rafael Moro Martins, and I agreed. His insights would prove invaluable.

Over the next two weeks, all of us with archive access pored over the chat logs. What we found was stunning. The truth of the most extreme conspiracy theories that loyalists of Lula's party had long harbored about these prosecutors and Moro—many of which I had doubted—was fully evident from what they were doing and saying in secret.

The most explosive revelations we found in those first two weeks were in chat logs between Judge Moro and Dallagnol. Their chats spanned years, from the time the task force first began its work in 2014 through 2019. This was just one among thousands of chat groups, which in turn was just one file among hundreds of thousands of files. But the conversations between Moro and Dallagnol were utterly incriminating.

For years, there was suspicion that Moro was not acting as a neutral judge, but instead secretly collaborating with the prosecutors to direct them how best to prove the guilt of the defendants he was judging. Indeed, as the years went on in the Car Wash saga, Moro looked more and more like the latter: a zealous prosecutor intent on imprisoning the powerful leftist politicians and their rich funders who came into his court.

Up to this point, however, nobody had been able to prove this collaboration. It had all taken place in secret. And with both Moro and Dallagnol repeatedly and vehemently denying any such collusion, those who suggested they were guilty of this were easily dismissed as leftist conspiracy theorists.

Roughly one year before accepting Bolsonaro's offer to become minister of justice and public security, Judge Moro gave a speech in which he directly addressed these suspicions and insisted that he was nothing more than a "passive" observer of the prosecutors' cases against defendants:

> Let me make something very clear. You hear a lot about "Judge Moro's investigative strategy." I often make clear that it is the Public Prosecutor's office and the Federal Police who are the ones responsible for that. I don't have any "investigative strategy" at all. The people who investigate and decide what to do are the prosecutors and the Federal Police.
>
> The judge is reactive. We say that a judge should cultivate passive virtues. And I even get irritated sometimes. I see somewhat unfounded criticism of my work, saying that I am a judge-investigator. I say: then go ahead and identify in my judicial decisions where I determined the production of a legal proof without provocation.

All of that was a lie. And we now had proof.

Far from being a passive observer of the prosecutions before him, Moro was actively involved in shaping the cases against the very criminal defendants he was ethically and legally required to judge as a neutral, objective arbiter. In sum, he had been doing—not in isolated instances, but continually, over the course of years—exactly that which he so sanctimoniously denied in that speech and in countless other interviews.

The chats between Moro and Dallagnol took place in a private Telegram chat. Oddly, or perhaps revealingly, Moro was one of the very few people whose telephone number Dallagnol had not stored in his phone, likely because he wanted to conceal the fact that the two of them were in such constant, clandestine communications. When they spoke of Moro, the prosecutors never used his name but instead called him by a code name—*Russo* ("Russian")—reflecting their knowledge that such collaboration was improper.

Far more important than the frequency of their communications was their content. As we read through their conversations, we found countless instances, over many years, where the judge and chief prosecutor collaborated in secret as to how best to build the case against the defendants, all to ensure that Moro's guilty findings—which he knew in advance he would issue—would survive appellate scrutiny.

Reading these secret chats with Dallagnol, one got the clear impression that Moro was not only part of the prosecutorial task force but its leader, boss, and mastermind.

As we read through the hundreds of pages of secret conversations between them, we were genuinely stunned by the brazen and undisguised directives from Moro about how Dallagnol should prosecute these cases. While Dallagnol was typically reserved and cautious, Moro was unconstrained, paying virtually no attention to the ethical requirements of neutrality and objectivity, and exhibiting indifference, indeed contempt, for legal limitations on his judicial power.

Moreover, their exchanges were anything but professional, objective, and neutral. This was a partnership, a friendship, an ongoing collaboration. Dallagnol's eagerness and excitement when talking to Moro was palpable. He came across like a needy adult son craving the approval of his stern and distant father.

In US courts, there is an ironclad prohibition on judges speaking in secret about pending cases with lawyers who appear before them. Except in rare and narrow exceptions, the principle that a judge can communicate with the parties before him only when all are present is fundamental to the US justice system. It is simply inconceivable that a US judge would ever secretly chat with a prosecutor about a pending case, even about the most insignificant matters—let alone continuously, about every meaningful aspect of the prosecutors' case, over the course of many years, in the weightiest and most consequential judicial proceedings.

Yet here we had proof that Judge Moro did exactly that. If one didn't know the identity of the parties to this chat group, one would have assumed that Moro was a prosecutorial colleague of Dallagnol's on the Car Wash task force—coordinating the construct of their cases, debating the best prosecutorial strategies, mocking the defendants and their lawyers, and commanding the public messaging campaigns against the defendants—rather than a judicial official duty bound to judge their cases with neutrality and fairness.

Though the collaboration between the judge and the chief prosecutor extended to dozens of criminal defendants who were ultimately found guilty by Moro, they had a particular fixation on the most prized target in their clutches: Lula. Long before his trial began, and extending through its conclusion, Moro and Dallagnol spent hours upon hours secretly colluding about the most effective means to find Lula guilty and ensure the verdict would survive appellate review. They also plotted how to construct the most effective messaging campaign to persuade the public of Lula's guilt.

I began matching the dates of their conversations to the publicly reported events that took place inside Judge Moro's courtroom during Lula's trial. The two of them would plot in secret the night before or the morning of the proceedings in that trial, and then Moro would don a robe, walk into his courtroom, and pretend he was an objective evaluator ruling on evidence he was hearing the first time, rather than an active, aggressive, and secret collaborator in Lula's prosecution.

Unlike in the United States, where criminal defendants almost always have their guilt determined by a jury of their peers, in Brazil, with rare exceptions, it is a judge who determines guilt or innocence. That makes it all the more offensive to basic notions of fairness if a judge departs from their required role of neutral arbiter to become a member of the prosecutorial team.

As I read what Judge Moro—now Justice Minister Moro—spent all those years doing in the highest-profile and most consequential criminal cases, including the one that springboarded President Bolsonaro's victory by removing his primary adversary, it became clear that the magnitude of the corruption that was materializing in these documents was explosive beyond what I could appreciate. Extreme secrecy was paramount if we were going to be able to report this material without first being stopped—either by prepublication judicial censorship, police seizure, or some other drastic means. So how could we find lawyers or other legal experts who had the skill and expertise we needed, but who were also trustworthy enough to view this evidence?

Discussing this quandary with Leandro, he advocated that we work with the legal team the Intercept Brasil had been using to review our most sensitive stories. In particular, Leandro sung the praises of two lawyers, Rafael Borges and Rafael Fagundes, who worked at the law firm founded by one of country's most famous and prestigious criminal lawyers and human rights activists, Nilo Batista, now the Intercept Brasil's outside counsel.

I gave Leandro my consent to share specific chats between Moro and Dallagnol with the Intercept Brasil's lawyers to seek their preliminary assessment on what it showed. And I also asked him to arrange an in-person meeting with them to discuss the legal risks of my dealing with the source and this material.

Early the next morning, Victor and I went to downtown Rio, to a high-rise building overlooking the water. We met in a conference room with the two Rafaels—the "Rafas," we called them—and Leandro, as well as Leandro's deputy editor, Alexandre de Santi, and an Intercept editor, Andrew Fishman, who had worked as my assistant during the Snowden reporting and thus had experience with the security and administrative aspects of this kind of reporting.

We also invited the videographer we had hired to film all of the work, in anticipation of a documentary. It is, to put it mildly, unusual to authorize someone to film you while you're engaged in cloak-and-dagger activities that may very well be considered a crime by some. It's even more uncommon, and probably rather risky, to have your conversations with your own lawyers filmed before you even know the lay of the legal landscape you're navigating.

David, in particular, was adamant that it was precisely this type of gamble that made *Citizenfour* so powerful and successful. That Snowden was willing to be filmed from the very first time he met me and Laura Poitras in that cramped Hong Kong hotel room was itself quite unconventional, but ultimately it was that mindset that produced an outstanding film and, more broadly, a style of reporting and discourse that changed the world. I viewed that as a highly successful model and was willing to take the risk of trying to replicate it.

With the videographer already rolling, we entered the conference room and met the Rafas for the first time. Tensions were high for everyone. We began by putting our cell phones in another room—never a soothing way to begin a meeting.

They were young—both in their mid-thirties—and told me they had known each other since their law school days. The criminal defense bar in Brazil, as is true of most countries, is naturally hostile to prosecutors and law-and-order judges, but the most prominent Brazilian criminal defense lawyers—including the Rafas' boss, Nilo Batista—had become collectively alarmed by the virtually unstoppable popularity and power of Moro and the task force as they ushered in unprecedented powers to be used against criminal defendants. From the start, those who warned most vocally of the dangers of the Car Wash excesses were the criminal lawyers who represented defendants appearing before Moro and who watched as their rights were continually disregarded. That knowledge gave me comfort that we were in the right place.

I was eager to talk about the legal framework governing what I legally could and could not do when speaking to the source. I began by explaining the legal framework in the United States—in essence, that a journalist has never been charged with a crime for passively receiving stolen material and then publishing it. There are criminal laws on the books in the United States that likely encompass such journalistic activity and could render it criminal—particularly the Espionage Act of 1917—but they have never been used against a journalist in these types of circumstances.

On many occasions, the US Department of Justice (DOJ) has certainly wanted to prosecute journalists for publishing classified information or other material illegally obtained from a source. From the Pentagon Papers, to the WikiLeaks disclosures of war logs and diplomatic cables, to the Snowden NSA materials, the US government has threatened this and come close on several occasions. The DOJ's reluctance stemmed from their concern that while valid laws likely rendered journalistic publication of at least some types of top secret documents criminal, the First Amendment's free press guarantee could be invoked by a court to invalidate those laws, and the DOJ preferred to leave journalists in a permanent state of uncertainty rather than risk a precedent that could forever protect journalists who report on such materials. (The Trump administration's 2019 unsealing of an indictment against WikiLeaks founder Julian Assange, though masquerading as something other than an attempt to criminalize the publication of secret documents, was uncomfortably close to finally doing this.)

The US government's reluctance to test this proposition is almost certainly grounded, at least in part, by the stinging defeat suffered by the Nixon administration in 1971 when it tried to obtain an order of prior restraint against the *New York Times*, which would bar the paper from publishing the Pentagon Papers. Nixon was rebuffed by the Supreme Court on the ground that such prior restraint censorship orders are inconsistent with the First Amendment. But the court ruling explicitly left open the question of whether the US government, after the fact, could criminally prosecute the *New York Times* and its reporters and editors. They never tried, and have not tried since, because the uncertainty itself is a potent weapon. This I know firsthand: it was that legal uncertainty that allowed the US government to threaten me with arrest and prosecution over the Snowden reporting.

After explaining this, I asked the Rafas how the legal and constitutional framework in Brazil compares. Is it clear that journalists cannot be criminalized for working with sources who themselves have committed crimes? Are there legal and constitutional protections to prevent the prosecution of journalists for receiving and then publishing material that is illegally obtained from sources?

The short answer, they said, is that the Brazilian Constitution explicitly protects the right of journalists to protect the anonymity of their sources—a "shield law" that press advocates in the United States have tried but failed to enact at the federal level for decades. That was good news.

They also said there were court rulings from fairly high appellate courts that had rejected previous attempts by various governmental bodies to criminally prosecute journalists. In doing so, these courts had established a principle that journalists cannot be accused of committing crimes merely by reporting on materials that had been illegally obtained by the source. That was also good news.

The key to all of this, the two lawyers stressed, was *passivity*. These legal protections applied to journalists who did not participate in any way in the criminal acts that allowed the source to obtain the information. That included any attempt to direct or encourage the source to obtain specific information.

As a result, they emphasized, I had to exercise the greatest caution when speaking to the source. One wrong sentence, they emphasized, could be seized on to construe something I said as constituting encouragement or direction and could thus, in an instant, convert me from journalist to coconspirator. Especially in a case with stakes as high as these—I was at that very moment receiving vast troves of private conversations and documents implicating the country's most powerful people while simultaneously communicating with the source who had obtained it illegally, by his own reckoning—it was absolutely imperative that I avoid saying anything that was even vague enough to be exploited by potentially vindictive law enforcement authorities.

I assured them that this was my working assumption from the moment I began talking with the source, and that I had tried hard to say little to the source beyond empty banalities—such as "That makes sense" and "Okay"—to indicate my interest to him and build a climate of rapport, but without ever saying anything that could be exploited. Fortunately, I had an extremely talkative source who was quite wound up about the material he was giving me and needed little encouragement to proceed.

The meeting provided as much legal and technical reassurance as I could have hoped to hear. It seemed that the legal framework in Brazil was at least as protective for journalists as was the US framework, and probably even more so. But the Rafas were quick to point out that all of these legal doctrines and constitutional phrases were just words. The Brazilian Supreme Court itself had never ruled on this question of journalistic rights, so the protections were short of absolute. But even if they had been secure, we were in an entirely new era in Brazil; with Bolsonaro in power, none of the old assumptions could be safely treated as certainties.

With the legal issues out of the way, the Rafas were eager to discuss the chats they had already read between Moro and Dallagnol. They were indignant about what they had read. Even while maintaining their cautious tone, as lawyers they were deeply offended by the full-scale violation of ethical boundaries and limits.

When I asked them whether there was any possible argument to justify the collaboration and collusion revealed by these chats, they were adamant: "Absolutely not." They repeated the phrase "completely improper" multiple times, seeming genuinely appalled by Moro's actions.

We agreed that we would spend more time poring over these chats to find the most relevant and incriminating exchanges. Because we lacked the capacity to search the archive in a focused way, we would do as much as we could separately to find important stories, and to regularly share what we found. We also talked about our need for the Rafas to continue to view the material as we found it, not only to give legal advice but also to offer journalistic input on the critical legal issues, helping to illuminate which materials revealed serious improprieties and abuses of judicial and prosecutorial power.

Despite some good news about the legal landscape and the determination of everyone to take the plunge together, the mood in that meeting was far more tense and edgy than it was reassuring and confident. At the end of the meeting, Leandro and I talked about how the small team comprised of Victor and myself would start working on the archive together but also in parallel with the Intercept Brasil. Though the chats file I had shared with them was only a tiny part of the archive, it was one that had massive value.

Victor and I left the meeting and returned to my house to work on the archive. I tried hard to read through as many chats as possible, but I was frequently distracted by the need to speak with the source, who bombarded my phone with questions, observations, and claims about the material. As always, our conversation was punctuated by more and more documents rolling into the chat window.

— — — — — — — — — —

Now that we had the legal green light, we spent the next three weeks identifying the first set of stories we would publish. We ultimately settled on three articles that we concluded were blockbuster revelations, with a common theme of serious corruption and bias in the anti-corruption task force and Judge Moro's conduct.

The first detailed the years' worth of secret and obviously corrupt collaboration between Judge Moro and the Car Wash prosecutors to ensure conviction of the defendants Moro was judging. The second concerned the plotting by Car Wash prosecutors to use their prosecutorial power in the weeks before the 2018 election to impede a victory by the

Workers' Party—a goal they spent years vehemently denying. The third involved extensive admissions by the prosecutors of the massive evidentiary and jurisdictional holes in their case against Lula in the days before announcing their decision to prosecute him.

During the first week of June, we worked frenetically and in extreme secrecy to finalize these articles, with the intention of publishing them the following week. Each day, our concern intensified that Justice Minister Moro, armed with powerful instruments of state surveillance and law enforcement, would learn about what we were doing. For that reason—along with our belief that the public urgently had a right to learn about these stories—we were determined to get these stories published as quickly as possible consistent with journalistic reliability.

Now we had to confront a difficult but crucial question: Would we seek comment from Moro and the Car Wash prosecutors in advance of publication? Ordinarily, this is not even a question journalists ask. It's a given that a reporter allows a subject of a story, especially an incriminating one, to respond and provide their side for inclusion. There are, however, exceptions—narrow and rare, but important ones.

In countries where prior restraint is practiced, journalists can and do exercise the right to publish stories that might be censored without notifying the authorities beforehand. In the United Kingdom, for instance, there is no constitutional guarantee of a free press, and the British government wields numerous legislative authorities to threaten and even censor news outlets to deter them from publishing information it deems harmful to national security. When I was reporting for the *Guardian* in 2013 to reveal the ways the British spy agency GCHQ was working with the NSA to surveil Internet activities, the government warned the *Guardian* and other news outlets that if we did not curb our revelations, it would begin invoking prepublication censorship authorities, including D-Notices that "advise" against the publication of certain material, and even court-ordered prepublication injunctions. Prime Minister David Cameron said of our NSA reporting, "I don't want to have to use injunctions or D notices or the other tougher measures. I think it's much better to appeal to newspapers' sense of social responsibility. But if they don't demonstrate some social responsibility it would be very difficult for the government to stand back and not to act."

These were no empty threats: it was only weeks earlier that the British government had detained my husband David, and that they had also sent armed agents into the *Guardian* newsroom to force editors to physically destroy the computers on which their copy of the Snowden archive was kept. Throughout the months following publication of the first set of Snowden stories, right-wing and even centrist newspapers frequently featured demands that *Guardian* editors and reporters be arrested and prosecuted.

When it came to our concerns about prepublication censorship in Brazil, we were more worried about the potential of judicial censorship than anything the Bolsonaro government might do, on account of the courts' history of extreme deference to Moro. The prospect that the justice minister would be able to find a friendly judge willing to censor us seemed quite high, particularly since Brazil had never really seen leaks of this magnitude or type before and therefore had little legal tradition protecting them.

It is true that had a Brazilian court tried to enjoin publication of these materials, we still could have used the Intercept in the United States to publish them with reporting in English. But any attempt to publish them in Portuguese—which would have been necessary to reach the Brazilian population, which had the greatest right to know of them—would have almost certainly been viewed by judicial authorities as an attempt by the Intercept Brasil to flout a court order enjoining their publication. That could have jeopardized the ongoing ability of the Intercept Brasil to report in Brazil, a risk we were unwilling to take.

After much deliberation, we decided in the week prior to publication that we would notify neither Justice Minister Moro nor the Car Wash prosecutorial task force of the stories we were preparing, which meant, of course, that we could not seek their comment. We resolved, instead, that we would publish an editors' note explaining the general framework for how we decided to report on these materials. It would include our rationale for not seeking prepublication comment, offer both Moro and the Car Wash task force the opportunity to have their comments included as soon as the first set of articles was published, and then, once the threat of censorship had been thwarted, seek their prepublication comment on all stories going forward.

Chapter 7

— — — — — — — — — —

AN UNLIKELY ALLIANCE

A s we began to finalize our stories and plan our initial publication
date, I realized that despite the firm legal ground we were on technically, the recency of the Intercept Brasil's creation would be a source
of political and journalistic vulnerability. While we had rapidly grown
our audience over our three years of existence, the site was still unknown
to the majority of the population. That would make it easier for the Bolsonaro government and supporters of Justice Minister Moro to isolate
and demonize us as more hackers, foreign operatives, or leftist activists
than traditional Brazilian journalists, and thus as criminals rather than
professional reporters.

That the site was founded by and most associated not with a Brazilian journalist but a foreign one—myself, one married to a gay socialist
member of Congress no less—only added to my concern that doing this
story alone would be a gift to the targets of our journalism. And if we
did the story alone, completely freezing out the Brazilian media, it would
generate a high degree of professional resentment and competitive jeal-
ousy that would provide further incentive for the vehemently pro-Moro
Brazilian media to lead the way in vilifying our work.

As a result, I decided to use a strategy that we used during the
Snowden reporting: partnering with the most established media outlets in order to co-opt them into the reporting. In the Snowden case,

that worked to prevent the government from depicting our reporting as un-journalistic and, as importantly, to turn the large media outlets from likely adversaries into participants and therefore allies and defenders. When Snowden first spoke with myself and Laura Poitras, I had been a *Guardian* columnist for only a few months, while Laura was a documentary filmmaker unaffiliated with any media outlet. We knew we had to rope in large media organizations to provide us protection, and we ended up working with the largest and oldest news brands in the world—the *Guardian*, the *Washington Post*, the *New York Times*, NBC News, *Der Spiegel* in Germany, *Le Monde* in France, the CBC in Canada, and others.

One of my most prolific and successful media partnerships during the Snowden reporting was with Brazil's *Globo* media empire. The first two stories I did about NSA spying on Brazil—specifically mass surveillance of ordinary Brazilians—were done in partnership with *Globo's* flagship newspaper in Rio. And the next two stories I did in Brazil—involving NSA spying on the United Nations and other international institutions—were done in partnership with *Globo's* leading newsweekly, *Época*, including one that was featured as its cover story.

But the most consequential Snowden reporting I did in Brazil was with *Globo's* all-dominant television network, *Rede Globo*, specifically, its flagship Sunday night program *Fantástico*, a *60 Minutes*–style program that has long been the most watched broadcast of any kind in the country. Working with one of *Fantástico's* star investigative reporters, Sônia Bridi, we revealed in successive prime-time stories that the NSA and its British and Canadian allies were spying on Dilma, on its state-owned oil giant Petrobras, and on its Ministry of Mines and Energy. Ultimately, the stories dominated headlines, made a huge impact on its national politics, and won numerous reporting awards for myself and *Globo*.

Through this partnership, I had built excellent relationships with the senior leadership of the media group, including the powerful billionaire heir to the *Globo* empire, João Roberto Marinho. Long viewed as the country's most powerful person, he had been steadfastly supportive of the Snowden reporting.

So as I contemplated partnering with large media outlets—to maximize both protection and impact—*Globo* was the obvious first choice. Roping in *Globo* to the reporting was particularly tantalizing to me because the media empire had been Sérgio Moro's biggest booster by far. For years it had treated him like a deity, lending its multi-platform editorial line to the defense of everything he did, serving as a clearinghouse for the devastating leaks strategically employed by Car Wash prosecutors, and in general doing more than any other entity to construct the imagery of Judge Moro and the Car Wash prosecutors as high priests of anti-corruption ethics, and Lula and the Workers' Party as corruption-laden plagues. It would be a huge journalistic coup to lure *Globo*, of all outlets, into working with us to reveal the corruption that had for years underlaid the entire fraudulent operation.

Feeling inspired, I emailed Sônia, the *Globo* journalist with whom I had forged a great working relationship and ultimately a friendship. Without revealing any details, I told her that we had a truly earth-shattering story that I wanted to talk to her about to see if we could renew our partnership. She said she was traveling on assignment in India, but put me in touch with her colleague, another highly regarded investigative journalist with *Fantástico*.

Her colleague and I made a date to meet the next day at *Globo*'s headquarters. Prior to doing so, I met with Leandro, whom I invited to the meeting. We discussed what would likely be a major obstacle to forging a partnership with *Globo*—namely, that because they had virtually acted as the propaganda arm of Moro and Operation Car Wash, they had a great deal at stake in their reputation. Would they really turn on a dime and reveal highly incriminating information when doing so would undermine the reputation of Moro, now installed as all-powerful justice minister, and his prosecutors?

But there was a separate, possibly even more serious obstacle to creating this partnership. As I explained to Leandro, less than eighteen months earlier, I had obtained from a different source the itemized telephone bills of numerous powerful Brazilian politicians, including the Bolsonaro family. But making sense of them was a deeply labor-intensive task—the bills simply listed all the cell phone numbers these politicians had either called or been called from—and a large team of skilled technicians and deeply sourced reporters would be necessary to identify the numbers, find patterns, and report them.

I had contacted *Fantástico* about the possibility of working together on these materials, which were unquestionably of high journalistic significance. The response I got back was amazing: Marinho, the billionaire heir who runs *Globo*, along with its longtime news director, Ali Kamel, had imposed an absolute bar against any *Globo* journalists working with me or the Intercept ever again. (They were, secondarily, concerned about the legality of reporting on these hacked phone bills.)

Why was this prohibition imposed? Because, I learned, Marinho had been furious with me and David ever since David published an article in the *Guardian* in 2016 that denounced the attempt to impeach Dilma and that blamed *Globo* for inciting the protests against her. In response, Marinho had sent an angry letter to the *Guardian* that contained a stinging and unhinged personal attack on David—which the *Guardian* promptly published, not as a standalone article but relegated to the comment section under David's article.

Writing in Portuguese and English in the Intercept, David then wrote his own very acerbic reply to Marinho, someone extremely unaccustomed to being addressed in this manner. The fact that David's article became one of the most viral and well read in the Intercept's history made Marinho furious, particularly because he thought it was unfair that we were criticizing *Globo* after his media empire had worked so well with us on the Snowden story three years earlier. To Marinho, this was a personal betrayal: he apparently thought we owed him and *Globo* a lifetime of deference.

When we met with the *Fantástico* reporter, I explained that we had a massive scoop and were interested in the possibility of renewing our partnership with *Globo* to report it. Naturally, he was curious to know more, but I explained that before I could tell him anything specific, I had to obtain confirmation that Marinho's bar against working with us would not preclude a partnership.

Part of my reluctance to share details with *Globo* was the standard journalistic concern that you do not want other media outlets to learn of sensitive scoops in advance, for fear that they could report them first in their own way. But I had a much larger and more specific concern: given *Globo*'s very close and long-standing relationship with Moro and the Car Wash prosecutors, I was very worried that if I revealed what we had, they would march over to Moro and tell him, enabling the justice minister to secure a prepublication censorship order from a court or take other actions to impede or preempt the reporting. I trusted *Globo* enough that

I was willing to gamble that their journalistic instincts would lead them to report the story once they were on board. I also knew, as the custodian of the archive, that I could retain control over the materials as I had done with the Snowden archive. But until I had confirmation that this veto from on high had been lifted, I did not trust them enough to tell them what I had.

For two weeks we played a silly, semantic cat-and-mouse game in which *Globo* kept telling me they had not heard of any veto imposed by Marinho and Kamel, with us continually responding that such a claim was insufficient. Before we could tell them what we had, we needed affirmative confirmation directly from the top executives that there was no longer an institutional prohibition on working with us. Those assurances never came, and we concluded that a partnership with *Globo* would be impossible.

We resolved that instead, we would approach other media outlets—the nation's largest newspaper, *Folha* of São Paulo, and the newsweekly *Veja*, both almost as pro-Moro as *Globo*, once we had published our first set of stories and they had seen how significant they were.

— — — — — — — — —

We decided that our publication date would be Tuesday, June 11. With a date finally in place, excitement was building. Leandro mobilized the entire newsroom to begin working feverishly to have all three stories, plus our editors' note, ready for publication.

But at the last minute—on Friday, as we were in what we thought was the final stage of preparations to publish—a massive monkey wrench was thrown into our plans. It was one that sent us into hours of conference calls, debates, and conversations with lawyers to decide how we would react.

From the start of my discussions with our source a month before, he had been extremely consistent in his motives and message. He had presented himself as a whistleblower, pure and simple, whose only objective was to inform the public about grave corruption on the part of powerful officials carried out in the dark. He had repeatedly emphasized that he sought no personal attention or financial gain from having provided it to me.

On that Friday, however, the source made what seemed to be a joke that suggested an alternative motive. As we chatted, I advised him that we were nearing the date of publication, and he said, completely out of nowhere, "Please let me know in advance exactly what you intend to publish and when, so that we can profit off the stock market."

When he said this, I recalled that he had made a similar joke a few weeks prior, but only in passing and with a clearly frivolous tone. I ignored the first comment, but now that he said it a second time, this time with more specific expression, I knew I could not be so dismissive. I still believed he was being facetious, but I also had to assume that every word exchanged between myself and the source would be available at some point to authorities, who would dissect it in the hope of finding something incriminating. Someone could, in the future, try to craft a case that by publishing on a weekday, when the markets were open, we deliberately aided the source's corrupt financial motives.

I sent urgent messages to Leandro and the two Rafas, saying we needed to speak right away. Once I explained the joke made by the source, we all recognized how potentially damaging it could be if we ignored the text and simply published as scheduled. We agreed that we could not proceed with our Tuesday publication date. To protect ourselves against any future bad faith accusations, we had to publish the stories on a weekend, when the stock market was closed. Waiting until the next weekend was not viable. Indeed, we were already concerned that the chances Moro would discover what we had were increasing with each passing day. And given how close we were to having the stories ready for publication, waiting five more days contradicted the journalistic impulse to publish vital information of great public importance.

So, as we spoke late Friday afternoon, we decided we would publish the first three articles, along with our editors' note, on Sunday, less than forty-eight hours away. That meant we were eliminating two full days of preparation time for our newsroom. The abrupt shift in the publication date meant that everyone on our team could do nothing else, and would be unable to sleep, from that moment until publication time.

Leandro informed the team of the change, while Victor Pougy and I got to work at my house on the article we were writing, along with the editors' note I would byline with Leandro and Intercept editor in chief Betsy Reed. Despite the extreme pressure this decision engendered, I was secretly happy. When I have a huge story, I'm impatient about any delays. The sooner the better, as I see it—provided, of course, one can publish at a high level of professionalism and accuracy.

On Sunday morning, June 9, I did something atypical: I went to the Intercept Brasil newsroom in downtown Rio. I knew the moment of publication would be historic, and I wanted to be with the team that worked with us to get the stories ready.

The first thing I saw when I arrived was the art for the series. It was stunning. Created by two young staffers in their mid-twenties, Rodrigo Bento and João Brizzi, the graphics accompanying the story were perfect, viscerally conveying the clandestine and profound wrongdoing exposed by the Telegram conversations, as well as the historic nature of this massive leak for Brazil, while invoking design elements of the chats themselves.

Deltan Dallagnol, lead prosecutor of Operation Car Wash, depicted in one of the graphics accompanying the Vaza Jato story. Courtesy of João Brizzi.

But the moment my prepublication excitement reached its peak was when I saw the hashtag that Bento and our communications director, Marianna Araujo, had created to serve as the title of the series of exposés: "#VazaJato." It was a remarkably creative play on words, stitching together the Portuguese terms for "leak" (*vazamento*) and the Car Wash anti-corruption probe (Lava Jato), whose own corrupt underbelly we were about to expose. What this hashtag so effectively and cleverly conveyed was that now the tables had turned. As opposed to the task force's use of leaks against their enemies, a massive leak was now going to expose the truth about the Car Wash prosecutors and Sérgio Moro.

As we made the final preparations, two old but very familiar anxieties emerged in me. As I learned when I obtained the Snowden archive six years earlier, when you have a story that you know *should* be huge, shock the public, and make an enormous impact, you can never really be sure whether your evaluation of its significance is accurate until you publish it.

But then there's another, more serious, doubt: What if some part of the archive is not authentic? In both cases—the Snowden archive and the #VazaJato archive—I rigorously verified the authenticity of the materials. With the Snowden archive, we were able to consult with insiders who confirmed that numerous documents were real, and the sheer size and technical complexity of the archive strongly suggested it could not be fraudulently created. The same was true of the #VazaJato archive. Beyond consulting experts and insiders who confirmed the authenticity of multiple nonpublic facts contained in the archive, we obtained a level of proof unattainable for the Snowden archive: our own reporters had communicated over the years with several of the Car Wash prosecutors by Telegram. As a result, we were able to compare the chat records in those reporters' phones with the same chats in the archive provided by our source. They were identical, word for word. This was very strong evidence that the archive was real.

But in the moments prior to publication, both of those concerns paled in comparison to our excitement that we were about to publish journalistic revelations of historic importance. Dozens of people, including Lula, were unjustly lingering in prison as a result of the judicial and prosecutorial corruption revealed by these stories, and Brazilian democracy had been fundamentally reshaped by myths about the corrupt officials whom this journalism would expose. It is not an exaggeration to say that this anti-corruption probe was the primary cause of Bolsonaro's ascent to the presidency, and that Moro's popularity had become the anchor of the government's legitimacy.

The newsroom worked through Sunday morning and afternoon to finalize the stories. At roughly 5:30 p.m., we agreed we were ready to publish. All four stories had been fact-checked, copyedited, carefully laid out—in both Portuguese and English—and all the bylined journalists had signed off on them. (My byline was on all eight, in both languages, so there was tremendous pressure that day to approve all the articles).

An hour before they were ready for publication, I teased the story on Twitter. The lead Car Wash prosecutor, Deltan Dallagnol, had boasted in a late April tweet that his team of prosecutors were "technical, impartial, and nonpartisan" and that he had pursued all defendants without regard to bias or ideology—exactly what our stories disproved. I found his tweet, and, after consulting with Leandro, posted my own on top of it, questioning whether his claim was true. "We're about to find out," I wrote, and then added the then-unknown hashtag created by our team:

Glenn Greenwald ✔
@ggreenwald

Isso é verdade? Estamos prestes a descobrir! #VazaJato

Translated from Portuguese by Google

That's true? We're about to find out! #VazaJato

🔵 **Deltan Dallagnol** ✔ @deltanmd · Apr 25, 2019
O trabalho do MPF na Lava Jato, de novo, é técnico, imparcial e apartidário, buscando a responsabilização quem quer que tenha praticado crimes no contexto do megaesquema de corrupção na Petrobras.
Show this thread

4:34 PM · Jun 9, 2019 · Twitter Web Client

ılı View Tweet activity

2K Retweets   **9.3K** Likes   **207** Quotes

Tweet from Glenn Greenwald ninety minutes before the publication of the first Vaza Jato story.

The tweet quickly went viral. If a cryptic, vague tweet attracted that level of excitement—with a hashtag nobody had yet heard of—I was reasonably certain that the archive itself and our reporting would generate more than enough attention.

At 5:57 pm, we were finally ready, and the managing editor hit "publish" on all four stories in Portuguese, followed by all four stories in English. #VazaJato was live.

After we announced the stories, I posted, above my previous tweet, a description of the sheer size and breadth of the archive that we had obtained, explaining that these four stories were merely the beginning. That tweet, like all the ones posted that day by the Intercept Brasil, went super-viral:

Glenn Greenwald ✓
@ggreenwald

O arquivo fornecido pela nossa fonte sobre o Brasil é um dos maiores da história do jornalismo. Ele contém segredos explosivos em chats, áudios, vídeos, fotos e documentos sobre @deltanmd, @SF_Moro e muitas facções poderosas. Nossas reportagens acabaram de começar. #VazaJato

Translated from Portuguese by Google

The file provided by our source about Brazil is one of the largest in the history of journalism. It contains explosive secrets in chats, audios, videos, photos and documents about @deltanmd , @SF_Moro and many powerful factions. Our reports have just started. #VazaJato

Glenn Greenwald ✓ @ggreenwald · Jun 9, 2019
Isso é verdade? Estamos prestes a descobrir! #VazaJato
twitter.com/deltanmd/statu...

6:29 PM · Jun 9, 2019 · Twitter Web Client

ı|ı View Tweet activity

10.7K Retweets   **31.9K** Likes   **2.3K** Quotes

Tweet of Glenn Greenwald moments after first Vaza Jato story

On a wall in the Intercept Brasil newsroom were several large television screens. They were all tuned to a program that monitors traffic to our site. Within a few minutes, page views were exploding. Very shortly thereafter, more people, by many multiples, were visiting the Intercept

Brasil's site than at any time since our launch. Within a few more minutes, all previous traffic records, not just for the Intercept Brasil but the Intercept itself, were shattered, and then shattered more.

We could see the story ricocheting throughout social media far faster and more vibrantly than we had dreamed. In less than an hour, the term #VazaJato—one that nobody had ever used until that day—was the top trending Twitter hashtag in Brazil. An hour after that, it was the fastest trending term in the world.

How the articles would be received in English was a different concern. Whether anyone in the Western world would care about an investigation into figures they knew little about—if they had heard of them at all—was a complete mystery. But there, too, the reaction was immense. The traffic to our English-language articles was enormous, among our biggest stories ever. The English-language tweets announcing the investigative series also quickly went viral online.

Recognition of the stories' importance came quickly from journalists both in Brazil and around the world, even among previous defenders of Moro and Operation Car Wash, as well as longtime critics of both myself and the Intercept. "This Intercept expose on Brazil's FUBAR political situation should be everywhere," wrote the *Atlantic*'s Derek Thompson, adding, "The president of the world's 6th biggest country reportedly plotted with his justice minister and prosecutors to imprison the opposing party's popular ex-president on the way to getting elected!" The Latin American historian Patrick Iber observed, "I disagree with Glenn on many things but this is a huge story that should be considered separately." Brazil-based journalist Will Carless declared #VazaJato the "biggest story in the world right now," while the editor in chief of *Americas Quarterly*, a longtime defender of Moro and Operation Car Wash, Brian Winter, acknowledged, "I've read these stories twice now and—there's no doubt— it's an awful day for reputation of Car Wash probe & its protagonists." And the *Guardian*'s Latin American correspondent Tom Phillips, referring to the Brazilian capital, said simply: "I suspect there is rather a lot of xingando [cursing] going on in Brasília tonight."

In the week that followed, media reaction in Brazil was far greater than we had hoped for. The center-right newsweekly *Veja*, one of the most loyal media supporters of Moro, quickly published a remarkable cover that depicted Moro as a crumbling statute of a Roman Emperor, with a play on his name that means "disintegration." The cover also proclaimed that the "compromising" evidence we published demonstrates "clear transgressions of law." This was especially significant because the covers of newsweeklies are displayed on virtually every corner and have a major impact on popular consciousness.

Writing on June 11, just two days after publication, one of the nation's largest center-right newspapers, *Estadão* of São Paulo, also long supportive of Moro and the Car Wash task force, editorialized that our findings "indicate a totally unacceptable—and perhaps illegal—relationship between [Moro] and the public prosecutors, with political and legal implications that are still difficult to measure. For much less, other ministers have previously been fired." The *Estadão* editorial concluded: "If Sérgio Moro continues to say that what is evidently not normal is normal, his stay in the government will become unsustainable. The minister and the prosecutors involved in this scandal would do well, the first if he resigned and the others if they stepped away from the task force until everything is clarified."

Both the Car Wash task force and Moro issued lengthy statements that night in response to our reporting, posted on their official sites and sent to media outlets requesting comment. Both expressed anger that they had been apparently victimized by hackers who obtained their private messages. They denied that the messages we published demonstrated any wrongdoing. And they complained that they had not been asked for comment ahead of publication.

These were standard denial and self-victimization tactics, which we expected. But what was most notable about each response is what they did *not* say. At no point in their initial statements did either the Car Wash task force or Moro deny the authenticity of the materials. Indeed, the task force implicitly acknowledged that they were genuine, noting, in an official statement:

> Lava Jato prosecutors in Curitiba have held discussions in groups of messages over the past five years on various topics, some complex, in parallel with personal meetings that give them context. Several of the members of the prosecutors' task force are close friends and, in this environment,

outbursts and jokes are common. Many conversations, without the proper context, can give rise to misinterpretations. The task force deeply regrets the discomfort of those who may have been affected.

Moro also implicitly acknowledged the archive's authenticity by denying that they showed wrongdoing. "No abnormality or coordination is demonstrated by these messages in my actions as a judge, despite having been removed from the context and the sensationalism of the materials, which ignore the gigantic corruption scheme revealed by Operation Lava Jato."

That night, *Globo's* agenda-setting flagship nightly news program, *Jornal Nacional,* extensively covered our reporting and the denials by Moro and the task force. The last thing *Globo* wanted to do was report on our journalism, particularly given their animosity toward us and how incriminating our reporting was for their beloved justice minister, but they could not ignore it.

— — — — — — — — — —

With the first stage of the series having gone so exceedingly well, we now turned our attention to finding the right media partners. Since *Globo* was out of the picture, left to report on our stories but not participate in them, Leandro and I agreed that the first partner we should seek out was Brazil's largest newspaper, *Folha* of São Paulo. Its mainstream stature aside—it is essentially the *New York Times* of Brazil—*Folha* has always been a bit feistier, more heterodox, and more independent than other corporate media conglomerates. They have some truly great journalists, including several who are among the country's most knowledgeable reporters on the Car Wash probe, which we knew would be a great journalistic asset for us in reporting the archive. Perhaps most importantly, they were the only big Brazilian media outlet to have at least occasionally expressed skepticism or even opposition toward the more extreme transgressions of Moro and the Car Wash prosecutors.

A few days after we published our first set of #VazaJato articles, I called *Folha's* editor in chief, Sérgio Dávila, to ask if the paper would be interested in working with us on reporting new stories. By then, the four articles we published were dominating headlines, and #VazaJato was by far the biggest story in Brazil. Still, it would be a leap for an establishment outlet like *Folha* not only to partner with us but to participate in reporting on an archive the Bolsonaro government was already starting to call "criminal."

Sérgio said he'd be happy to meet with us as soon as possible. The next day Leandro and I flew to São Paulo, along with the security team we had been forced to hire that week. We met with Sérgio and the paper's top editors and lawyers for roughly an hour to discuss the terms of a possible partnership and how we envisioned working together on the archive. They seemed very enthusiastic, but asked for forty-eight hours to decide.

We left the meeting optimistic but anxious. We could already see the hostility and counterattacks from the pro-Bolsonaro and pro-Moro factions, independently powerful camps that had fully merged once Moro joined Bolsonaro's government. We knew strategically that it would be foolish to stand alone, and that we needed a mainstream partner to sanction and participate in the reporting—the bigger, the better.

Folha did not take forty-eight hours. The day after we met, Sérgio called to say *Folha* was excited to partner with us. This was a crucial development: it would be much harder for the Bolsonaro government to claim we were not journalists when we were working hand in hand with Brazil's largest and most influential newspaper. We had specifically asked that one of the *Folha* reporters with an encyclopedic knowledge of Operation Car Wash, Ricardo Balthazar, be assigned as the lead reporter to work with our team, and Sérgio said Ricardo would fly to Rio as soon as we were ready to begin.

Folha's first article in partnership with us appeared on June 23, just two weeks after our first series of articles. It was devastating for Moro, detailing how Car Wash prosecutors, with Moro's approval, had conspired to manipulate decisions from the Supreme Court by concealing vital information from the court's justices. The byline reflected our joint reporting:

FOLHA DE S.PAULO
★ ★ ★

As important as that first article was, the accompanying editorial from *Folha*, explaining the rationale behind our new partnership, was even more impactful. Crucially, the subheader explained, "Examination of the material did not detect any evidence that it might have been altered." The editorial itself noted that "reporters . . . searched for the names of *Folha* journalists and found several messages that our reporters have in fact exchanged with members of the Car Wash task force in recent years, thus providing convincing evidence of the integrity of the material." *Folha* added, "Given the vastness of the archive, journalists [at *Folha*] have spent significant time analyzing the dialogues, examining the context of the discussions in the various message groups and checking the information found in order to verify the consistency of the materials obtained by Intercept."

The editorial also underlined a crucial fact: "After the first reports on the messages, published by the Intercept on June 9, Moro and the prosecutors responded by defending their performance in Car Wash, but without contesting the authenticity of the revealed dialogues." Indeed, it was clear from their initial, sputtering, and unfocused responses that both Moro and the prosecutorial task force were knocked on their heels by these abrupt revelations. Once they found their footing, however, Moro and the task force began to use rhetorical sleight of hand to raise doubts about the archive's authenticity, claiming—quite improbably—that they had all deleted all Telegram messages from their phones, and therefore had no way of determining whether the messages were, in fact, accurate. With increasing aggression, they tried to sow public doubt about whether these messages were real. Their longtime allies, *Globo*, helped by always referring to the materials we were reporting as "the *alleged* messages."

To have *Folha* state definitively that they had investigated the archive and determined its authenticity was a major boost for us, and a big blow to Moro's and Bolsonaro's efforts to insinuate doubts about the material. That show of solidarity was critical. Over the next six months, *Folha*, in partnership with the Intercept Brasil, published well over a dozen different exposés about Moro and Operation Car Wash, including some of the most incriminating articles, spawning ethics investigations.

Ultimately, several other news outlets independently confirmed the authenticity of the messages we published. Prosecutors who had communicated in several of the Telegram groups and had kept their chats confirmed to those papers that they matched, word for word, our published versions.

Soon, we embarked on a second critical partnership with a major media outlet: the center-right newsweekly *Veja*. It is hard to overstate the influence of the magazine's cover. Displayed on every street corner at newsstands in every large and midsize city, people too poor to buy them nonetheless read the covers. The drumbeat on the cover of *Veja* of highly negative images of Dilma and Lula played a major role in laying the groundwork for her impeachment and his subsequent imprisonment. Conversely, the numerous magazine covers that depicted Sérgio Moro as a superhero single-handedly vanquishing corrupt politicians were indispensable to the triumphal image he enjoyed.

To have *Veja* on board would be formidable, we reasoned, given the magazine's reputation for being squarely on the center-right, and especially in light of its unyielding reverence of Moro. Shortly after we had sealed our partnership deal with *Folha*, I called a reporter I knew at *Veja* and asked if he could help arrange a meeting with the magazine's editor in chief, Maurício Lima. The next day, I spoke with Maurício, who said that he and the magazine's new owner, Fábio Carvalho, were extremely enthusiastic about working with us. The next day, they both flew to Rio to meet with me in my home.

After hearing their expressions of excitement and support for our reporting, I voiced my major concern about working with them: the magazine had been such an unflinching and vocal fan of Moro and Operation Car Wash that I wondered whether they would publish highly incriminating information about them in the manner the journalism required. Both of them, but particularly Carvalho, sought to allay my concerns, speaking for roughly an hour.

They told me that because Carvalho was a new owner (having purchased the publishing company that owns *Veja* just a few months earlier) and Lima was a new editorial director (having assumed that position at roughly the same time), this was "a new *Veja*." They assured me that the magazine's team was eager to report the truth about Moro and the Car Wash task force, no matter where it might lead. Carvalho stressed that before becoming an investor, he had been a practicing lawyer and was thus highly concerned with the precedents being set by Moro and the Car Wash prosecutors that ran roughshod over long-standing Brazilian criminal justice protections.

By the time of our meeting, they had already published the initial cover story that showed Moro as a crumbling, decrepit statue, which was highly favorable toward our first series of reports and equally critical of Moro. They argued, persuasively, that this was proof they were willing not to pull punches.

Though I was still feeling a bit cautious, even at the end of their pitch, they convinced me that they meant what they said. We agreed to work together, and they wasted no time dispatching a large team of reporters to work on the archive from my house (the Intercept's Rio newsroom was currently occupied by the *Folha* reporters). We were not willing to hand over full copies of the archive to anyone—we felt we had a strong obligation to protect its contents and secure our right to control how it was used—but we gave our partners unfettered access to the materials from the newsroom and my house.

On July 5—less than a month after our reporting began—*Veja* dropped the equivalent of a journalistic nuclear bomb on Moro and the Car Wash prosecutors. The longtime Moro boosters published a second highly critical cover story on the justice minister. *Veja* depicted Moro with his finger tipping the scales of justice. "Justice with His Own Hands," read the headline, stating underneath: "Exclusive dialogues show that Sérgio Moro committed irregularities, tilting the balance in favor of the prosecution in the Car Wash probe."

Sergio Moro featured on the cover of Veja for the first joint Intercept Brasil / Veja reporting

The article itself, spread out over eight full magazine pages, complete with graphics of previously secret chats, used even harsher language. Indeed, *Veja* used more severe language in the story's headline than the Intercept Brasil's lawyers had authorized us to use regarding Moro up to that point: "New Dialogues Reveal That Moro Illegally Guided Lava Jato Actions." We had avoided "illegalities," opting instead for the softer terms "irregularities" and "improprieties." But *Veja* editors were adamant that they had the goods and that the material left no doubt that Moro had crossed clear legal lines. I agreed.

First article jointly published by Glenn Greenwald and Veja, July 5, 2019

The beginning of the *Veja* article quoted a highly respected former Supreme Court justice, Eros Grau: "When the judge loses impartiality, he ceases to be a judge." To see the nation's most prominent jurists now openly slamming Moro's conduct in such unflinching terms demonstrated how radically and quickly the climate had transformed.

One striking aspect of the article was the inclusion of my name as the first in the byline. The *Veja* editors and I shared several laughs about how we would have reacted had someone told us a few months earlier that we would soon be uniting to publish highly incriminating exposés about Moro and Operation Car Wash with my name in the lead. Yet here it was: a significant proclamation by *Veja*, following *Folha*'s own, of their investment in #VazaJato.

Like *Folha*, *Veja* published a separate editorial that explained why they had decided to partner with the Intercept Brasil in this increasingly controversial and polarizing reporting. But what they had to say was even more startling than the *Folha* editorial. Entitled "Letter to Our Readers: About Our Principles and Values," the *Veja* editorial read like a confession of past journalistic wrongdoing. Knowing that its partnership with us and its exposés on Moro would likely come as a shock to readers who had spent years reading hagiographic coverage of the justice minister in its pages, and who had spent the past several weeks consuming a diet of increasingly vitriolic attacks on myself and the Intercept, *Veja*'s subheader read: "Unlike those who foment hatred or take advantage of it, *Veja*'s commitments are not to political figures or parties."

The editors made a remarkable admission: they acknowledged that *Veja* had been central to the campaign to lionize Judge Moro with their series of highly flattering magazine covers. In explaining why they were participating in the #VazaJato reporting, *Veja* displayed five of those covers with this caption: "TREATED AS A HERO—Former judge Sérgio Moro was on the cover of *Veja* on several occasions, most in his favor: although he was instrumental in the fight against corruption, one cannot turn a blind eye."

Veja's "Letter to the Reader" accompanying the first Vaza Jato story.

The magazine noted that "*Veja* has always been—and continues to be—in favor of Lava Jato, but the dialogues we publish in this edition violate due process, a cornerstone of the rule of law—which, by the way, is more fragile than is presumed, even more so in our young democracy." "Anyone who thinks we're against Sérgio Moro is also wrong," *Veja* added. "Few media outlets have celebrated the work of the former judge in the fight against corruption (see the covers above)"; but, "one day, the vigilante knocks on the door and, without the right to a fair defense, the person is summarily condemned."

Like *Folha*, the magazine confirmed the authenticity of the material, explaining: "We analyzed dozens of messages exchanged over the years between members of our newsroom and prosecutors. All communications are true—word for word (which reveals strong evidence of the archive's veracity)." *Veja* would join the São Paulo newspaper in publishing numerous #VazaJato articles over the course of the next several months. While *Folha's* tended to be shorter and newsier, *Veja's* were deep dives into the corruption that permeated the Car Wash operation.

Eventually, close to a dozen major mainstream outlets joined in the reporting—including Universo Online, *El País* of Brazil, BuzzFeed of Brazil, Agência Pública, and prominent conservative analyst Reinaldo Azevedo of *BandNews*—representing an ideological and political cross section of media entities that made it increasingly difficult to depict the reporting as an ideological crusade or to isolate us as rogues or criminals.

Working with our partners, we ended up publishing, over the course of the next six months, more than one hundred stories based on the archive, showing serious corruption and improprieties on the part of the once-revered Car Wash team and the once-untouchable justice minister, Sérgio Moro.

The stories came fast and furious, and were all proven by their own once-secret conversations. Among our other key findings were these:

- Moro told the Car Wash prosecutorial team not to pursue former center-right president Fernando Henrique Cardoso on corruption charges very similar to those against Lula, because he was "an important political ally" who should "not be alienated."

- Car Wash prosecutors routinely talked about Moro as someone who was unethical and violated basic defendant rights in order to achieve his desired outcomes, but got away with it because the political class was happy with those results. They also openly and angrily objected that Moro's appointment by the Bolsonaro government would look like it was a quid pro quo for Lula's imprisonment and would permanently destroy the legacy and legitimacy of the Car Wash task force.

- Showing how personalized was their contempt for Lula, leading Car Wash prosecutors mocked the death of Lula's seven-year-old grandson from meningitis while he was in prison. (One of those involved in those discussions publicly apologized when we reported this, but most stayed silent.)

- Car Wash prosecutors plotted to convert their newfound celebrity into profit, often in ways that ran afoul of ethical guidelines, such as the receipt of payments for speeches from companies under investigation.

- The task force conspired to conceal information from the Supreme Court.

- Moro violated judicial guidelines and his own practices to release damaging tapes he obtained of conversations between Lula and Dilma, which he did purely for political reasons.

- The chief of the task force, Deltan Dallagnol, had improper conversations with a key judge on the appellate court immediately above Moro to ensure the affirmation of convictions.

- Car Wash prosecutors warned that Moro, as Bolsonaro's justice minister, would protect criminality on the part of Bolsonaro's family in order to secure his spot on the Supreme Court, which had been promised to him by Bolsonaro.

- Car Wash prosecutors, including Dallagnol, oversaw political messaging and social media campaigns against Supreme Court justices they perceived as adversarial.

- Prosecutors leaked information to friendly media outlets while publicly denying they had done so, all to pressure defendants into accusing higher-ups of crimes.

As these revelations washed over the Brazilian public and media, how the public perceived Moro, Dallagnol, and the Car Wash probe, and how the media talked about them, changed quickly and perceptibly.

Polling data quickly reflected both the reach and impact of the reporting. After the first week of publication, a survey by the firm Atlas Político revealed that 73.4 percent of Brazilians had heard about the Intercept's reports. Moro's once-invulnerable popularity was also shaken in the first month, dropping from 60 percent in the previous month to 50.4 percent.

The man who knew best how consequential was this reporting was Sérgio Moro himself. The week after we began publication, *Estadão*—long a pro-Moro outlet—reported that "those who spoke to Moro in the past few days found a dejected man" who "seemed embarrassed to have his name involved in scandal." Most poignantly, the article reported, "He who long passed judgment on others has now himself become the judged."

In retrospect, the anxiety I had that the revelations would not make the impact I believe, they deserved seems quaint. On the contrary, they rocked Brazilian politics to their core. Our reporting destabilized the Bolsonaro government by revealing that its most important member, and the path that was paved for Bolsonaro to the presidency, were corrupt. The revelations also severely altered public opinion about the most significant anti-corruption operation in modern Brazilian history, casting doubt on the prosecution and imprisonment of numerous defendants, including Lula. And they galvanized nationwide debates over criminal justice and the role of journalism and leakers.

Our journalism also radically, and permanently, changed the lives of all of us who were at the center of the reporting.

Chapter 8

— — — — — — — — —

BOLSONARO'S COUNTERATTACKS AND THE FALLOUT

When we began the reporting on the #VazaJato archive, I knew that the Bolsonaro movement had a very potent and well-orchestrated online attack machine. It was obvious during the 2018 election, and it played a big role in enabling Bolsonaro to win despite being opposed, at least in the first round of voting, by most of the political establishment and Brazil's leading media outlets.

The first sign of the movement's profound toxicity came in late 2018, when it was activated against *Folha* reporter Patrícia Campos Mello, who had just broken the bombshell story that the Bolsonaro campaign was being illegally financed by right-wing business interests. But Bolsonaro's victory in January catapulted them to the levers of power, thus enabling that movement to grow rapidly and become fortified in new ways.

After my colleagues and I published our exposés, we became the primary sworn enemies of the Bolsonaro movement. And it did not take long for this elaborate machine to be mobilized against us.

On June 10, the day after we published our first set of stories, the president's youngest son, Eduardo Bolsonaro, resurfaced a conspiracy theory about myself and David that had long lurked on the Brazilian far right. Specifically, they claimed—based on nothing—that LGBT congressman Jean Wyllys fled Brazil after Bolsonaro's victory not because he feared for his life, but rather because I had paid him $700,000 to leave, along with a monthly stipend of $10,000 a month, so that he could live in Europe and David could take his place in Congress.

Eduardo, in a tweet that went mega-viral on social media and the phones of millions of Brazilians via WhatsApp, posted a video from a far-right commentator (eventually hired by CNN Brasil in 2020) who hinted at this conspiracy, which then galvanized countless pro-Bolsonaro websites and YouTube channels to spend the next several months disseminating the absurd slander as fact.

The next day, a petition emerged online that demanded my deportation, claiming that I was a threat to the national security of Brazil. Within twenty-four hours, the hashtag #DeportaGreenwald rose to the top of Twitter, and the petition quickly accumulated more than 100,000 signatures.

Memes branding me an "enemy of brazil" ricocheted throughout right-wing echo chambers. One read: "GRAVE: Glenn uses the Intercept to try to create a pro-Lula narrative using illegally obtained archives."

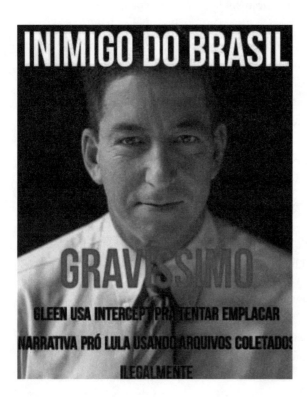

A widely circulated meme depicting Glenn Greenwald as an enemy of Brazil.

Because most of my attention was devoted to preparing the next series of exposés and securing our partnerships with *Folha* and *Veja*, I was only vaguely aware of these attacks. But each day there was a new variant of a hashtag aimed at me sitting atop Twitter's trending topics, which soon included demands that I be imprisoned: the most popular and frequently deployed of these was #GlennNaCadeia (#GlennInPrison).

However, the growing attacks on social media were dwarfed by very specific, graphic, and detailed threats both David and I began receiving, often directed at our kids. On June 11—two days after the first publication date—we received one particularly disturbing email with our two sons' names in the subject line. The message contained a great deal of private information about our family—where we lived, where our kids went to school, personal data about both of us—along with extremely gruesome and demented threats about what they would do to our children.

As people who had for years been in the public eye as part of intense political controversies, David and I were well accustomed to the sort of standard, nonserious threats everyone with a public platform has to endure, of the "I hope you die" or "You will pay" variety. But these threats of violence were markedly different.

Given that the email came from someone with considerable inside information, we took the situation very seriously. We decided our best protection would be to go public. David took that message, along with the dozens of similarly alarming ones we had received after it was announced he would replace Jean in Congress, and brought them to the Federal Police (now, it should be noted, under the command of Sérgio Moro).

Ever since he entered Congress and became the target of antigay bile and violent threats, David, with Marielle Franco's assassination obviously on his mind, had urged me to use security whenever I leave the house. Despite my reluctance to do so, the visibility—and surging hatred—this reporting had suddenly provoked for our family left me no choice. Senior management at First Look Media and the Intercept told me to obtain whatever security we believed was necessary. Stories of people being betrayed by their own security are legion in Brazil, so we had to choose carefully. We consulted with David's party, which gave us a list of trusted police officers and other armed security experts. Thiago, a police officer in the municipality of Niterói of great integrity, became the head of my security team. He quickly assembled a team of four security experts, all police officers, and procured a bulletproof vehicle of the kind that could have saved Marielle's life.

I now followed David's protocol: I could only leave the house accompanied by armed guards in an armored car. Our two sons went to school that way. We tried as best we could to explain to them in a reassuring manner why our house was being quickly converted into an armored fortress. Shortly after, the center-right speaker of the lower house decided that the threats directed at our family were so severe that Congress had a responsibility to pay for David's security detail. Our lives were lived behind walls of electric gates, armored cars, and armed men whom we trusted with our lives. A year and some months later, as this book goes to print, neither of us has left our house without this security protection.

The attacks from the Bolsonaro family continued to escalate in the week after we published the first #VazaJato revelations. On June 13, Eduardo Bolsonaro commented on a joint appearance his father had made with Sérgio Moro at a highly watched soccer game, widely interpreted as the president's expression of support for the justice minister in the wake of our reporting. Eduardo said that the cheers for the duo from the crowd demonstrated that "the illegal leak provoked by the Intercept and Greenwald" was having the opposite effect of the one we intended.

The next day, the president himself spoke about our stories. He vehemently defended his justice minister, emphasizing that our reporting was based on "a criminal invasion." Contradicting himself, he cast doubt on whether the messages were genuine ("whether what is being leaked is true or not"). He heralded Moro as a national hero whose service "is priceless," emphasizing that Moro imprisoned corrupt leaders—meaning Lula, his principal opponent. And he emphasized that the evidence showing Lula's guilt "was not forged."

As intended, those comments sent an unmistakable signal to the Bolsonaro movement that they should back Moro. Videos began to appear on YouTube calling for my arrest. They encouraged the use of the hashtags to demand my arrest or imprisonment, which kept them at the top of social media feeds for weeks. Trumpeted by both pro-Bolsonaro and pro-Moro websites, some of them piled up hundreds of thousands of views in a few days. We began hearing from friends that their apolitical parents were receiving videos and other messaging through WhatsApp and Facebook accusing me of being a criminal and insisting that I belonged in prison for having "hacked" the phones of Brazilian authorities.

Meanwhile, friends, and even acquaintances of ours, also began telling us that they were receiving monetary offers from anonymous operatives to say things about our personal lives, whether true or not. Before the first week was over, it was clear that we were not only engulfed in all-out war, but that it would be even dirtier and more extreme than we had imagined.

— — — — — — — — —

The attacks reached an entirely new level on June 15—six days after publication of our first stories. The previous day, I had noticed a flurry of excitement in right-wing media over the appearance of a new, anonymous Twitter account calling itself Pavão Misterioso ("mysterious peacock"), which announced that it was going to release "extremely incriminating bombshells" about me the next day, beginning at 2:00 p.m. Before the day was over, the account had close to 150,000 followers, all eagerly waiting to see whatever dirt had been dug up about me.

Pavão Misterioso
@oppavaomisterio
Entrou em junho de 2019
0 Seguindo **146.804** Seguidores

Tweets   Tweets e respostas   Mídia

Anonymous Twitter account prior to the first tweet

I knew from experience how these smear campaigns worked. In the first phase of the Snowden reporting, the *New York Times* and the *New York Daily News* had both contacted me to say they were preparing reporting about various aspects of my past, including old tax debts and a corporate interest I had in a company that provided consulting services to numerous companies, one of which distributed adult films. The *New York Times* ultimately decided the reporting was not in the public interest, and I was able to preempt the *Daily News* by writing my own article in the *Guardian*. The attempt by the *Daily News* to embarrass me fell flat, as most of the Internet mocked their trivial and irrelevant revelations.

I had stayed up much of the night on June 15 trying to finish our next story, so by the afternoon of June 16, as the time of the Pavão approached, I was fighting off the desire for a nap. That a large part of the country was waiting for some promised "bombshell" about me helped stave off sleep.

At exactly 2:00 p.m., as promised, the Pavão account began tweeting. After the first few tweets, I breathed a sigh of relief. It was baseless and conspiratorial garbage.

Pavão began by announcing that the central figures in the plot about to be revealed were Pierre Omidyar, the billionaire founder of eBay who also funds the Intercept; someone named Evgeniy Mikhailovich Bogavech, who the Pavão account said was a mastermind Russian hacker wanted by the FBI; myself; David; and Jean Wyllys, the gay congressman who fled Brazil.

In the first several tweets, it laid out an elaborate plot under which I had paid Bogavech hundreds of thousands of dollars in bitcoins to hack the phones of Brazilian authorities. It included several obviously fake documents purporting to be the bitcoin receipts of my payments to the Russian hacker. It was a cheap and obvious forgery, replete with all sorts of typos and spelling errors.

The forged bitcoin transaction document was purportedly written in English yet contained basic errors that only Brazilians who are not perfectly fluent in English would make. For instance, it spelled the word "transferred" wrong and used the Portuguese word for "rubles" rather than the English one. It also used the Brazilian format for expressing large numbers (in which a period rather than a comma is used to separate thousands, while the comma rather than the period is used to separate cents). Most absurdly, it claimed to be able to identify the bitcoin transaction as mine, despite the fact that the whole point of bitcoin transactions is anonymity, because I had conveniently named my account (the one I was supposedly using to commit major international crimes) with identifying initials of "INT" (for Intercept), "BR" (for Brazil), and "GG" (my initials):

TRANSACTION 982019-0 BRA-PAN-RUS STATUS: EXTINGUISHED

CF INTBRGG 8748479920002991 FXBT-BRA 84 BTC TO COINBASE-PAN (TIC)

02-13-2019 08:02:11 GMT DAILY VALUE BTC US$ 3.624,54 TOTAL TRANSFERED IN US DOLLARS 308.085,90 STATUS: COMPLETED

02-13-2019 09:03:49 GMT FULL CONVERSION TO ETHEREUM COIN (ETH) IN A POSITION DAILY OF US$ 121,96 CASH STATUS AT TIME: ETH 2.526,1225 NO CHANGE IN US DOLLARS VALUE STATUS: CONVERTED AND COMPLETED

PAN CHACBS 7730019002039 SEND ETH VALUE 2.526,1225 TO ANAPA-KRASNODARSKIY KRAY-RUS FIKSIK129-RUS (TIC)

02-13-2019 11:02:34 GMT ETH 2.526,1225 CONVERTED TO RUSSIAN RUBLOS RUB 20.539,070,30 CASH STATUS AT TIME: CONVERTED AND WAITING OWNER DECISION

02-14-2019 10:02:58 GMT MONEY TRANSFERRED TO SHANGHAI COMMERCIAL BANK LIMITED BY PERMISSION 392884885-MGR CREATED BY VIKTOR POLLSON

IN TOTAL VALUE, ANAPA, KRASNODARSKIY KRAY, RUSSIA ZENIT SOCHI BANK SIGNED THE E-TRANSACTION AT ULITSA LENINA PLACE.

NO MORE PATHS IN THIS TOOL. STATUS: FINISHED

Forged document posted by the new Twitter account "Pavão Misterioso," June 16, 2019.

Knowing that this was all a complete fabrication—I had never used bitcoins in my life, never heard of Bogavech, and never paid any source for any information—I dozed off, content in the knowledge that this was not some devastating bombshell revealing incriminating information about me, but a dreary, primitive, empty fraud by some low-level, attention-seeking Bolsonarista.

But when I awoke from my nap two hours later, the Internet had a big surprise in store for me. Pavão's accusations—which ultimately included the claim that I had paid Jean to flee the country to secure David's seat in Congress—were the biggest story in Brazil. All sorts of people were taking them seriously. That I had paid a Russian hacker for the documents, and paid Jean to flee, was being repeated as fact by YouTubers, as well as by key Bolsonaro figures, including his sons.

The so-called #ShowDoPavão of June 16 ended with several tweets that strongly implied the anonymous author was an officer with the Federal Police. It claimed that I would be summoned by them that Thursday, instructed me which computers to bring (implying that the author had in-depth knowledge of the various computers I used), and ended by saying, "Until Thursday, my dude."

← **Sequência**

Pavão Misterioso ⌄
@oppavaomisterio

Agora o principal: vc,
@ggreenwald apareça na
Rodrigues Alves número 1 no
Rio de janeiro, vc já esteve aqui
diversas vezes renovando sua
carteira de estrangeiro, com seu
notebook Dell, na quinta feira e o
apresente, não no Apple que usa
para ver pornografia,

16:00 · 16 jun 19 · Twitter Web App

1.968 Retweets   **4.497** Curtidas

Pavão Misterioso @oppav... · 44 min ⌄
Em resposta a @oppavaomisterio
Mas o Dell onde fica teu Cryptobank, que
um de nós pessoalmente esclarecerá as
denúncias e possivelmente te dê voz de

Tweete sua resposta

Now, the key: you, @ggreenwald, will appear at Rodrigues Alves 1 in Rio de
Janeiro, you were here many times to renew your visa, with your Dell notebook, and on Thursday you'll present not the Apple you use to watch por-
nography, but the Dell where your Cryptobank is kept. . . .

Soon, #ShowDoPavão was the number one trending Twitter term in Brazil by far. Within an hour, it was the top trending term globally, which it remained for at least the next twenty-four hours, as conspiratorial accusations continued to spread throughout Brazil. One congressman from Bolsonaro's party—using an infantile play on my name that would become a staple of the pro-Bolsonaro right, *Verdevaldo*—put it this way on June 17:

Carlos Jordy ✓
@carlosjordy

O Show do Pavão ficou nos trending topics mundial ontem. Hoje, o assunto continua em 1o, assombrando o Verdevaldo e demais inimigos da lava jato e do Brasil. In Pavão We Trust!

#PavaoMisterioso
#InPavaoWeTrust

Translated from Portuguese by Google

The Pavão Show was on the global trending topics yesterday. Today, the subject continues in 1st place, haunting Verdevaldo and other enemies of the lava jet and of Brazil. In Peacock We Trust!

#PavaoMisterioso
#InPavaoWeTrust

12:25 PM · Jun 17, 2019 · Twitter for iPhone

1.8K Retweets   **124** Quote Tweets   **8.1K** Likes

Tweet from pro-Bolsonaro congressman Carlos Jordy

Numerous mainstream news outlets reported on the Pavão claims, but mostly to debunk them. *Estadão*, for instance, published a June 19 article headlined "Crypto-currency Specialists Point to Inconsistencies in

'Pavão Misterioso' Report." It detailed the numerous errors in the forged bitcoin document and quoted the chief technological officer of Zro Bank as saying, "I've never seen a blockchain system like that one," adding, "It doesn't appear professional."

But the facts did not matter. The Bolsonaro right had long ago tuned out mainstream media outlets and constructed their own information ecosystem. The accusations against me spread unchecked throughout the same networks on WhatsApp, Facebook, and YouTube that had propelled Bolsonaro to the presidency in 2018.

— — — — — — — — — —

On June 19, Sérgio Moro was summoned to the Senate to testify about the improper conduct revealed by our reporting. It was a major event, with the room packed and all television networks covering the testimony of the justice minister. During Moro's nine-hour testimony, he never once referred to us as journalists. Instead he repeatedly used the phrases "allies of the hackers" or "allies of the organized crime ring that hacked the phones of Brazilian authorities"—an obvious attempt to lay the foundation for our prosecution as criminals.

When it came time for Bolsonaro's son Flavio to question Moro, he used his time to vest credibility in the deranged Pavão conspiracy theories, asking Moro about them:

> An accusation has been raised that is extremely grave, in the event it is confirmed. It is part of this plot that is underway to destabilize our democracy, against the head of state, the president who has been democratically elected. In this case, Glenn Greenwald may have paid a Russian hacker to invade the cell phones of Brazilian authorities, and this payment may have been made in bitcoins, a currency that is encrypted and leaves no tracks. [...]
>
> We also have the accusation that the money circulating between the Intercept and [the Russian hacker] was used for another crime. Greenwald and his partner [sic], federal Congressman David Miranda of PSOL, may have bought the term of former Congressman Jean Wyllys, of the same party, for $700,000, along with a monthly payment of $10,000.

These are extremely grave accusations. I'd like to ask you if the
Federal Police is investigating these cases?

This wild storyline had everything it needed to stimulate the primal hatreds
of the Bolsonaro movement. It featured a clandestine plot by three gay
men—myself, David, and Jean, long a prime enemy of the Bolsonaros—
to engage in political fraud. It tried to implicate Omidyar, an Iranian-born
billionaire who was raised in France and now lives in the United States,
where he is a citizen. And Flavio Bolsonaro, using cryptic and barely co-
gent reasoning I still don't understand, even managed to claim that money
I ostensibly paid was somehow linked not only to Russia but China, a bête
noire of the fanatically anti-Communist Bolsonaro movement despite also
being Brazil's largest trading partner.

Like the original Pavão conspiracy theory, it was hard to believe that
anyone took seriously Flavio Bolsonaro's attempts to elevate these ram-
blings to the level of the Senate and the Federal Police. But they succeeded.

On June 19, the newsweekly *Istoé*—long a mainstay, with *Veja* and
Época, on the street corner newsstands of Brazilian cities—published
a cover story claiming that federal investigators were closing in on the
criminal enterprise to hack the phones of Moro and the Car Wash prosecutors. It mirrored the Pavão fiction almost entirely, but added some
amazing new flourishes. The central claim was that I had wired money
to Russian hackers using bitcoins, then used my friendship with Edward
Snowden, and his friendship with the two brothers who founded Telegram, to access the app's servers.

The conspiracy theory was self-contradictory and incoherent: if I
had access to the Telegram servers through my association with Snowden
and the Durov brothers, why would I need to pay a Russian hacker to ac-
quire those same files?

Even more inane was the motive *Istoé* attributed to the brothers. Why
would two people who founded Telegram—which centrally relies on its
promise of providing secure communications—risk their entire company
to give me and Snowden access to the communications of Brazilian judges
and prosecutors? The answer provided by the magazine makes me laugh
to this very day. It was, they said, because the brothers reside in Dubai
after having fled Russia—which means they likely have Muslim leanings,

which would in turn make them hostile to the pro-Israel Bolsonaro. The convoluted theory is hilarious for many reasons, not least of which is the idea that Dubai is a pious Islamic city, rather than the playground of debauchery and gluttony for transnational, secular elites.

Yet this conspiracy theory—originated by an anonymous Twitter account—was now given credence by a magazine with national reach, on its cover, complete with a complicated flow chart showing the plot that included me, Snowden, the Durov brothers, Lula, and hundreds of thousands of dollars flying around between us:

ON THE TRAIL OF MORO'S HACKER
EXCLUSIVE
The Federal Police Have Clues That Led Them to the Criminals Who Violated Justice Minister Sérgio Moro's Conversations.

There Are Possible Connections in Russia and Dubai, and Suspects Involved in the Crime Ring of Santa Catarina.

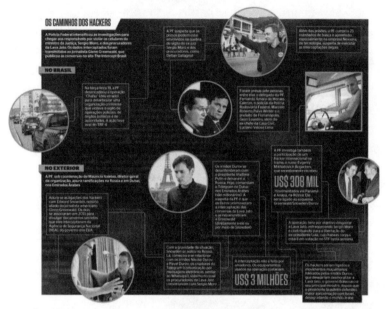

Isto É graphic depicting a vast conspiracy behind the Vaza Jato reporting, involving Glenn Greenwald, Edward Snowden, and Russian hackers.

The attacks continued to escalate. One particularly disturbing report came from one of the nation's most prominent right-wing journalists, Alexandre Garcia. Before working as a *Globo* television journalist for three decades and then being hired as a commentator in 2020 by CNN Brasil, he was the official spokesman for Brazil's last military dictator in the 1980s. In mid-June, Garcia reported that generals in the Brazilian military were discussing how to use one of the most repressive dictatorship-era laws still on the books—the National Security Law—to characterize my reporting as a crime against the state, and prosecute me.

My instinct to laugh off the vapid Pavão forgeries was dampened significantly by how widespread this coverage had become, and especially by how many powerful people in Brazil were speaking openly of my imprisonment.

During the second week of our #VazaJato reporting, members of Bolsonaro's party in Congress introduced a motion requiring me to appear to testify, as Moro had just done. When they saw that left-wing members of

Congress (including my husband's colleagues in his party) were supporting their motion—believing it would be beneficial for me to have this national platform to discuss our revelations—the pro-Bolsonaro lawmakers quickly tried to withdraw it, realizing the mistake they had made. But by then it was too late: centrists in Congress joined with the liberals and leftists to approve a hearing. The date for my testimony was set for June 25.

Along with one of our lawyers, Rafael Borges, I flew to Brasilia the night before the hearing and stayed with David. When I arrived in Congress the next morning, the halls were packed, and had a suffocating feeling: media were everywhere, the public was lined up to get in, and there were more lawmakers in attendance than the room could accommodate. David decided he would not participate—we have both learned how difficult it is to remain calm and rational when people are publicly attacking your husband—but he stayed for most of the hearing to give moral support.

Because the Bolsonaristas had tried to abandon their effort to subpoena me, the left was able to pick the committee before which I would testify. They chose the Human Rights and Minorities Commission, chaired by a member of the Workers' Party. But the hearing was also filled with pro-Bolsonaro members, ensuring that my eight hours of testimony would be constantly sidetracked by screaming matches, accusations, and recriminations. It was, in one sense, a circus, but I also recognized what a valuable platform I had been given and did my best to use it.

I was given ten minutes for an opening statement. I used this time to make two points I believed most critical. The first was to explain to a country that had little or no history of these kinds of leaks that the most important and consequential journalism in the democratic world is often enabled by civil disobedience or other forms of lawbreaking by a journalist's sources. I cited the Pentagon Papers, explaining that the *New York Times* and *Washington Post* were able to show the US public proof that the government was lying to them about the Vietnam War only because a military insider, Daniel Ellsberg, provided top secret documents to them in violation of the law.

I also reminded Brazilian legislators of their own history with such reporting. In 2013, when I used Snowden's documents to show Brazilians how their government institutions, their corporations, and their population was being spied on by the NSA and its allies, I was twice called by the Senate to testify about this reporting. At no point, I reminded them, did a single senator suggest that I was guilty of any wrongdoing, let alone a crime, by using materials "stolen" by my source. To the contrary, all the senators and most of Brazilian civic society—left, right, and center— expressed gratitude to Snowden and support for my journalism. Why, I asked rhetorically, should the principle they recognized then, when they perceived the reporting as in their national interest, be different now?

The other point I stressed was the reason a free press is so necessary for securing democracy: without it, powerful officials—including judges and prosecutors—will have no limit on their ability to abuse their power in the dark. The Brazilian Constitution, enacted during redemocratization, en- shrines protections for press freedom even more robust than does the US Constitution. That's because, I explained, citing Brazilian legal specialists, the Constitution's framers recognized that the tyrannical abuses they were seeking to escape would be repeated if a free press wasn't fully protected.

I enjoy engaging in important public debates, even if they are con- tentious (perhaps especially then). My experience as a high school and college debater, and the decade I spent in the savagely conflictual world of Manhattan litigation, prepared me well for such events. But this day- long hearing was unlike anything I had previously experienced. I felt somewhat like a yo-yo: while the leftist members of Congress spent their time praising my work and heralding it as heroic, the pro-Bolsonaro members, almost to a person, branded me a criminal and said I should be arrested—preferably before I even concluded my testimony. An Associ- ated Press article—entitled "Glenn Greenwald Becomes Focus of Brazil Press Freedom Debate"—aptly described the scene:

> Several weeks after publishing explosive reports about a key member of Brazil's far-right government, U.S. journalist Glenn Greenwald was called before a congressional committee to face hostile questions.
>
> "Who should be judged, convicted and in prison is the journal- ist!" shouted congresswoman Katia Sastre, an ally of President Jair Bolsonaro. . . . The Pulitzer Prize–winning journalist and his Brazilian husband also say they have been receiving detailed death threats, calls for his deportation and homophobic comments in an increasingly hostile political environment. [. . .]

During the June 25 hearing at the chamber's Human Rights and Minorities Commission, lawmaker Carla Zambelli told Greenwald: "If you don't prove this information, it is fake and you're a liar. If it's true, then you're a criminal because you hacked someone's phone." Greenwald responded: "The government's party evidently has a lot of confusion about the journalism we did."

As intense as these attacks were, the support we received was just as intense and spirited, and provided a surreal counterbalance. But the threats that came from the Bolsonaro faction in the Congress were powerful and chilling.

A week after the congressional hearing, it seemed that these threats were becoming realities. On July 2, a right-wing site long used as a favorite dumping ground for leaks by Moro and the Car Wash prosecutors announced that an agency responsible for detecting improper financial transactions by politicians and their families—one under the direct command of Moro—had opened an investigation into my finances, based on allegedly suspicious transactions.

That the investigation was retaliatory was self-evident. I had lived in Brazil for fifteen years without, to my knowledge, ever being investigated by any agency. Now suddenly, less than a month after I began reporting extremely incriminating revelations about the Bolsonaro government, an agency reporting directly to Moro not only opened an investigation into my finances but leaked to their favorite website that they had done so, ensuring the public would hear of the "suspicions."

News of this investigation prompted widespread condemnations from press freedom groups and politicians across the spectrum. As the *Guardian* reported, "Brazil's Bar Association, journalists and opposition lawmakers have reacted with outrage to reports that the country's federal police plan to investigate the bank accounts of [Glenn Greenwald] who published leaked conversations between prosecutors and the graft-busting judge who is now Jair Bolsonaro's justice minister." The center-left party REDE petitioned the Supreme Court for an order barring any investigations of me in retaliation for my reporting.

Yet the onslaught of attacks from the various appendages of the Bolsonaro movement continued unabated. On July 5, the Pavão account, now with many hundreds of thousands of followers, announced that it was returning with far more serious "bombshells." The pro-Bolsonaro and pro-Moro media were frenzied with anticipation. True to its word, the next day the account posted very intricate forgeries of WhatsApp conversations between David, Jean, multiple left-wing members of Congress, and Intercept Brasil executive editor Leandro Demori.

Pavão—seeking to draw a parallel between our reporting and what he was doing—purported to have hacked all of their cell phones and obtained conversations in which Jean complained to David and Leandro that the payments I promised him to leave Brazil were late. Far more work and effort were put into these forgeries than the first ones about bitcoin transfers. They had somehow managed to clone the chip to Leandro's telephone. Though there were numerous flaws that proved these chats to be fake to anyone who cared about the truth, they were spread far and wide. The top three trending topics on Twitter soon became #VoltaDoPavão (#ThePavãoReturns), #Pavão, and #GlennPagaJean (#GlennPayJean).

Mainstream news outlets quickly debunked the forgeries, but once again, it did not matter. The Bolsonaro and Moro factions treated them as true. One of Globo's biggest stars, the hugely successful soap opera writer Glória Perez, posted a tweet celebrating: "Wow. Saturday has begun very excitingly, with the return of the Pavão!"

In a mega-viral tweet, another Bolsonaro son, Carlos, who oversees the family's communications strategies, posted "Fly Pavão" in Morse code, along with a video of a peacock menacingly spreading its feathers. Pavão had taken on cult status for the Bolsonaro and Moro movements, and they were spreading every one of its scurrilous accusations about me, David, and the Intercept without any concern for their truth, leading millions of Brazilians—even apolitical ones—to believe them.

Carlos Bolsonaro ☑ @CarlosBolsonaro · Jul 6, 2019   ⌄

...- --- .-/.--. .- ...- .- ---

♡ 2.9K   ↺ 5.6K   ♡ 33.1K   ↑

All of this took place during the lead-up to my appearance at a famed biennial international literary event held in the bucolic town of Paraty, in the interior of Brazil. I had spoken there once before, at the height of the Snowden reporting, and it was a delightfully inspiring, if quaint, event, with artists, activists, and literary figures making pilgrimages from around the world to the old Portuguese colony for high-minded discussions about culture, art, politics, and literature.

The Bolsonaro movement had learned of my invitation two weeks in advance and were plotting on social media how to organize a massive protest against my participation. Our own security advisers had told us there was a chance the protests could be aggressive or even violent. I thought about withdrawing, but I knew doing so would only embolden the Bolsonaristas. And most importantly, we wanted to adhere to the message we had conveyed from the start: *We are not afraid.* I constantly emphasized in interviews and in public appearances that I would never leave Brazil or go into hiding as a result of threats, whether ones of persecution from the government or violence from its supporters. I felt that withdrawal from the Paraty biennial would be a betrayal of our commitment to show the country that we need not fear this movement—that we all have the ability to exercise our legal and constitutional rights free of intimidation.

The event organizers—highly unaccustomed to having to deal with threats of this sort at their normally harmonious event—spoke to my security team about rather unconventional measures they wanted to adopt. They believed that they could not guarantee my safety if they held the event in their usual venue, so they said they wanted me to speak from a boat in the middle of the water, with the crowd gathered at a distance on land. They also said that they had arranged for my arrival via a small, inconspicuous fishing boat. They assured us the local police would be extremely vigilant in keeping order, given how important the literary event is for the town.

On July 11, the night before, I arrived with my security team. One of the first things we saw upon arriving in Paraty was a sign declaring that I was not welcome in that town:

Indignation is a noble thing! Get out of Paraty, Glenn Greenwald.
Photo by Glenn Greenwald.

The event was scheduled to begin at 7:00 p.m. Along with my security team, I arrived at the pier at 6:30. Accompanying us was Patrícia Campos

Mello, the *Folha* reporter who had been targeted after breaking the story of illegal financing of the Bolsonaro campaign, who was writing for the paper about the extreme security measures needed for my participation. After being told that the event was delayed by protesters, at 7:00 p.m., we were finally given the go-ahead to board the tiny single-motor boat.

By this time, it was already dark. But as we approached the shore where the boat-stage was, we saw fireworks being shot into the air. "I wonder if those are your supporters?" Patrícia asked me earnestly. But just a couple moments later, we began noticing that the fireworks were being shot horizontally *at our boat*, and began falling closer and closer to it. Patrícia sardonically observed, "I'm starting to think that those are not supporters of yours." We laughed, a bit nervously.

Despite some close calls, we arrived at the boat-stage without being hit by fireworks. When I ascended the stage, I saw the thousands of people who had gathered for the event, and they were highly energized. Also highly energized were the dozens of pro-Bolsonaro protesters who had gathered on the riverbank behind the boat and who continued shooting fireworks at the boat.

Drone photo of the boat-stage at the event in Paraty. Photo by Guido Nietmann.

Speaking along with me was a panel composed of HBO Brasil host Gregório Duvivier, the left-wing writer Sabrina Fernandes, and two well-known scholars, Alceu Luís Castilho and Sérgio Amadeu. When we all arrived on the stage, complete with camera and sound people, the boat was rocking so much that we were certain we would tip. On the few occasions any of us tried to stand, the waves immediately pushed us to the floor.

As soon as I was given the mic to speak, the Bolsonaro supporters began blasting the Brazilian national anthem on a loop through gigantic speakers. Even with the sound system we had, and me yelling into the mic, it was clear that the crowd was struggling to hear me. Indeed, I couldn't even hear myself speaking. The protesters continued shooting fireworks into the air and horizontally at the boat and crowd. Once again, they began exploding closer and closer to our boat. Roughly thirty minutes into the event, fireworks landed in the crowd and set a banner on fire. The entire event felt like being in the middle of a civil war.

Once the event was over, I descended into the small fishing boat that was waiting to take us back to the pier. By now it was pitch black. As we sped through the dark, this did not seem to me like a very effective safety plan. At one point, the driver was headed straight for a large wooden buoy protruding out of the water; one of my security officers saw it and yelled, leading him to slow down at the last second. We crashed into it, causing a very sudden jolt, but the impact could have been much worse.

The next day, all the major Brazilian newspapers reported on the evening's chaos. *Folha* published photos that accompanied Patrícia's first-person account of accompanying me on the boat.

A picture of me in a life vest spread all over Bolsonaro's online networks, as his supporters gloated that they had interrupted the event and forced me to flee. It wasn't true—we finished the event—but they had succeeded in making it difficult for the audience to hear me, while creating a climate of hostility and intimidation.

Glenn Greenwald leaves the Paraty event by boat. Photo by Eduardo Anizelli / Folhapress.

That event presaged a growing climate of intimidation for Bolsonaro critics and other journalists. The following week, one of Brazil's most influential journalists, *Globo's* Míriam Leitão, was forced to cancel a long-planned book event due to threats of violence. Felipe Neto—the country's most influential YouTube personality, and a virulent enemy of the Bolsonaro movement because of his outspoken criticisms of the president—also canceled a September event for the same reason. And when the Intercept Brasil's deputy editor, Alexandre de Santi, was invited to speak at a college in his home state, members of the state legislature tried to stop it. When that failed, a protest was organized. The Intercept Brasil announced that not only would de Santi attend, but Leandro would join him in a show of solidarity.

— — — — — — — — — —

Less than two weeks after the events in Paraty, a major development oc-
curred in the law enforcement investigation into our sources. On July 23,
Justice Minister Moro announced that the Federal Police had arrested
four people who they claimed were responsible for hacking into the telephones of the Car Wash prosecutors and providing us with the contents.

The individual they named as the main hacker was found in the interior of São Paulo state and had a criminal history of low-level fraud. The
others were said to have helped him in various ways. The Federal Police
leaked the information that one of them, whose alias they said was "Red,"
had confessed to the hacking. Because I never knew the identity of my
source (or sources), I had no idea whether the people they arrested were
really involved in the hacking or providing the archive to us.

When I first heard the news, my primary concern was that federal authorities would try to coerce them into falsely implicating me in crimes.
This, after all, was the modus operandi of the Car Wash probe Moro oversaw: the concoction of pretexts to coerce imprisoned defendants into accusing others as a condition for release or leniency.

I was thus relieved when news reports said that the accused hacker
was adamant that I had never paid or even offered him money; that I had
no foreknowledge of the hacking; that I did not know his identity; and,
citing the example of Snowden, that his sole motivation was to expose
corruption that he believed the public had the right to know. (The person
alleged to be the chief hacker who had communicated with me most,
Walter Delgatti Neto, told CNN Brasil in a December 2020 interview
that from the moment he was arrested, he was continuously pressured
by authorities to implicate me in crimes, and promised his freedom from
preventative imprisonment in exchange for signing a document accusing
me of having been his coconspirator. He refused that corrupt deal. I was
fortunate that my alleged source had more integrity than the law enforcement officials presiding over this investigation.)

By hyping these dramatic arrests along with their media allies, Moro
and the Federal Police succeeded, at least temporarily, in shifting attention
away from the revelations we were publishing and toward their criminal
investigation. Now that they had names and faces, they could dramatize

as the villains, the possibility that they would depict us as coconspirators of a criminal enterprise became much more tangible. From that point forward, *Globo*'s television coverage mostly focused on the "hackers" and the "crime ring," while barely acknowledging the revelations about Moro and Car Wash we were reporting with our media partners.

Concerns over the government's intentions escalated significantly three days later, on July 26. Seemingly out of nowhere, Justice Minister Moro issued a unilateral "decree" that purported to vest him with new powers: namely, to direct the "summary expulsion of foreigners" deemed, in Moro's sole and unreviewable discretion, "dangerous to the security of Brazil."

The decree, comically bearing the number 666, prompted a vocal and immediate backlash from legal experts and people across the political spectrum. It was assumed almost universally that its impetus was to convey that Moro now had the power to expel me from the country, at any moment, with no recourse. For instance, the normally neutral BBC said that Moro's decree "commits a series of illegalities and unconstitutional acts in establishing conditions for the deportation of foreigners from Brazil. This is the assessment of six experts on the topic heard by BBC News Brasil."

That same day, a congressman from Bolsonaro's party, Filipe Barros, filed a formal request with the federal prosecutors' office for my immediate "preventive" arrest. In a statement issued to the public, he falsely accused me of a wide array of crimes, including having paid the hackers, and said that national security required my immediate imprisonment.

All of that was the increasingly alarming backdrop against which Bolsonaro made his first direct comments about me since we had begun the reporting. Asked during a press conference about whether Moro's new deportation decree was aimed at me, Bolsonaro denied this, explaining—correctly—that Brazilian law prohibits the deportation of any foreigner who is either married to a Brazilian national or is the legal custodian of Brazilian children. Since I'm both, Bolsonaro lamented, "That's the problem: he can't be kicked out, so he can be calm about that." Bolsonaro's precise familiarity with the intricacies of deportation law as they applied to me left little doubt that the normally incurious president had participated in discussions about whether I could be deported.

Bolsonaro quickly added that both David and I were "fraudsters" because we had married and adopted "two boys"—emphasis on the *boys*, by a president who built his career claiming gay men want to recruit and molest children—as a ruse to avoid deportation. "Glenn does not fit the [deportation] decree," he said, "because he is married to another man and has adopted boys in Brazil. Trickster, trickster [*malandro*], to avoid such a problem, he marries another trickster and adopts children in Brazil."

The president's public declaration that we adopted our two children not out of love but out of a desire to exploit them as a shield against deportation was odious. The theory itself was blatantly nonsensical: my fifteen-year marriage to David was already an absolute legal bar against my deportation; I did not need Brazilian children to be exempt from the law. But far worse was his depiction of our family as fraudulent, in a climate where the Bolsonaro movement had spent years stimulating extreme anti-LGBT animus—one that could easily expose our children to all sorts of recriminations and dangers.

As hateful as those comments about our family were, what Bolsonaro said next dramatically transformed the political and legal landscape. "He doesn't need to worry about being deported, but maybe he'll spend some time in the slammer here in Brazil," he told the reporters with a smirk.

I had spent almost two full months as the target of every weapon the Bolsonaro movement had—fake news, forged chats and bitcoin documents, leaked financial investigations, detailed death threats, fireworks shot at me, formal requests for my imprisonment from federal lawmakers, hashtag campaigns calling for my arrest that trended virtually daily on Twitter. But the combination of Moro's chilling deportation decree and Bolsonaro's explicit threat of imprisonment changed everything. It caused a serious backlash from both Brazilian civic society and the international press, who realized that the government's acts were becoming genuinely menacing, not just to me but to press freedom generally.

Among the responses that emerged was a *Washington Post* article that described how "the public threats against Greenwald represent an early test for Brazil under Bolsonaro, the right-wing former military officer who won the presidency last year with appeals to nationalism, homophobia and nostalgia for the country's two-decade military dictatorship." Even more pointedly, the *New York Times* published a profile of David and me entitled "'The Antithesis of Bolsonaro': A Gay Couple Roils Brazil's Far Right," which said that we were "on the front lines of the country's increasingly bitter political divide" and "under attack by Mr. Bolsonaro and his allies." The *Times* concluded, "The scandal has also become the first test of the resilience of Brazil's democratic institutions under the leadership of a president who has spent much of his political career railing against democracy."

Journalistic light is always a helpful tonic against authoritarianism, especially in a country for which a positive international image is an economic necessity. But as relieved as I was that the international media was now paying serious attention to these mounting threats, the fierce, angry reaction inside Brazil to the threats against me was far more important.

The day after the president's public threats to imprison me, several leading civic organizations devoted to press freedom, as well as the generally cautious Brazilian Bar Association, contacted us to say that they wanted to hold a major event in Rio de Janeiro to express support for press freedom and solidarity with the reporting being done by the Intercept Brasil. I quickly agreed, and we scheduled the event for just three days later, in order to capitalize on the momentum and the anger generated by Bolsonaro's threats and Moro's despotic decree.

Those groups began promoting the event, originally titled "Support for Glenn Greenwald," which was then amended to include "the Intercept Brasil." All fifteen hundred tickets were reserved online within a matter of minutes. Excitement over the event was palpable. Brazilians seemed to understand that, as the Associated Press had noted, this was the first real test case under the five-month-old Bolsonaro government, not only for press freedoms but for civic freedoms and democratic values generally. It had become clear, much to my relief, that many Brazilians were ready to take a stand in their defense.

For the first time since we began, I felt there was widespread recognition that the reporting we were doing was not only an exposé of rampant prosecutorial and judicial corruption within the Car Wash probe, but, far more broadly, a challenge to the Bolsonaro government's efforts to infringe core political liberties. And the support for my reporting and the defense of me against these threats was now at least as impassioned and widespread as the attacks we had been enduring for weeks.

The evening of July 31 was one of the most inspiring and gratifying of my life. I arrived with David and our sons, along with our security teams, and saw a large crowd of pro-Intercept marchers outside the arena where the event was being held. They carry placards with my face and slogans in defense of press freedom and against dictatorship. We had heard that thousands of people who could not get tickets planned to gather outside. As we passed by in our car and into the basement, we could see and hear that the crowd was large, unruly, and boisterous. I saw a few stray pro-Bolsonaro protesters, but they were massively outnumbered.

Once inside, I gave a press conference to the Brazilian media who had assembled. David, who was scheduled to introduce me to speak, was brought to the stage while I waited in a regal back room with our kids. I don't think I've ever appreciated them more. While thousands of people were gathered to hear me speak, some of them screaming slogans of support, the boys—at the time nine and eleven years old—could hardly have cared less. They used the occasion to aim spitballs at me through a straw and then pretend they were not, giggling to each other when I looked at them with irritation after they hit their target.

When I was brought up to the stage, seated next to David and our kids, the energy of the crowd was infectious. On the roster of speakers were more than two dozen members of Congress and some of the nation's most influential cultural figures, including the actor Wagner Moura, best known for his role in the Netflix series *Narcos*. But what moved me most was the presence of older activists, artists, journalists, and dissidents who had confronted the Brazilian military dictatorship, some of whom were imprisoned and exiled for having done so, including the singer Chico Buarque (forced out of Brazil by its junta in 1969) and the left-wing journalist Cid Benjamin (imprisoned by the dictatorship).

For two hours, one speaker after the next roused the crowd with defiant speeches. Included among them were video remarks from my journalistic colleagues in the United States, including James Risen and Naomi Klein. The Brazilian left (and the Bolsonaro right) was quite shocked when one of the videos denouncing the Bolsonaro government's attacks on me and defending my press freedoms came from none other than Fox News host Tucker Carlson. Perhaps the most significant video was from Rodrigo Maia, the very powerful center-right speaker of the lower house, who made clear that while he was no fan of mine, he regarded the threats from the government as a profound assault on a free press.

In David's introduction of me, he spoke pointedly about our marriage and, gesturing to our children, the family we had built together. That was of particular importance given the increasing antigay attacks on us and our family from the Bolsonaro movement, which had relied on homophobia to propel him to the presidency. The speech David gave was rousing and emotional, as usual. When he was done with his introduction, I stood up to speak and, completely unplanned, we kissed for an extended period of time as the crowd, recognizing its political significance, cheered us on. Photos of us in that embrace were widely circulated.

Brazilians show support for American journalist Greenwald

By Associated Press
2019/07/31 10:28

Glenn Greenwald and David Miranda kiss after speaking at a free press rally in Rio de Janeiro

What was most important about the ethos of the event, which I tried to emphasize in my own thirty-minute speech, was the virtue of fearlessness. The fear created by the sweeping election victory of Bolsonaro and his far-right movement was particularly acute given barbaric events like the assassination of Marielle Franco, Jean Wyllys's flight from Brazil, and the revelations of links between the Bolsonaros and the country's most

terrifying militias. Combined with trepidations over explicit antidemocratic threats, for those first few months after Bolsonaro's win, most had
felt the instinct to tread lightly and keep one's head down. In the immediate aftermath of the election, I had certainly felt that temptation myself. The massive far-right tidal wave had generated an unhealthy mix of
importance and anxiety. This event was an opportunity, with strength in
numbers, to unite to fundamentally change that climate.

The energy we created together that night was the opposite of fear
and helplessness. One person after the next vowed to fight Moro and the
Bolsonaro movement. I devoted most of my speech to this theme, bran-
dishing the US passport that I had in my jacket pocket to explain that, at
any moment, I could—but never would—leave Brazil in order to publish
the Telegram archive documents from the safety of the United States or
other foreign soil. "I will never leave this country," I said. "I will never
allow the country of my children to revert to dictatorship."

Glenn Greenwald speaks at a free press rally in Rio de Janeiro. Photo by Lu-
cas Landau / Reuters.

"Fascists want you to have fear of them," I said, but "together, we will
defeat them."

It was tremendously fortifying to hear affirmations, stories, and expressions of support and solidarity from people who had so courageously confronted an actual military dictatorship and not only survived, but thrived—and even to hear the stories of their comrades who had done so and were killed. I felt a responsibility to this heritage, to the people who had sacrificed so much to usher in democracy in Brazil. As we left this extraordinary event, we were as energized as we had been at any point since the first day of publication.

News reports subsequently revealed that on our way out, our cars were followed by unmarked units of the state military police. They claimed, dubiously, that this was for our own protection, but we paid little attention to that. That event had provided all the courage we needed to report without fear. Up until this moment, our labors had felt like trench warfare, like we were constantly besieged and on the verge of being destroyed. After that night, I never felt that way again.

Another landscape-changing event took place one week later, ten days after Bolsonaro's public threats to imprison me. On August 8, Supreme Court Justice Gilmar Mendes issued an order barring any investigations by the Bolsonaro government or agencies reporting to Moro in connection with, or retaliation for, my reporting. It was a stinging rebuke to the government and to Moro's repeated efforts to threaten and intimidate me with legal or criminal reprisals. In that ruling, Mendes issued a stirring defense of the importance of the press freedoms robustly protected by the 1988 Brazilian Constitution:

> Despite speculation about how the journalist obtained the material he released . . . freedom of expression and the press cannot be vilified by investigative acts directed at the journalist in the regular exercise of his profession. . . . [The recent history of constitutional democracies] has warned us that the protections of freedom of expression and the press must be preserved for the benefit of obtaining information by the whole society, even though sometimes the exercise of these rights is in tension with the circumstantial interests of governments and rulers.

For the first time, I was now able to focus on reporting the rest of the archive without being constantly distracted by attacks from Bolsonaro and threats of investigation or prosecution emanating from Moro's multiple agencies.

That's not to say that we were thereafter free of attempted recriminations and remarkably ugly attacks. In late July, my mother, who lived
in the United States and had been battling lung cancer for several years,
had learned that her radiation treatments were no longer working. After
deciding to forego the more radical and debilitating chemotherapies, she
had received a prognosis of two to three months of survival.

David and I had never been able to bring our two kids to meet my
mother in the United States, because we were not legally permitted to
travel outside of Brazil with them until their adoption was fully finalized,
which had happened only in March of that year. Two months later, the
#VazaJato source had contacted me, which meant there was simply no
time to visit her. But now we were determined that our sons should get
to know their grandmother, and she was, of course, eager to meet them.
However, when we applied at the US consulate in Rio for emergency
visas for them on the grounds that their grandmother had terminal cancer, the visas were rejected—something quite bizarre for the children of
a US citizen.

After the Brazilian media reported on the denial of visas for our children, a pro-Bolsonaro blogger notorious for lowlife fake news, and whose
wife was a top aide to one of Bolsonaro's ministers, published an article
accusing me, David, and my mother of all lying about her cancer diagnosis, suggesting that our real motive for trying to get visas was to flee Brazil
in fear of arrest. He found my mother's Facebook page and noted that she
was posting jokes and other humorous content, which he took as proof
that she did not really have terminal cancer. Countless Bolsonaro supporters flooded my mother's Facebook page in the last stage of her life,
accusing her of lying about her health and demanding, in Portuguese and
broken or Google-translated English, that she post proof of her cancer
diagnosis. In the midst of this news about my mother's imminent death,
I posted a tweet critical of Bolsonaro, to which the president's son Carlos
responded with a tweet telling me to "ask my mother."

As a result of all the media attention, the consulate reversed its decision and issued visas to our sons, enabling us to travel to meet my mother
while she was still doing well. She passed away three months later.

We sued the pro-Bolsonaro blogger, and a court ruled in our favor,
ordering him to pay fifteen thousand reals (around three thousand US

dollars) plus our attorneys' fees. (In 2020, the blogger would be imprisoned, after a judgment by the Supreme Court, for helping oversee a fake news network against Bolsonaro's adversaries and for being part of a plot to usher in a coup against Brazil's democratic institutions. Despite this, some online operatives of the Democratic Party in the United States—angered over criticisms I have lodged of their party's leaders—would take to using his articles, now offline by virtue of these legal proceedings, against me.)

In September, the agency controlled by Moro that leaked that it had commenced an investigation into my finances, only to be barred by the Supreme Court from proceeding, did the same to David. On September 11, *Globo*, carrying out their standard role as functionaries for Moro, trumpeted headlines that this agency had detected financial movements into and out of David's bank account from before he entered Congress that it described as "atypical" in light of the salary of a city council member. The intent was obvious: to dirty David's name once they were barred from investigating me, and to try to posit an equivalency between the scandal engulfing Bolsonaro's son—who was credibly accused of receiving kickbacks from phantom employees—and David.

The explanation for these monies, which *Globo* did not bother to solicit from me before publishing, was obvious. Of course the sums of money going into and out of David's account were atypical. That's because my salary with the Intercept—which was publicly disclosed—was much greater than the public salary of a Brazilian city council member, and we transferred my salary each month from the United States to our Brazilian bank accounts to pay our family's bills. In response, David and I both opened our bank records and provided full transparency to the court, then demanded that the Bolsonaro family do the same. Of course, with this proof provided, this supposed "investigation" never went anywhere. The intent, rather, was to remind us that Moro still wielded power and that he, working in conjunction with his servants at *Globo*, could still tarnish our reputations.

At roughly the same time as this leak against David, in early September, one of the ugliest attacks of all was launched against our family. It came from one of Brazil's most prominent mainstream journalists, Augusto Nunes. Over the decades, he has been editor in chief of the newsweekly *Veja*, as well as the host of an iconic political roundtable television program called *Roda Viva*. But in recent years, Nunes has relinquished any pretense of journalistic credibility to become a full-throated supporter of Bolsonaro. On his popular program on the Jovem Pan radio network and YouTube channel, Nunes spewed a bizarre rant about our family, saying we are unfit parents. Because both David and I work, he suggested that we are guilty of neglecting our children and that perhaps a judge should return them to the orphanage on the grounds of parental neglect. "Who is taking care of these boys?" he asked rhetorically. "I think a children's judge should investigate this question."

That Nunes's comments were bigoted and cowardly was self-evident. Millions of people, including Nunes's own bosses and colleagues, raise children either as single parents or as part of a couple where both partners work. But Nunes would never suggest they were guilty of parental neglect. He did so only because we are a prominent gay couple who had been reporting on and politically working against the corruption of his beloved Bolsonaro government. LGBT groups and even *Globo* journalists condemned his remarks and rushed to our defense, but it was a reminder of what was still in the air.

Chapter 9

- - - - - - - - - -

THE LAST BATTLES

Throughout August, September, and October, I tried to stay focused exclusively on our reporting, ensuring that the crucial documents from the archive continued to be vetted and responsibly reported.

The changes this reporting was ushering in—not least the damage to Moro's public reputation—were of critical importance. The aura of intimidation and invincibility that Moro had long wielded had been severely eroded by our steady flow of revelations. The broad popular army of supportive citizens and media voices he once commanded had shrunk to a nub of far-right Bolsonaro supporters. Moro's stature had been radically diminished, from apolitical hero to a hardened ideologue embroiled in scandal. And the other branches of government, tormented for years by his seeming invincibility, had now finally smelled his blood in the water and begun pushing back against his excesses.

In the fall 2019 session of Congress, Moro suffered a series of once-unthinkable legislative defeats. His anti-crime package—the heart of what he had promised when he joined the Bolsonaro government— was stripped of its worst authoritarian excesses and enacted only as a shadow of its original form. Congress then passed a direct repudiation of Moro, an "Abuse of Authority" law designed to punish judicial and prosecutorial corruption and overzealousness, the explicit result of our reporting. Moro lobbied hard against the legislation, insisting that it was an attack on Car Wash, but to no avail. That David could be one of the votes in Congress against Moro's authoritarian anti-crime package and in favor of a law finally reeling in prosecutorial excess only made these results more gratifying.

But the most significant change came in the Supreme Court. In late August, the high court annulled one of the most prized convictions of the Car Wash probe, a guilty verdict for the former president of Petrobras, on the grounds that Moro violated the rights of defendants in how he presided over the trial. The court subsequently used that ruling to overturn the conviction of more than a dozen high-profile individuals who had been imprisoned as part of Operation Car Wash.

For years, no higher court had dared rule that Moro's conduct was illegal, even when it was blatantly so. Popular opinion had been solidly in his corner, and they had feared public wrath if they impeded the decrees of the omnipotent judge and the oligarchical media united in support of him. But by now, everything had changed. Moro was little more than a discredited apparatchik, dependent on Bolsonaro's movement for his ongoing popularity. And the Supreme Court began upholding the Constitution without fear of how Moro and his (now sharply reduced) fanatical band of followers would react.

But by far the most significant outcome of our reporting—and the greatest blow to the legacy of Moro and Operation Car Wash—came in November when the Supreme Court ordered the immediate release of Lula from the prison cell in Curitiba where he had spent the last eighteen months of his nine-year sentence. Although the court's ruling rested on a constitutional issue distinct from whether Moro had corruptly presided over his trial (namely, the court ruled it unconstitutional to imprison citizens while they still have appeals pending, and Lula had at least two more), nobody doubted that it was #VazaJato that had created the climate enabling the court to take such a politically fraught step. Moro's highest-profile and most prized prisoner would be free.

One person who had no doubt about the link to our reporting was Lula himself. Lula called me on the night he was freed, as soon as he arrived home after his flight from Curitiba to São Paulo. It was easily one of the most gratifying moments of my journalistic career. To hear so much appreciation from a person who had been unjustly kept in a cage made me feel, in that moment, that everything we had endured was worth it. Outcomes like this were the reason I had become a journalist in the first place. That it was someone who had overcome so much, who had risen to such heights, and whose work had improved the lives of millions of people and the country I have come to love made that phone call that much more fulfilling.

I did not know, and still do not know, whether Lula ever actually had any involvement in corruption. Only a fair trial with due process can and will determine that—and that's exactly what Lula was deprived of. But I know for certain that the judicial proceedings that concluded he was corrupt were fundamentally unjust, and rife with corruption, improprieties, and violations of basic rights. Lula himself always said that he would belong in prison if his guilt were proven in a fair judicial process, and I agree. But our reporting showed that the judicial process to which he was subjected was anything but fair.

There could scarcely have been a more polarizing event for Brazil than the release of Lula from prison. His supporters regarded us as heroes. But his enemies, of which there were many, reached a peak of hatred and anger toward us, holding us responsible for his resurrection at a time they thought that, after two decades of trying, they had finally slayed the Workers' Party beast.

On the eve of Lula's liberation from prison, I traveled to São Paulo to speak at one of the city's universities. In the midst of the event's promotion, producers with Jovem Pan—the highly popular right-wing radio network and YouTube channel—asked me if I would appear on their morning show, called *Pânico*, the next day.

I had appeared on the program twice before: once when David dramatically replaced Jean Wyllys in Congress, and then again shortly after we began publishing #VazaJato. *Pânico* is a widely watched program that reaches millions. My view is that if you're a journalist whose work affects the whole country, you have an obligation to address not just your supporters but also your critics. I also believe in debating those who hold different views and ideologies, as I have done in the United States, where I have appeared on Fox News and other right-wing outlets. With this in mind, I agreed to appear on their panel.

The next morning, I arrived at *Pânico*'s downtown studio with Victor Pougy. Just a few moments before the program was to begin, one of the producers told me that they wanted to include on the panel Augusto Nunes—the pro-Bolsonaro fanatic who had a couple of weeks earlier suggested, on that very same network, that David and I were guilty of neglecting our children, calling for a judge to investigate whether they should be removed from our home.

Based on an instinctive confidence in the benefits of dialogue, I said I had no problem with his inclusion. Once the producer left, I told Victor that I was going to immediately raise the comments he had made about our family and demand a response or apology. I was not going to treat someone who had dragged my young kids into a political dispute and suggested they should be taken away from us as some kind of good faith colleague or debate adversary, unless he was willing to retract and apologize for, or at least clarify, what he meant by his attacks on my family.

When I entered the studio, Nunes wasn't yet there. I greeted the host and panelists, whom I knew from my prior appearances. Moments later, they bought in Nunes and sat him down in the chair immediately to my left, with just a few inches of distance separating us. We neither exchanged pleasantries nor looked at one another.

The program began—it is broadcast live—and as soon as the host asked me the first question, I ignored it, saying that before we could discuss any other issues, I needed first to resolve something. I recounted how Nunes had, only weeks earlier, invoked our young sons as part of his rant. I then turned to Nunes, looking directly at him, and asked a very specific question: "Do you still think that a children's judge should investigate our family to determine whether our children should be returned to the orphanage from which we adopted them?"

Perhaps it was naivete, but I honestly expected that Nunes would, if not apologize, at least acknowledge that we all say things in the heat of the moment that we do not mean—something to diffuse his comments so that we could proceed with the show. Instead, he did the opposite. He claimed that I was too dense to recognize the "irony" that he had employed in his remarks—there was absolutely nothing ironic about what he had said—and he then proceeded to insult me.

Greenwald appearing on Pânico with far-right Bolsonaro journalist
Augusto Nunes.

As I listened, I felt my anger growing, in a way I had never experienced before. I almost never feel rage in political debate. I can express
righteous anger, but I always maintain emotional control. This was different. It was rage, and it was purely *paternal*. I was sitting just inches from
someone who was calling for our children to be taken out of our homes
and returned to a life of parentless deprivation in an orphanage.

I listened to him justify what he said, and pretend he meant it ironically, for as long as I could. When I couldn't take it anymore, I interrupted
him and said he was a "coward," intending to explain that his cowardice
was composed both of his involvement of our young children in a political dispute and, even more so, of his fear to say the same thing about
his bosses and colleagues who also work, yet raise children. But when I
called him a coward, he raised his voice, cutting in to demand that I take
it back. Instead, I repeated it several times, trying, with futility because of
his interruptions, to explain my rationale.

I could feel the tensions rising quickly. We were yelling at each other
with just inches between us, our fingers practically touching while pointed

at each other's faces, and so there was only one place to which this alter-
cation could escalate: physical violence, live on the air. I was controlled
enough to know I would not initiate it, but also not to back away.

I saw Nunes's arm rising to hit me and instinctively held up my arm,
blocking his swing at my face. Once I realized he had initiated physical
force, I immediately stood up and walked toward him.

When I did, he used his hand to push my face away. By now, the
panelists on the show had run over to separate us. As soon as we were
separated, I felt an uncontrollable surge of rage—it was partly instinctual
and partly based on what he had said about our kids—and I took a swing
at his head, but only brushed it due to the distance of our separation and
the fact that the panelists were holding both of us back. As soon as I did
that, Victor, who was in the studio, angrily chided me, "Don't do that.
You're better than him. He's dragging you down to his level." I told him
he was right—he was—but that it was simply an uncontrollable instinct.

The show host immediately went to commercial. The producers
came over quickly and said that the director of the network and its lawyers wanted to speak to me. That made sense; they were obviously worried about a lawsuit or other repercussions.

I went back to the office of the Jovem Pan director, who was there
with their general counsel. They were deeply apologetic, and did not hide

the fact that they feared a lawsuit. After all, the person who had attacked me was their employee, on their premises, after they had invited him on the show. I was not interested in any lawsuit. I was unhurt and did not want to waste my time and energy on dumb litigation. But I wanted them to think it was a possibility so that they would feel duty bound to do the right thing: apologize to me not just privately, but publicly, and require that Nunes do the same. They promised that would happen.

After the meeting, the producers said they would have their car service take me back to my hotel. I told them there was no need, as I wanted to go back into the studio to finish the show. Why should I be barred from a show because one of their on-air personalities had attacked me? So I went back into the studio, without Nunes, and finished the ninety-minute show. On the breaks, I checked my phone. Predictably, the live footage had spread all over the Internet, and the messages from media outlets all over the world, as well as from friends and colleagues worried about me, already numbered in the hundreds.

Once I was back in my hotel room, I recorded videos in both English and Portuguese explaining what had happened, and why. I emphasized what I thought was truly important about this incident, which was not that I had been physically attacked by another journalist. Though obviously very unusual and bizarre, the assault was more symbolic than violent. Far more significant, and revealing, was the reaction to it. The country's leading Bolsonaro supporters—including his sons and the movement's US-based "guru," Olavo de Carvalho—celebrated Nunes's attack on me, with many saying that it should have been more violent, with a closed fist or worse. "Augusto Nunes giving a punch to Verdevaldo [sic] was the most beautiful thing ever on Brazilian TV," Carvalho tweeted.

President Bolsonaro's son Eduardo announced that Augusto Nunes had "acted in legitimate defense of his honor" and "reacted the way any normal person would with blood in his veins." Another of Bolsonaro's sons, Carlos, pledged, "All my solidarity to the man: Augusto Nunes." Yet another tweet declared, "Augusto Nunes is a hero but erred when slapping Verdevaldo's face: he should have thrown a chair at his face!" A pro-Bolsonaro member of the São Paulo state legislature introduced a formal motion of "praise for Augusto Nunes for the excellent services provided to the Brazilian population."

Several hours after the confrontation, Jovem Pan issued a mealy-mouthed statement that more or less apologized to me for what happened, but without making clear that the blame lay with Nunes. Contrary to the commitments of the station's management, Nunes issued a boastful rant, praising himself and saying explicitly that he would attack me if he were in that same situation again. Petrified of angering the Bolsonaro movement, Jovem Pan put Nunes back on the air the following day, leaving no doubt that a physical attack against another person was acceptable behavior for their far-right on-air personalities.

As I emphasized in the videos I published that day, all of this demonstrated that the Bolsonaro movement—like all authoritarian factions—craves violence in lieu of discourse in the resolution of political differences. Beyond that, what they most want is civic disorder, civil conflict, to justify the repressive dictatorship-era measures they advocate. Key Bolsonoro supporters, including his son Eduardo, were explicit about the fact that it was civic unrest that would facilitate a return of dictatorship-era decrees of repression—the express goal of Bolsonaro himself for decades. They want to foment that unrest to reach that goal.

But this episode revealed something else: uncontrolled rage over the fact that our work had resulted in Lula's freedom. Lula understood the significance of the attack on me. In the jailhouse letter he wrote to me the following day, hours before he walked out of Moro's prison, he prefaced his praise for the reporting I had done with reference to the assault, knowing that Nunes—a devoted Lula hater for years—was motivated at least in part by my role in Lula's imminent freedom: "Dear comrade Glenn: I was proud to see you face that disgusting figure in rotten Brazilian journalism."

The following day, November 8, Lula walked out of Sérgio Moro's prison. It was one of the most emotional and polarizing moments in Brazil in years, as the once-towering figure left the dreary federal building where he had been confined for eighteen months, before a large crowd of admirers who cheered, chanted, and cried. Aware as always of the media imagery he was conveying, the seventy-four-year-old embraced and kissed his fiancée in cinematic fashion, and greeted the crowd of Workers' Party loyalists.

What made the scene even more poignant and powerful was that, two months earlier, Moro's prosecutors—fearful of exactly this kind of scene—had told Lula he could leave prison, but only if he did so quietly and served the remainder of his sentence under house arrest. However, Lula had made a public show of refusing this arrangement, insisting that he would leave prison only on unconditional terms, and if he were fully exonerated.

Although he would lack the power to directly refuse a court order to vacate jail for home detention, Lula, ever the crafty strategist, had drained their plan of its political vibrancy, leading them to abandon it. It was a real risk on his part, since there was no guarantee that he would be released. But, as was often the case in Lula's storied political career, it was a risk that paid off. All the news outlets covered his dramatic, triumphant exit from Moro's prison live, and photos of him with his fiancée, surrounded by adoring crowds and looking younger and more spritely than he had in years, adorned the cover of every newspaper and magazine in Brazil. Lula did not merely leave prison. He strode back in national view as a virtual conqueror, having vanquished his once-invulnerable but now severely diminished and scandal-plagued adversary, Sérgio Moro.

In one sense, Lula's release represented a culmination of our months of reporting. While the goal of the reporting was never to free Lula, there was no doubt in my mind, especially after having spent months reading the truth about his prosecutors and his judge, that his imprisonment was deeply unjust. And regardless of the criticisms I had of his politics and the uncertainty about whether he was in fact guilty of crimes, he was still a leader with an extraordinary story—a very Brazilian story—who had done immense good for millions of people with very little opportunity in their lives.

When he called me that night, I tried to maintain an emotional distance, a journalistic detachment, but it was difficult. Above all else, I was talking to a person who had been kept in a cage for the eighteen months as the result of unjust processes and corrupt officials, and it was hard not to feel joy for him and gratification at what our journalism had accomplished.

But what was particularly striking about our conversation was that Lula had little interest in the emotion of the moment. Each time I tried to express happiness for his freedom or ask him how he felt, he brushed off my questions. Instead, he was focused on how the left could prevail over the Bolsonaro movement in the 2020 municipal elections. It was as if Lula had not just left prison, after eighteen months. Instead, I was talking to Lula the master political strategist. Lula did not even enjoy his new freedom for a day before diving back into strategizing over how to change Brazilian politics—something that, in retrospect, should not have surprised me. Perhaps, I pondered, that may have been his way of normalizing his life after his unjust imprisonment by his political enemies; or perhaps his life of hardship had taught him how to brush that kind of adversity aside. Whatever the motives, I realized in the moment that it was this single-minded devotion to political change that made Lula the monumental figure he is.

Lula's liberation certainly felt like a major turning point. Similar to the way I felt when US federal courts began ruling that the domestic surveillance programs we revealed during the Snowden reporting were illegal and unconstitutional—it would be much harder for the US government to prosecute us for having revealed illegalities and fostered reforms—I felt that the ability of the Bolsonaro government to make good on its threats to prosecute me was severely diminished once our reporting had resulted in major changes in the Supreme Court, culminating in the freeing of Moro and the Car Wash probe's most prized prisoner.

But what finally made me believe the threat of imprisonment was extinguished was, ironically, the conclusion of the comprehensive investigation into the hacking operation by the Federal Police, the Brazilian equivalent of the FBI, which reported directly to Justice Minister Moro.

On December 19—just over six months after we published our first series of articles—the Federal Police issued a detailed 177-page report of the findings of their investigation, which they called Operation Spoofing. Leaked to the news outlet *Metrópoles*, the report made clear that the Federal Police found no evidence of criminality on my part.

Among other specific legal breaches, the investigators attempted to determine whether I had conspired with or given advice to the hackers that could constitute encouragement to commit further crimes or advice on how to do so. The investigators concluded that I had never done so, emphasizing instead that I had at all times maintained a "careful and distant posture regarding" the hacks and the hackers. This was a decisive exoneration.

Headlines from news outlets emphasized the emphatic finding—a somewhat surprising one given that it came from a police agency under Moro's command—that I did not have any relationship to, let alone participation in, any crimes. The article that broke the story of the police report was illustrative of how the news was framed:

JUSTIÇA

Spoofing: PF buscou crimes em conduta de Glenn, mas não encontrou

Em relatório, delegado mostra que o jornalista fundador do The Intercept
Brasil foi investigado e lamenta não ter podido interrogá-lo

RAPHAEL VELEDA
20/12/2019 18 33.ATUALIZADO 20/12/2019 20 01

IGO ESTRELA/METRÓPOLES

Spoofing: Federal Police searched for crimes in Glenn's conduct, but found none

I felt like 2019 was ending with as close to a guarantee as possible that I would not face criminal charges and that I would be able to start the new year, and continue the #VazaJato reporting, without that threat hovering over my head. After all, if even Moro's Federal Police were explicitly exonerating me, after a comprehensive investigation, it seemed virtually impossible that the Bolsonaro government or high-level prosecutors could find a way to ignore these findings.

That is what made the next series of events so startling.

In mid-January, having spent the previous six months working without pause under the most stressful circumstances of my career, I finally arranged for time away with my family. David and I traveled with our sons, a few other family members and friends, and our security team to a farm resort in the interior of Rio state, where we intended to stay for a week. It was the first time I felt I could afford to disengage from the war we had initiated with those first articles back on June 9.

On the second full day of the trip, at roughly noon, I was preparing to

go horseback riding with my youngest son. As we were waiting for the sad-
dles to be secured, I casually scrolled through Twitter, having been blissful-
ly unaware of the news cycle since our arrival a couple days earlier. Within
seconds I saw a tweet—from the right-wing blog most closely linked to
Moro, the one that had originally reported the start of an official investigation into my finances—that began "URGENT" and, in all caps, announced
that the Federal Public Ministry (MPF), the rough Brazilian equivalent of
the US Department of Justice, had officially "denounced" me, along with
six others, for the hacks of Brazilian authorities' communications.

O Antagonista ✔
@o_antagonista

URGENTE: MPF DENUNCIA GLENN GREENWALD E
MAIS SEIS POR INVASÃO HACKER.
oantagonista.com/brasil/urgente...

o antagon sta

URGENTE

12:03 PM · Jan 21, 2020 · TweetDeck

**Tweet from the pro-Moro site announcing criminal charges against Glenn
Greenwald**

I did not immediately react with much alarm. For one thing, this
Moro-worshipping site had been by far the most hostile to our reporting
and to me in particular, so I assumed it was exaggerating the significance
of the news. For another, the English translation of *denuncia* is ambig-
uous, so it was unclear to me from the tweet whether the ministry had
merely issued some kind of statement condemning my actions, or if the
situation was more serious. The site is notorious for the extreme brevi-

ty of its "articles"—which are almost never more than a couple of sentences—and, true to form, the only new information this particular post added was that "according to the complaint, Greenwald 'directly assisted, encouraged and guided the criminal group.'"

Despite my lack of alarm, my interest was piqued for obvious reasons. I began scrolling to see if other more credible sites had similar news. I immediately discovered that they did. The reports from *Folha*, *Veja*, and other major news outlets left no doubt as to what had happened. I had been formally charged with multiple crimes, along with the six individuals accused of participating in the hacking itself.

I realized that this meant the end of our family vacation. But I also slowly began to process the fact that I was now officially charged with multiple felony accounts, which cumulatively carried the possibility of more than one hundred years in prison.

That the charges were legally frivolous and politically motivated was obvious, but the question from the start had been whether justice in Bolsonaro's Brazil would be determined by legal principles and precedent, or by brute force and corrupt power.

After showing David the news, the first call I made was to our lawyers, the two Rafas, who explained the specific theory used to justify the criminal charges against me. The prosecutors conceded that I had not participated in the original hack of the Car Wash prosecutors' phones that enabled the reporting, which was completed before the source first contacted me. But they claimed that I became part of the criminal conspiracy based on a telephone call, recorded by the alleged hacker and recovered by the police when they arrested him, in which my source asked whether he should keep copies of our conversations. I replied that it was up to him, but that I saw no need for this, given that we were keeping our own copies. The criminal complaint claimed that my answer to him constituted implicit encouragement to destroy the evidence of our communications, not only making me guilty of obstruction of justice but also converting me into a full-fledged conspirator in the hacking plot itself. I was therefore rendered criminally liable for everything my "coconspirators" did in advancement of that conspiracy.

The irony was stunning. To justify the multiple felony charges, the prosecutors relied on the exact same passage the Federal Police had cited to conclude that I was unfailingly cautious and professional in the reporting I had done. The prosecutorial theory was that I had implicitly encouraged my source to "destroy evidence" (namely, the chats we were having) by letting him know that we were keeping copies ourselves. They asserted this despite the fact that I had explicitly told the source that I could not provide him any advice about what to do and that he should keep copies if he felt more comfortable doing so.

Shortly after I spoke with my lawyers, they called back with more information that clarified what had happened. The high-level federal prosecutor responsible for the charges against me was Wellington Divino Marques de Oliveira—the same prosecutor who had sought to criminally indict the head of the Brazilian Bar Association, Felipe Santa Cruz, on charges that Santa Cruz's criticisms of Justice Minister Moro for his corrupt conduct as a judge constituted "criminal calumny." The prosecutor was clearly a devoted loyalist to Moro, bent on abusing the prosecutorial power of the state to punish critics and adversaries of the justice minister and the Bolsonaro government.

Unlike in the United States, where the Department of Justice has the unilateral power to indict and criminally charge a defendant, prosecutors in Brazil can only level charges. They do not become a formal indictment unless a judge accepts them. It is extremely rare for a judge to reject criminal charges at the start of the proceedings, and the standard for doing so is high: the defendant has to prove that the charges have no conceivable validity. On that particular occasion, however, Santa Cruz succeeded in convincing the judge to throw out Oliveira's spurious charges.

Following the January 21 news of the criminal charges against me, the reaction in Brazil was swift and close to unanimous. Mainstream journalists united to condemn it, and legal experts from across the spectrum denounced it as a politically motivated and legally baseless abuse of power.

On the day the charges were announced, BBC Brasil published an article headlined "According to Legal Specialists, the Complaint against Glenn Greenwald Must Be Rejected," quoting a retired federal appellate judge who said: "This complaint is baseless. It seems to me that it is political retaliation due to Vaza Jato and the anger of the Federal Public Ministry." The most respected news outlet for judicial and legal matters, Consultor Jurídico, headlined its article "For Lawyers, MPF Complaint against Glenn Greenwald Is Legal Nonsense," and said the consensus of legal and judicial experts was that the formal complaint was one "that violates constitutional guarantees, freedom of the press and democracy."

The big Brazilian press did not hide its opposition to the charges, either. *Globo*'s flagship nightly news program, *Jornal Nacional*, led off its broadcast with the story and devoted close to ten minutes to numerous denunciations of the Public Ministry. *Folha* published multiple articles highlighting the legal flaws of the charges and the politicized history of the prosecutor. Most major newspapers, including *Folha*, editorialized in my defense.

And perhaps most significantly of all, lower house speaker Rodrigo Maia again expressed his support for my press freedom, just as he had done in the video he recorded for the Rio rally a few months earlier, in an emphatic and highly viral tweet:

Rodrigo Maia ✓
@RodrigoMaia

A denúncia contra o jornalista @ggreenwald é uma ameaça à liberdade de imprensa. Jornalismo não é crime. Sem jornalismo livre não há democracia.

Translated from Portuguese by Google

The complaint against the journalist @ggreenwald it is a threat to press freedom. Journalism is not a crime. Without free journalism there is no democracy.

Para PF, não há evidência de participação de Glenn em ação de hackers - Painel
🔗 painel.blogfolha.uol.com.br

4:51 PM · Jan 21, 2020 · Twitter for iPhone

6.2K Retweets   **2.4K** Quote Tweets   **39.8K** Likes

Lula tweeted, in both English and Portuguese, "All my solidarity to journalist Glenn Greenwald who was a victim of another blatant abuse of authority against freedom of press and democracy." Dilma Rousseff echoed that sentiment, posting that "the Public Ministry's complaint against Glenn Greenwald is a serious attack on press freedom. It is unacceptable in a democratic country, and it is also a clear affront to the injunction to the contrary granted by the Supreme Court." Ciro Gomes, the former governor and minister in Lula's cabinet who came in third place in the 2018 presidential election, posted a long video condemning the charges, tweeting, "Journalism is an essential task for democracy and individual and public freedoms. What Glenn did was the most genuine journalism."

The reaction internationally was similarly united and vocal in my defense. Media outlets and prominent figures from across the political spectrum, including several 2020 presidential candidates, denounced the charges against me.

My relationship with the *New York Times* is similar in many ways to my relationship with *Globo* in Brazil: rocky in the best of times, bitterly adversarial in the worst. But the paper's editorial on the day I was charged was adamant in condemning the Brazilian government. Headlined "Brazil Calls Glenn Greenwald's Reporting a Crime," it began: "The Brazilian government's filing of criminal charges against the American journalist Glenn Greenwald is an increasingly familiar case of shooting the messenger and ignoring the message." The *Times* depicted these charges as part of a broader trend. "Sadly, assailing a free and critical press has become a cornerstone of the new breed of illiberal leaders in Brazil, as in the United States and elsewhere around the world." And it concluded with this dramatic pronouncement:

> Mr. Greenwald's articles did what a free press is supposed to do: They revealed a painful truth about those in power. Puncturing the heroic image of Mr. Moro was obviously a shock for Brazilians, and damaging to Mr. Bolsonaro, but demanding that defenders of the law be scrupulous in their adherence to it is essential for democracy. Attacking the bearers of that message is a serious disservice and a dangerous threat to the rule of law.

Similar editorials appeared in the *Washington Post*, the *Guardian*, the *Wall Street Journal*, and other news outlets. The right-wing journal *National Review* also published a ringing defense of me, under the headline "Bolsonaro v. Greenwald." It argued, "Greenwald is not being targeted because he is publishing work based on documents that were acquired through illegal means but because that work embarrasses the government of Brazil. That is his crime." Fox News host Tucker Carlson covered the story on his show—one religiously watched by many Trump-loving Bolsonaristas in Brazil—with a tribute to my character and journalism, concluding with this proclamation: "Glenn Greenwald, we're rooting for you." MSNBC's Rachel Maddow tweeted a similar message of support.

The charges were brought in mid-January, as the Democratic primary was heating up in the United States. Press freedom activists began pressuring candidates to speak out. The first presidential candidate to show support was Bernie Sanders, who tweeted: "The free press is never more important than when it exposes wrongdoing by the powerful. That is why President Bolsonaro is threatening Glenn Greenwald for the 'crime' of doing journalism. I call on Brazil to end its authoritarian attack on press freedom and the rule of law." The same day, congresswoman and presidential candidate Tulsi Gabbard posted: "For years, @ggreenwald has exposed abuses at the highest levels of government and his investigative journalism deserves our support. If we allow the powerful to silence such journalists, our democracy and freedom is in peril. #StandWithGreenwald." The following day, presidential candidate and Democratic senator Elizabeth Warren also weighed in, tweeting: "The Bolsonaro government is pursuing state retaliation against Glenn Greenwald because of his work as a journalist to expose public abuse and corruption. Brazil should drop the charges immediately and stop its attacks on a free and open press."

All of that international condemnation, and domestic protest, provided some comfort. But I did not believe that either of these would be a sufficient bulwark against prosecution. The Brazilians who wielded power under Bolsonaro regarded mainstream domestic and international opinion, human rights groups, and civil libertarians as their enemy. Given the hatred that had been cultivated against me by the Bolsonaro movement for months, I was convinced that they would not be easily deterred in their drive to imprison me.

Indeed, President Bolsonaro and his key supporters could barely contain their glee over news that I had been charged. Asked by journalists about the charges at a press gathering outside the presidential palace, Bolsonaro mocked the media for its objections: "He was accused by the justice system. Do you not believe in justice?"

The Bolsonaro movement predictably celebrated the criminal charges on all of its platforms, predicting my imminent arrest, holding parties on their YouTube channels, and making homophobic jokes about what would happen to me in prison.

I spent the next several days of my "vacation" on the phone with lawyers and giving interviews to the press in Brazil and internationally. When I went to breakfast at the resort restaurant the next day, I sat with my husband, children, and friends, as other guests nearby held newspapers whose front pages detailed the crimes of which I was accused.

My lawyers told me that they would immediately prepare a petition to the court to reject the charges. They felt optimistic about our chances—based on the grounds that the prosecutor's charges violated not only the Supreme Court prohibition from the prior year on investigating me, but also the free press guarantee in the Constitution—and said they expected a very quick ruling, within a matter of days. Still, they reminded me that it was highly unusual for a judge to reject criminal charges at this initial stage, and that it was far from guaranteed that we would prevail on this petition.

Their prediction that we would have a court ruling within the week, however, proved to be inaccurate. Each day that went by without a ruling compounded the stress. I was trying to work on our next set of stories on the #VazaJato archive, but the possibility of having to battle dozens of felony charges and a lengthy prison sentence made it somewhat difficult to focus.

Finally, on February 6, we received a court ruling. The judge had declined to indict me, rejecting the criminal charges.

But the rationale in the decision was anything but a clear success. The judge—Ricardo Leite, known as a right-wing jurist with loyalties to Moro—emphasized that the only reason he was dismissing the charges against me was because they conflicted with the August 2019 Supreme Court ruling. Had it not been for that decision, the judge made explicitly clear, he would have accepted the charges.

Indeed, the judge went further than that, concluding that the evidence demonstrated that I was "as an instigator of the conduct of the other defendants and not merely a receiver of illegal content." Citing the same conversation with my source flagged by the prosecutors regarding retention of our conversations, the judge wrote that I seemed to be encouraging the source to engage in obstruction of justice, and that that could justify not only my ultimate conviction but even my immediate arrest and imprisonment, pending a trial, in order to protect the sanctity of the investigation.

This was an odd claim, to put it mildly, given that the Federal Police investigation had already concluded that there was no evidence to suggest criminality on my part. That the judge specifically raised the possibility of my preventative imprisonment was also darky ironic. After all, this was one of the radical, previously rare tactics that Moro and the Car Wash prosecutors had dangerously normalized as a feature of Brazilian justice.

In declining to formally indict me, the judge pointedly said he was doing so "for now," contingent on whether the Supreme Court maintained the prohibition against holding me liable for the reporting. The judge was essentially inviting the Supreme Court to vacate its constitutional protections of me so the prosecution could proceed.

In response, the prosecutors appealed the judge's ruling, asking the appellate court to reinstate the charges. Because we had technically won—the charges were dismissed—we were not permitted to make an appeal of our own. But our strategy in defending against the prosecutor's appeal was to induce a far broader ruling than the cramped, technical victory we had obtained—a ruling that would affirm the right of journalists to work with their sources as an indispensable component of reporting, and in my case, would find the attempt to criminalize this right to be a violation of the constitutional guarantee of a free press. I wanted to ensure that the precedent the Bolsonaro government and its loyalists tried to use against me not only failed when it came to my case, but would be barred as a tool against other journalists.

As this book goes to print, the appellate court has not ruled on the appeal. Technically, the government is still seeking to imprison me for the reporting we did. There has been pressure from pro-Bolsonaro prosecutors on the chief prosecutor (himself a Bolsonaro appointee) to formally request that the Supreme Court vacate its protections of my press freedom rights. But so far the court has refused, and the ruling remains in effect.

— — — — — — — — — —

I won't pretend that being criminally charged was free of stress and anxiety. But in a very real way, I was glad that the reporting culminated in a legal battle and the attempt to criminalize my journalism. It meant the mask worn by the Bolsonaro government dropped, in front of Brazil and the world. The government's extreme reaction underscored how effective our journalism had been in revealing profound corruption on the part of major Bolsonaro officials, and how that corruption had played a vital role in Bolsonaro's rise to the presidency, calling into question the legitimacy of his victory.

Above all, I was gratified for the opportunity to wage this free press battle. Just as was true for the Snowden story—before the reporting began, Edward and I spent as much time talking about media strategies as we did surveillance and privacy, because we knew the story would test the outer boundaries of press freedom—from the start, I viewed #Vaza-Jato as being at least as much about the viability of a free press and democratic values in the Bolsonaro era as it was corruption and improprieties within the judiciary and prosecutorial branches.

In the most difficult moments, I often thought about what David said in a widely watched *Globo* TV interview after he replaced Jean Wyllys in Congress. When asked by the host whether he was scared, given that Jean had fled Brazil under death threats that were due in large part to antigay animus, David courageously acknowledged that he was scared, but quickly added: "If I'm not willing to go to Brasilia and represent the community I came from and the people who voted for me, with all of the privileges and resources I now have, who is willing to do it? How can I expect others to do it if I'm not?"

David's poignant comments inspired my own resolve and captured perfectly how I felt. Brazil has given me everything—my husband, my children, my career, my friends, new ways of thinking about life and what matters. I love the country and its people. I am grateful that I was able to play a role in what became the first real test of the Bolsonaro government's ability to crush civic freedoms, and of the willingness of democratic institutions and civic society to fight back.

We endured a lot of attacks, suffered several harsh blows, and ended up with numerous scratches and scars, some of which are likely never to fully heal. But I believe that in many critical respects, we also won. We won by revealing the truth about the fraudulent image cultivated about Moro and the Car Wash probe; by establishing the right of journalists to report without being turned into felons; by showing Brazil that vital journalism is often possible through massive digital leaks and acts of conscience by a source, even if they undertake illegal acts to enable that reporting; and, most of all, by demonstrating that one need not fear the Bolsonaro government and its movement, which relies above all on intimidation. Instead, we demonstrated that courage is contagious. When all those who believe in democratic values unite, we are stronger than the regressive forces that seek to drag the country back to its darkest days.

All of those questions were very much in doubt when we began our reporting, just months after the stunning presidential victory of Bolsonaro and the empowerment of his movement. That our journalism helped resolve those questions so decisively, in a way that I believe will endure, was a testament to the power of journalism and, ultimately, the most gratifying thing I've done in my life.

AFTERWORD

n the months after my indictment was rejected, with our #VazaJato reporting largely concluded, Brazilian politics and its justice system were
reshaped even further. Many of these changes came from the reporting and its aftermath, while other changes were reflective of the serious
threats and dangers posed by the Bolsonaro government that had shaped
the climate in which we undertook this reporting.

In September 2020, the chief prosecutor and public face of the Car
Wash task force from its 2014 inception, Deltan Dallagnol, left his position. He did so while facing numerous disciplinary proceedings for unethical conduct, many based on the revelations we reported. It is hard to
overstate what a symbolic blow Dallagnol's departure was to the legacy of
Operation Car Wash. Dallagnol was the second-most important symbol
of the Car Wash probe, after Moro, and it was Dallagnol who had led the
prosecution—in court and publicly—of Lula. Although he had become
a highly divisive and polarizing figure, for the faction of the political and
media elite whose worldview came to be defined by Car Wash loyalties,
Dallagnol was their most admired leader.

Dallagnol's end came in discredit and disgrace. Though he claimed
he left due to health issues affecting one of his children, few believed
that was the cause. Shortly after his departure was announced, he was
found by an ethics panel to have abused his prosecutorial position for
political and partisan ends, after a complaint brought by Senator Renan
Calheiros, long a prime target of the Car Wash prosecutors. And he faces
numerous other pending disciplinary actions, some of which carry seri-

217

ous professional sanctions that could restrict, or end, his future prospects as a prosecutor.

The end of the alliance between Bolsonaro and Moro was even more dramatic than Dallagnol's fall. Throughout the close of 2019 and into 2020, the criminal investigations targeting Bolsonaro's sons over financial improprieties and ties to paramilitary militias were escalating, coming closer and closer not just to Flavio but also to the rest of the Bolsonaro family and the president himself.

Simultaneously, media leaks began reflecting growing tensions between Bolsonaro and Moro. Given that each side's loyalists were leaking in the most self-serving way possible, it was hard to know which were true. The core claim from the pro-Moro side was that Bolsonaro was attempting to interfere in the police investigations of his family by demanding that Moro replace independent-minded chiefs with ones more loyal to Bolsonaro, who would shield his sons from ongoing investigations, and that Moro was resisting any incursions into police independence.

The pro-Bolsonaro leakers, on the other hand, claimed that Moro was deliberately abusing the investigations as a way to harm Bolsonaro, hoping to weaken the president so that he could run against him in 2022. Bolsonaro publicly insinuated on several occasions that Moro was refusing to follow his orders, which were not to impede investigations into Bolsonaro's family, but to improve police efficiency and rid police agencies of corrupt and inefficient bosses who Moro could control.

It was also clear that our reporting played at least a significant role, if not the primary role, in these mounting tensions. Bolsonaro was reportedly furious with Moro for not supporting him in his attempts to protect his corruption-plagued sons, given that Bolsonaro had publicly stood by Moro as he was engulfed in the scandal generated by our revelations.

Beyond that, the fact that #VazaJato had diminished Moro's stature and political support created an opening for Bolsonaro to demand more control over Moro's agencies. While at the beginning of his presidency Bolsonaro had needed Moro more than Moro needed Bolsonaro, our investigation left Moro in a highly vulnerable position, reliant on Bolsonaro and his movement as a primary source of support. And the specific reporting we did showing that even Moro's loyalists inside the Public Ministry believed he would abuse his position as justice minister to shield

Bolsonaro's sons from investigation (in order to curry favor with Bolsonaro and secure Moro's seat on the Supreme Court) undoubtedly placed
serious pressure on Moro to prove otherwise.

All of this was unfolding as the coronavirus crisis engulfed Brazil.
Bolsonaro embarrassed and infuriated even many of his most loyal supporters by becoming the consensus pick for world leader in denialism and
anti-science ignorance in his management of the pandemic. He openly
touted false cures, mocked the virus as no worse than a "little flu," flouted
isolation and distancing measures even after he contracted the virus, and
watched as Brazil became the second-leading country, after the United
States, in both confirmed coronaviruses cases and deaths (in mid-2020,
India, with a far larger population than either country, surpassed Brazil).

In April, Bolsonaro's health minister—a physician who for weeks
had been enraging Bolsonaro by giving daily press briefings that contradicted much of what Bolsonaro was saying—resigned or was fired. His
replacement, another medical doctor, resigned within a month of taking
office. After that, the position was vacant for weeks in the middle of a
pandemic, until Bolsonaro finally found his third health minister in less
than three months. Moro, always preoccupied with what bourgeois sectors thought of him, made it known through leaks that he was opposed to
Bolsonaro's botched response to the pandemic, only furthering height-
ening tensions.

Finally, in April, the conflict between Moro and Bolsonaro exploded in
the most dramatic and acerbic way imaginable. Moro held a press conference in which he announced that he was resigning from the government.
He accused Bolsonaro of a series of crimes, including attempts at corrupt
interference in police investigations and obstruction of justice. That the
man who was supposed to be the symbol of Bolsonaro's anti-corruption
bona fides was now accusing the president of criminality and corruption
was a major earthquake in the political world.

Now that Moro had not only quit, but accused Bolsonaro of serious
crimes on his way out the door, he became the prime target of the Bolsonaro movement's defamation machine. The same Bolsonaro supporters who, only a few months earlier, had been celebrating the prospect of
my arrest began citing our journalism and the leaked chats from Moro to
argue that their new enemy was corrupt and untrustworthy.

That Moro replaced me in that role was no small irony. When Moro, in response to being called a liar by Bolsonaro and his supporters, leaked his private WhatsApp chats with both the president and several of his key congressional allies, the irony was heightened further. Now Moro was leaking private communications to show the public the truth—the central method we used in our reporting—and Bolsonaristas wasted no time in pointing to those similarities.

It was both amusing and infuriating to watch Moro and his supporters spend the next several months complaining loudly about the fake news networks the Bolsonaro movement commanded, now that they were aimed at him. When he was justice minister, Moro had shown no interest in opposing, let alone investigating, these tactics when they were used against me and my colleagues. Even when a group of people created the anonymous "Pavão Misterioso" account to publish forged bitcoin transactions and WhatsApp conversations involving not only me but numerous members of Congress, Moro had never condemned these illegal acts, and apparently never directed the Federal Police to investigate those crimes, either.

It was a form of cosmic justice to watch Moro whine on a daily basis about the very tactics from which he had benefited when they were used to discredit me. And it further demonstrated that the highly cultivated media image of Moro was an utter fraud.

While Moro's complaints were clearly cynical and insincere, the same could not be said of the Brazilian Supreme Court. As the justices became one of the primary targets of these pro-Bolsonaro fake news networks— to the point that pro-Bolsonaro protesters fired fireworks at the Supreme Court building while it was in session—they became increasingly vocal in their efforts to protect Brazil's democratic institutions from assault.

Beginning in June 2020, the Supreme Court opened an investigation into the fake news network and antidemocratic plotting on the part of the Bolsonaro movement. They ordered the Federal Police to execute searches and seizures at the homes of more than a dozen pro-Bolsonaro bloggers, YouTubers, and activists. They seized their computers and phones, issued subpoenas for their bank records, and ordered social media companies, including Twitter and Facebook, to close their accounts.

One armed pro-Bolsonaro extremist, Sara Winter, was arrested after evidence turned up that she was actively plotting campaigns and protests demanding the closure of the Supreme Court. In July, the Supreme Court ordered the arrest of another pro-Bolsonaro blogger, Oswaldo Eustáquio, when he crossed the border into Paraguay, which authorities viewed as a preemptive attempt to avoid an imminent arrest warrant. (Eustáquio was the operative found guilty of defamation for claiming that my mother and I were lying about her having terminal cancer.) After spending almost two weeks in prison—in the same wing as the individual accused of hacking and providing me with the #VazaJato archive—Eustáquio was released into house arrest, on the condition that he not use social media. Two weeks later, however, he appeared on the YouTube program of a pro-Bolsonaro propagandist and, through tears, accused me and David of pedophilia and said that our two Brazilian children were "captives" in our home and that he was desperately concerned about how to rescue them. He claimed, not for the first time, that our adoption was illegal. So we sued him again.

The Supreme Court actions against Bolsonaro operatives were serious. In fact, there were aspects of these steps that I found troubling on civil liberties grounds, including their orders for suspects to be arrested prior to trial and for Facebook and Twitter to close their accounts. When I publicly expressed those concerns, Bolsonaristas were very confused: Why was the person they viewed as Satan for a full year speaking out in defense of their due process and free speech rights? Because they see politics as war, they couldn't understand the invocation of universally applied principles in defense of an adversary whose rights are being violated.

But my public concerns made little difference. Because it is illegal under Brazilian law to engage in antidemocratic plotting—a law instituted to prevent a return to the dark days of military rule—the Supreme Court believed, not without reason, that they were taking action not against dissidents but against subversives who were plotting the overthrow of democratic rule. In September, one of Bolsonaro's most prominent online supporters was caught actively plotting with the president's aides about how to provoke an "intervention" by the military—the term that was used for the 1964 coup—into Brazilian politics. That these conversations were leaked by police investigators and/or prosecutors showed how heightened was the concern about these antidemocratic maneuvers.

In late 2020, the accused hackers and sources of mine, who had been held in prison since their arrest almost a year earlier, were ordered released pending trial, based on a judicial ruling that their "preventative imprisonment"—one of Moro's signature abuses—had become legally intolerable due to the length of their detention without trial. As of this writing, they await trial on multiple charges of hacking.

At roughly the same time, Bolsonaro's son Flavio was finally indicted on multiple charges of kickbacks and money laundering, and awaits his own trial. A separate police investigation into another of Bolsonaro's sons, Carlos, the Rio de Janeiro city councilman, was reportedly headed toward the filing of numerous corruption charges against him as well.

As 2020 came to an end, Brazil was plagued by the coronavirus pandemic, the massive economic collapse that accompanied it, and extreme hostility between its political institutions. Nobody could meaningfully predict where Brazil was headed. Polls showed that Bolsonaro retained his core support almost completely, while many who did not support him were uncertain who to blame for their problems. Bolsonaro remains an effective demagogue, and with a besieged, though still powerful and well-organized, fake news network, he was able to control enough messaging to stave off impeachment and a full-scale collapse of his popular support.

— — — — — — — — — —

Perhaps the pinnacle of my experience at the center of one of Brazil's most intense political and journalistic controversies came when I received the Vladimir Herzog Award, the most prestigious and meaningful prize a journalist can receive in Brazil.

The award is named after the leftist Jewish immigrant journalist who was murdered in 1977 by Brazil's military regime, which faked his murder as a suicide. The prize is administered by the Herzog Institute, led by his son Ivo, who was seven years old at the time of his father's murder. Beyond working to preserve the real story of Herzog's murder, the institute is devoted to the defense of human rights and Brazilian democracy, ensuring that the military dictatorship never returns by memorializing its brutal history.

As Ivo told the *New York Review of Books* after Bolsonaro's first-round victory in 2018, he never expected that the threat of a restored military dictatorship would be as close and real as it now is. "I think we may be taking a huge step backwards. I'm very afraid," he said. "The political situation puts me under intense stress. I can't sleep without medication. But I've decided now is not the time to back down from the fight."

In its announcement that I would be a recipient of the 2019 prize, the Herzog Institute emphasized what it called the "violent reaction" to me and my reporting, provoked by the explicit threats from President Bolsonaro himself and the wave of vehemently antigay and xenophobic rhetoric against me and even my family.

The newly hostile and threatening climate for journalists in Bolsonaro-era Brazil was underscored by the institute's choice of the journalist who would share this award with me, Patrícia Campos Mello—the investigative reporter with São Paulo's *Folha* who revealed how Bolsonaro's presidential campaign had been funded by illegal, unreported expenditures from rich supporters. As the institute put it, "It's not a mere coincidence that the two journalists honored with the Vladimir Herzog Prize this year have been publicly embarrassed by the President of the Republic and threatened by his followers. Journalism that bothers almost always is good journalism."

The award ceremony in São Paulo, where we both gave acceptance speeches, was one of the most moving nights of my life. The Intercept's New York–based editor in chief, Betsy Reed, who had been steadfastly supportive of our reporting from the start, joined me, along with our Brazilian American communications chief, Rodrigo Brandão. The crowd was filled with people who had endured severe repression during the military dictatorship and had fought courageously against it, as well as with young journalists being honored for their own courageous, inventive reporting.

Patrícia and I both recounted, with a fair amount of emotion, how difficult the past months had been as we experienced a seemingly endless tidal wave of hatred, defamation, threats, and harassment from the president and his movement. There's no point in pretending that these attacks were not difficult. They were, for ourselves, our colleagues, and our families. By design, they made it seem that we would have no security, and no peace, as long as we were reporting in an adversarial and independent manner on Bolsonaro and his government.

As I explained in the preface, if I had to choose all over again, I would choose to do this work exactly as I did. I'm sure the same is true of Patrícia. I'm fortunate to have visibility, to have had a well-financed media outlet that was completely supportive of even the riskiest and most dangerous journalism, and to have worked with a team of incredibly brave and intrepid journalistic colleagues—both in Brazil and in the United States. If, with all of those tools, I'm not going to confront corrupt, powerful, and dangerous governments, and those who threaten Brazilian democracy, who should I expect will?

Brazilian democracy is only thirty-five years old. And the Bolsonaro regime poses a serious and explicit threat to it. Whether Brazilian democracy will survive, or instead be eroded and destroyed, is uncertain. The outcome will be determined not by fate but by the decisions and actions of those devoted to defending democratic values.

The abuses of the military regime in the 1960s and 1970s led thousands of young Brazilians to courageously oppose the dictatorship, resulting in their arbitrary detention, torture, and murder. Thousands of others were exiled, including some of the nation's most prominent artists, writers, actors, and scholars. It's impossible to speak to them, or read their stories, without being emboldened to follow their example.

The phrase "God is Brazilian" evokes many of the reasons I fell in love with Brazil and have rooted myself here for the last fifteen years. Central to Brazil's vibrancy is its freedom, its diversity, its democratic spirit. All of that is endangered by a government that has explicitly declared war on those values. But all of it remains uniquely worth fighting for.

ACKNOWLEDGMENTS

A s a result of the events described in this book, the last half of 2019 and first few months of 2020 were one of the most intense, difficult, exhilarating, pressurized, gratifying, and challenging periods of my life. It would have been impossible to endure and navigate without the support and collaboration of many people, to whom I owe enduring gratitude and appreciation.

I was very fortunate to have had colleagues at First Look Media and the Intercept in New York who never flinched in providing all the support we needed to do this reporting safely. From the start, Intercept editor in chief Betsy Reed, general counsel David Bralow, First Look president Michael Bloom, and the company's cofounder, Pierre Omidyar, never hesitated to stand behind the reporting, encouraging us in our most difficult moments, and making clear that they would provide whatever resources were needed for the physical security and legal protection of our entire team. Every journalist should enjoy this kind of editorial and corporate support, and knowing how rare it is, I am extremely appreciative of it.

My colleagues in the Intercept Brasil's newsroom, led by the charismatic and courageous Leandro Demori, were also crucial to the reporting of this archive. Composed almost entirely of young Brazilian journalists, most of whom had never worked on a story of such complexity and risk, the Intercept Brasil's staff produced journalism of the highest professionalism and quality, often under very difficult circumstances. When I founded the outlet in 2016, my primary goal was to give back to Brazil, a country that has given me so much, by enabling independent, courageous journalism beholden to and afraid of no powerful faction. After seeing firsthand the impressive, intrepid young team that Leandro has assembled, I am gratified that this objective has been fulfilled. Special thanks is due to Alexandre de Santi who, with wisdom and steadiness, assumed the not-always-enviable task of editing my own reports.

I owe the deepest thanks, as well, to the two lawyers who went so far beyond their duties as legal advisers in providing all kinds of invaluable support during this reporting. After leaving the legal profession back in 2007, I never imagined I would appreciate lawyers so much. But both Rafael Borges and Rafael Fagundes proved to be very wise, unfailingly trustworthy, and incredibly brave advisers and partners in the work we did. They saw this project not merely as work but as a cause, and for that, and their devotion, loyalty, and friendship, my gratitude is immeasurable.

My own team, with whom I worked and on whom I relied every day, was as smart, supportive, and skilled as it gets. My Brazilian journalism assistant, Victor Pougy, became a full-fledged, top-notch reporter by virtue of finding and bylining some of the most important exposés in the series. Victor is as great a friend and human as he is a journalist, and having someone like him, whom I could trust in every respect, was of immense value. Erick Dau, as usual, provided very wise counsel and unstinting friendship in the most challenging moments. Jonata Gomes, who works with me and my husband on numerous matters involving our security, worked day and night with great devotion to ensure that we could feel safe and secure; he also became one of my most valued friends. And our security team, led by Thiago and Apoena and several highly professional colleagues whose last names cannot be disclosed, demonstrated inspiring levels of devotion and sacrifice to our physical safety. For all of them, this was a cause as much as it was work, and I am indescribably grateful to each.

A group of friends and professionals with whom I have worked for years were, as they always are, critical to my ability to confront all of the difficulties posed by this story. My agent, Amanda "Binky" Urban; my editor and friend Sara Bershtel; my Intercept colleague Micah Lee, my friend and the leader of the Freedom of the Press Foundation, Trevor Timm; my best friend from childhood, Norman Fleisher; and my former source and lifelong friend Edward Snowden all contributed very wise counsel, guidance, and needed words of encouragement at the right moments.

Like the reporting itself, the writing of this book presented many challenges. A large amount of the credit for the final version that you're reading rests with my superb editor, Anthony Arnove of Haymarket Books, who used a laser-like knife to eliminate cumbersome and extraneous text, sharpen the prose used to tell the story, and shape a highly complex and unwieldy series of events into a compelling, focused story. I'm very appreciative to have an editor so skilled at preserving my voice and viewpoint while dramatically improving its expression.

Finally, my family played a central role in everything that I was able to do over the course of this reporting. My mother, Arlene, became a target of the Bolsonaro machine in a very ugly way as she was dying, yet handled it with stunning grace, strength, and humor—all of which she taught me through the power of her example throughout my life. While I miss her deeply, I am so happy to have been able to share this adventure with her. She was always my most devoted supporter and fan, and everything she gave me continues to be with me.

My children, João Vitor and Jonathas, endured a great deal: the virtual militarization of their house, the need for armed security just to go to school, and being always in the middle of intense and stressful situations. But the universe somehow gave me and David the children perfectly created for us and our lives, and having them at our side all the time lightened the mood, brought me unlimited joy, and always served as a reminder of why this work was worth pursuing.

And as I've said in every book I've written going back to the first one in 2006, everything that happens in my life is possible because of my husband, partner, and soul mate, David Miranda. Every year that goes by, our love and our bond deepens. Just as was true of the Snowden reporting, David was my indispensable partner for every part of the journalism we did here. I've run out of words to describe the central importance of David in my life except to say that everything I do is possible only because of him.

ABOUT HAYMARKET BOOKS

Haymarket Books is a radical, independent, nonprofit book publisher based in Chicago. Our mission is to publish books that contribute to struggles for social and economic justice. We strive to make our books a vibrant and organic part of social movements and the education and development of a critical, engaged, international left.

We take inspiration and courage from our namesakes, the Haymarket martyrs, who gave their lives fighting for a better world. Their 1886 struggle for the eight-hour day—which gave us May Day, the international workers' holiday—reminds workers around the world that ordinary people can organize and struggle for their own liberation. These struggles continue today across the globe—struggles against oppression, exploitation, poverty, and war.

Since our founding in 2001, Haymarket Books has published more than five hundred titles. Radically independent, we seek to drive a wedge into the risk-averse world of corporate book publishing. Our authors include Noam Chomsky, Arundhati Roy, Rebecca Solnit, Angela Y. Davis, Howard Zinn, Amy Goodman, Wallace Shawn, Mike Davis, Winona LaDuke, Ilan Pappé, Richard Wolff, Dave Zirin, Keeanga-Yamahtta Taylor, Nick Turse, Dahr Jamail, David Barsamian, Elizabeth Laird, Amira Hass, Mark Steel, Avi Lewis, Naomi Klein, and Neil Davidson. We are also the trade publishers of the acclaimed Historical Materialism Book Series and of Dispatch Books.